Chaotic – Harmony

Chronicles of Chaotic Minds

Chaotic – Harmony

Chronicles of Chaotic Minds

Stacy C. Kramer

ISBN: 9798333761439

Dedication

Chaotic-Harmony is dedicated to many people but especially my sister Patti Bird, who spent most of her adult life as a drug and alcohol counselor. She said what needed to be said without sugar coating and enabling. Her patients most always loved her and appreciated what she did for them. Patti always had answers for me as well, whether dealing with my own craziness or helping me understand the "why's" of life.

Chaotic – Harmony is also dedicated to the many people that I have met along my life's journey, which have given me insight to what it is like to be mentally ill and struggle with life in ways that are different from my own struggles. To my father, who is now in Heavan, who suffered from bouts of depression and who knows what else.

And to my Rock, my mother who is dam near perfect. No, really!

And most of all, my husband Ben, who always supported me for better or worse. I'm sure at times he would say it isn't always easy being married to me. However, I will be the first to say it isn't easy being me.

Preface

In 2003, my husband Ben and I owned a successful telecommunications company. We built our business from the ground up after relocating from the Bay Area to Sacramento, CA, not knowing a soul. My role involved marketing and selling equipment and services to businesses, and we pride ourselves on hiring driven individuals, even those without prior experience, and training them to succeed.

One of our employees joined us from Phoenix, AZ, bringing his two young daughters but leaving his wife behind. They were on the brink of calling it quits. When I learned why, I felt deeply saddened for this young family that was on the verge of splitting apart. His wife had been diagnosed with bipolar disorder and wasn't consistently taking her medication. Whatever challenges they faced had become too much for him, and he moved to be near his sister and other family members to create stability for himself and his girls.

At that time, I knew little about bipolar disorder. I mistakenly assumed it was similar to depression. As a strong Christian who believes in the sanctity of family, I couldn't understand why he wasn't doing everything possible to keep his family together.

I shared with him that I, too, have Major Depressive Disorder and that my husband had always been very supportive of me. While Ben didn't need to remind me to take my medication, I knew how crucial it was because I could always tell when I hadn't taken it by a certain time of day—I would start experiencing withdrawal symptoms.

I couldn't stay silent. I had to speak up on behalf of his

wife. I urged him to consider the vows they made when they married: "In sickness and in health." Did those vows not apply to mental illness as well? If she had cancer or another long-term illness, would he not care for her? I suggested that if he took the time to ensure she took her medication regularly and helped her manage refills before she ran out, it could make a significant difference in both of their lives. I also encouraged him to educate himself on bipolar disorder as much as he could so he would have a better understanding of it.

Eventually, they reconciled, raised their daughters together as a family, and are still together today. I don't claim that my words were the reason for their reunion, but perhaps, just maybe, something I said helped him realize that she needed his help, and he truly loved her.

It was because of that conversation that *Chaotic Harmony* was written. I felt a strong passion to create a book that could help partners, family members, and friends better understand the illness that plagues their loved ones. I've experienced it firsthand—when I mentioned I was on medication for depression, I often heard responses like, "What do you have to be depressed about?" or "Snap out of it!" If only it were that easy, we would all just snap out of it.

The more I wrote about mental illness, the more I wanted to share my experiences. Writing became a natural outlet for me. I would sit at my computer and type furiously about anything and everything. But then I realized that my thoughts were scattered, and I needed to put them in some sort of order.

So, I began to outline the characters, carefully crafting their descriptions. I found pictures of people in magazines that matched the images I had in mind for each character and glued them to the documents explaining their conditions. I needed to give the characters names that I knew I wouldn't forget. For 21 years, Dani was Stacy, yes, she was me. After all, I couldn't forget my own name.

Kathy was inspired by someone I knew who had narcolepsy. Although I never fully understood or witnessed the tragedies she endured, she shared many stories with me over the years that deeply affected me.

For Tammy's character, I drew inspiration from a girl I knew in the 5th and 6th grades. She was so sweet that if you knew her, you would never think she could do anything wrong. But when you learn her secrets, you see her in a whole new light.

Then there's Jackie—let me tell you about Jackie. She was someone from my past whom I loved with all my heart, almost as if she were my own child. People told me things about her that I didn't want to believe. One sad day, someone close to me showed me undeniable evidence of her actions. I began to hate her with every fiber of my being. When I wrote about her, I used what I believed was her true character and had a bit of fun with it in the book. Over the years, I've prayed for the strength to forgive her, which I did, but I could never forget the damage she caused. By the way, learning to forgive is crucial, you will find so much more peace within your soul.

I was able to write the manuscript very quickly, with high hopes that it would become a bestseller in no time, especially given the global epidemic of mental illness. I believed that offering insight into the mind of someone who suffers from mental illness might help, even if it was just one person.

But then it sat, untouched, for years. I would pick up what I initially called *Mental Illness: The Story*, read through it, get excited, and then put it down for another year or two. Whenever someone famous died from mental illness, drug addiction or suicide, I would pull it out again. Then there was Mental Illness Awareness Month in April, and I'd tell myself, "I have to get it ready for that." But it never happened.

Eventually, I got brave and thought it would be fun to send the manuscript to publishers, just to see what they thought. Even receiving rejection letters would tell me if I was onto something. I learned what publishers wanted to see when reviewing a manuscript and sent out some submissions. I was excited to receive my first NO! Yes, you read that right. I knew that if I got it out there in front of enough people, eventually, I might get a yes.

I had saved enough money to pay for a professional editor, Laura Matthews, from California. I couldn't wait to hear what she had to say. Her first comment was, "What a way to start a story, Stacy! Good Job"! But then came the critique—lots of it. I was both happy and discouraged, realizing that I would need to spend a lot more time fixing the manuscript. Laura would then edit it again—for more money, of course. And then we'd develop a plan, tweak it some more, and so on—all for more money! Spending money on myself or my ideas gives me major anxiety and so I put the manuscript down again.

Eventually I sat at my computer, trying to address the issues she pointed out. It felt like I needed to start the entire project over again. I was discouraged, so I stopped. I put the book away and let it sit. Meanwhile, I kept telling people about the book I wrote, and everyone always said they couldn't wait to read it. So, I would pull it out again and again. But eventually, the manuscript sat untouched for about four years straight. I would think about it from time to time, but I knew if I didn't follow through, I'd end up putting it away again.

Every so often, I would wish someone would come along and help me, someone who could just read my book, tweak it a bit, and use more sophisticated grammar. We could do this! But no one came.

In the spring of 2024, I visited my family in Southern California. My sister-in-law, Valerie, was excited to share something called AI that her school had just held a class on. I hadn't heard of the specific name, but I knew about AI in general. She showed me how it worked on her phone, and I was super excited about it. When I got back home, I remembered that I had installed AI on my smartphone. I decided to try it out on the first paragraph of my manuscript— the one I had received compliments on. I copied and pasted it into the AI, and seconds later, it spit out a version that blew me away. It took my words and enhanced them, making the paragraph so much more descriptive. I was one happy writer! This program worked with me to improve the grammar, spelling, and flow of almost my entire manuscript. I was able to edit what it generated, making the final product feel more natural when needed. It was my story, AI-enhanced. Yay! Then came the hard part—a whole new learning curve to get the book published. I chose Amazon because it seemed straightforward, with instructions and help readily available. So, if you're reading this right now, I did it! From the cover to the content inside completed!

Acknowledgments

Who would have thought a conversation at work in 2003 with an employee would open my eyes to how most people don't know how to deal with or recognize a person with mental illness? When Larry explained to me that he and his two young daughters had moved to be near his family without his wife, I for the life of me, couldn't understand why. As he explained that his wife had bipolar disorder and wasn't consistent in taking her medication, I had to ask, "Why haven't you helped her remember to take them?" I guess I was naive. All I could think of was marriage vows, "In sickness and in health." Wait, mental illness is a sickness, does it not apply? It is because of that conversation that *Chaotic – Harmony* was born.

I would like to thank several people for all the love and support throughout the years, supporting me and my crazy ideas. Thank you for never giving up on me and continuing to believe in me, even though I was not always consistent in my efforts.

Starting with my husband, Ben Kramer, who had to deal with me and what I thought was seasonal depression, which was later formally diagnosed as Major Depressive Disorder. Ben seemed to roll with my moods, probably due to him having a mother who needed her coffee first thing in the morning before anyone could talk to her. He would warn our sons, "Mom is having a B-Day," so they would leave the house and go do boy things. And B-Day wasn't short for birthday.

Thank you, Ben, for giving me the space I needed and always believing I could succeed at everything I set my mind on doing. I know it hasn't always been easy dealing with me, but trust me, it isn't easy being me.

To my mother, Flora, who believed in me more than I could ever believe in myself. She was a writer herself and worked on her stories throughout her lifetime. She wrote songs as well, hoping someday to be a published writer. She always inspired me, and if there's a gene tracing back to creative writing, then she gets the credit for it.

Thank you, sister Patti, for all the years of being one of my biggest mentors and best friends in life. When I didn't understand things, you did. You always had a way of teaching me without judging me, even when my ways were different from yours.

Thank you, sister Evelyn, for being the wonderful big sister, extra mother, and best friend a girl could ever have. You showed me love and taught me, "I have a voice, use it." And boy, do I!

Thank you, Laura Matthews, for professionally editing my manuscript. You were right on almost everything. I have to say, when I read your edits, I had hope, but I was also discouraged at the same time. It felt like I had to start over from scratch. I put the manuscript aside and brought it out many times over the years, trying very hard to follow your advice. There was so much work to be done.

I would also like to thank my dear friends who took the time to read my manuscript and provide honest feedback: Kathy Wolf, Angel Brooks, and my two sisters, Evelyn Smith, and Patti Bird. And, of course, my husband, Ben Kramer, who read the and edited the final draft.

A special thank you to all the family and friends who knew I was writing a book and always had something positive to say to encourage me. I would even like to include a thank you to the people I didn't know, who listened to me rant about the book I was writing and couldn't wait for a copy. Sorry you had to wait 21 years; however, you did inspire me to keep going.

And last but not least, Sylvester Stallone. I don't know him personally, but I watched a very inspiring video of him talking about writing *Rocky*. He kept getting turned down, but he pushed and pushed until someone believed in his work. When he became famous, he talked about getting up at 4:00 in the morning, going into his home office, and writing while his family was still asleep. I realized I was never going to be a successful writer if I kept sleeping in and dragging myself around until I felt motivated to get something done.

And if I can say I am proud of myself here, then I am proud of myself. Having one excuse after another is a good reason I had this book on hold for so long. Fear, anxiety, ADHD, not believing in myself or my work. How was I going to afford all the parts and pieces to get my book published? Who am I to think I can do this? I'm not college educated or certified on the subject. What makes me think I would have interest. Here's one: if my book becomes famous, I'll have to go talk to people, and I may not want to or be in the mood to. And then the crowds... big cities, anxiety, travel, anxiety, Bla Bla Bla! I am now ready for whatever happens. And if I have success, it's because there are a lot of people who can relate to the emotions and experiences in *Chaotic – Harmony*. So, here's to praying for success but mostly touching lives and making a difference.

Introduction

Mental illness affects millions, yet it is often misunderstood, stigmatized, and hidden away in the shadows. This book was born from a conversation that made me realize how little we understand mental illness and the people who live with it. My goal is to shed light on the experiences of those struggling with mental health disorders, and to foster empathy and understanding. This is not a medical book and should not be construed as one.

Drawing from my own journey with Major Depressive Disorder and Anxiety, as well as the stories of others, this book explores the complex realities of mental illness. I've learned that while mental illness can be isolating, it doesn't have to be a journey you take alone.

The book is divided into three sections: the first delves into personal narratives, the second offers insights into the broader implications of mental health issues, and the third gives practical advice through the story, for those supporting someone with a mental illness. While some of these stories are heartbreaking, they are also filled with resilience, hope, and the strength of the human spirit.

Whether you're dealing with mental illness yourself, supporting a loved one, or simply seeking to understand, this book is for you. Understanding mental illness isn't just about knowing the facts; it's about seeing the person behind the diagnosis, loving them anyway and realizing it is real. You may not be able to change them, but you can learn to deal with them or yourself. Let's begin this journey together!

Table of Contents

1 - The Accident

"Miss Jones, can you hear me? This is Francis with Star-Trak Monitoring Systems. Can you hear me?" Francis paused for a moment, trying to detect any movement or noise on the other end. "Ms. Jones, we've detected an accident with your vehicle. If you can hear me, please respond. We have requested an ambulance and a tow truck to assist you in case of an emergency. Miss Jones, we know your location and have sent help. Please stay with us if you can hear me."

As the paramedics arrived at the scene, they saw skid marks leading to a car wrapped around a tree, split into two pieces. Upon approaching, they noticed a woman still strapped into the driver's seat, the airbag inflated and blood everywhere. As she lay lifeless with her eyes open, the paramedics began checking her vitals.

"She's still alive!" one of the paramedics exclaimed. "Stay still, miss. We're going to get you out of here."

Though her condition seemed grave, the paramedics began to give everything they had to save her. They placed a neck brace around her to keep her head and neck stable and tried to keep her body still while trying to extricate her. After 20 minutes of painful manipulation of her body and the use of the Jaws of Life, they finally freed her from what was once a valuable convertible sports coupe. They placed her on a gurney, strapping her down for the trip to the hospital. She lay helpless, unable to speak or move, unable to feel her body as tears rolled down her face. "Stay with us" was all she could remember hearing that night.

As they rushed to the hospital, two EMTs worked on her, starting an IV and monitoring her vitals in the back of the ambulance. She drifted in and out of consciousness, barely able to understand their words.

"You're lucky to be alive, miss. Stay with us now. We're just a few minutes from the hospital," one paramedic said passionately. Upon arrival, the ambulance doors flew open even before the vehicle came to a complete stop. Nurses and doctors were already gathered as they pulled the gurney from the back of the ambulance and pushed it into the emergency room.

"According to her driver's license, she's 33-year-old Kathy Jones from Granite Bay," one of the EMTs reported. "We suspect this might be an alcohol-related accident, but we're not certain yet." The ER doctor frowned, his mind already racing through possible complications.

"Okay, let's move quickly. Get her on the table and start running tests and X-rays. We need to know what we're dealing with as soon as possible." As they moved her, Kathy's face flickered with brief awareness, her eyes darting around the room before closing again. The medical team worked with a sense of urgency, knowing that every second counted.

2 - Welcome Back Paul

"911, what is your emergency?"

"Hello, I just arrived home from a trip to find my girlfriend lying here unconscious! I can barely make out a pulse," Paul said, his voice trembling. "I think she has tried to commit suicide. God damn it! Dani, wake up! Paul shouted, clutching the phone with one and shaking Dani with the other.

Sir, can you tell me if she is breathing?"

"I can't tell!" Paul shouted.

"Sir, why do you think she tried to commit suicide? Sir?"

"It looks like she took pills. There's an empty prescription bottle here, and there's also a bottle of vodka that's almost gone. It spilled over on the table. Dani! Dani!" Paul Pleaded as he spoke.

"Sir, I need you to stay calm. Please tell me your exact address. We will have someone there in a matter of minutes."

Paul's heart pounded as he rattled off his address, his eyes never leaving Dani's pale, lifeless body. Paul was in shock and couldn't handle the stress of talking to the operator any longer, so he put the phone down, leaving the speaker on. He cradled Dani in his arms, crying profusely. "Dani, wake up, honey. Wake up. No! No! No! Dani, wake up, baby!"

Suddenly, the front door burst open, and three paramedics rushed in with their equipment. "Sir, we'll take over from here," said the one of the men, his voice calm but commanding.

Paul, trembling and tearful, stood to the side, his heart pounding as he watched the paramedic's work.

Two of the paramedics expertly administered CPR, their hands moving with practiced precision. One paramedic quickly inserted an IV into Dani's arm, while another checked her vitals. The third asked, "Is there anything we should know about her?"

"Not really, other than she is bipolar. Dani has been seeing a psychologist off and on for several years. She often forgets to take her medication. Sometimes, she runs out or doesn't refill her prescription, going months without it. She is also an alcoholic and smokes a little weed at times."

"OK, we got a heartbeat!" shouted one of the paramedics, his voice filled with relief and urgency. "Let's get her on a gurney and get her out of here," he said.

"I will come with you." Paul said, in desperation,

The paramedic standing closest to Paul said, "I am sorry, sir; you will have to drive your own vehicle. Our policy doesn't allow anyone to ride along due to insurance.

"What! That's crazy!" yelled Paul, his voice breaking with emotion. "I am her boyfriend! We live together, crying out loud! She'll need me if she wakes up!"

The paramedic repeated with a firm tone, "I understand, but sorry sir, we cannot take you with us. We are taking her to Rossville Memorial Hospital. You can check in at the emergency counter where they will assist you. That is all we can tell you. Please, sir, we need to get her to the hospital now!"

Paul felt a wave of helplessness washing over him. He watched, torn between frustration and fear, as they strapped Dani onto the gurney. The paramedics moved quickly, their faces set with determination, as they rushed her toward the waiting ambulance. Paul's mind raced, imagining the worst but hoping for the best, as he stumbled toward his car to follow them to the hospital.

Paul stood in the driveway, his heart aching, shocked as he watched the ambulance drive away with sirens blaring as they left his street. He felt a cold dread settle in his chest. He ran back into the house, grabbed his keys, and rushed out the door, dialing his cell phone as he got into his car.

"Hello, this is John."

"John, it's Paul. Dani was just taken to the hospital in an ambulance! I think she tried to kill herself!" Paul explained with panic in his voice, his words trembling with a mixture of fear and disbelief. His breath was heavy, and he struggled to stay composed as he continued, "I don't know what happened, but I found her unconscious. It doesn't look good, John."

"What! You're kidding me?" said John, his voice a mix of shock and disbelief.

"I can't believe this is happening," Paul explained frantically, with tears in his voice.

"Paul, pull yourself together," John urged. "C'mon, you need to settle down. Take a deep breath!"

"I just cannot believe this. I am heading to the hospital right now. I will call you back as soon as I know something."

"Wait!" said John. "Do you want me to come to the hospital and be with you?"

"No," said Paul, his voice quivering. "I will call you as soon as I know something." Paul hung up the phone and began to hit his steering wheel again and again, his knuckles reddening with each impact. "Why? Why? Just when things were going so well, why did she do this?" he shouted, his voice echoing in the car's confined space. As he drove to the hospital, he couldn't shake the feeling of guilt. "Why did it have to come to this?" he thought. "I should have seen the signs, done something sooner."

When Paul got to the emergency room, he ran in, leaving his car parked in the drop-off zone. The security guard standing by the door stepped forward. "Sir, you can't park your car there."

"But my girlfriend has just been brought here in an ambulance in critical condition," Paul said, his voice quivering with urgency and desperation.

Yes, sir, I understand, but you must park your car in the assigned parking, or it will be towed."

"Ah! Don't you people have any compassion for emergencies?" screamed Paul, his face red with anger.

"Sir, I am sorry, but we cannot have you park here," the guard replied firmly, maintaining his professionalism. Paul let out a growl of frustration, jumping back into his car and screeching his tires as he pulled away from the emergency room entrance. His hands gripped the steering wheel tightly, his mind racing with worry. He spotted someone pulling out of a spot in the parking garage and hurried to it.
As the previous person pulled out, Paul noticed a bumper sticker on the back of the car that read,

"LIVE YOUR DREAMS OR YOU'LL
LEAVE YOUR DREAMS BEHIND."

Paul pulled into the spot but sat in amazement, reflecting on different events and on those words. Amid his chaos and fear, the simple message struck a chord, offering a fleeting moment of introspection and clarity. Was this the price of his dream? He glanced at the empty passenger seat beside him, desperately wishing that Dani was there, healthy and happy. Despite his love for her, the constant emotional rollercoaster of their relationship left him feeling frustrated and exhausted.

Prior to his leaving on this last trip, he and Dani had some harsh words, and Dani threatened Paul with,

"If you leave me, I swear you are going to be sorry for it." Paul didn't take Dani's comments literally because she was always trying to use some form of manipulation to control him.

Paul was a musician who had recently signed a record deal with his band and was beginning to see success on the horizon. He and Dani had been together for several tumultuous years, marked by Dani's bipolar disorder and intense jealous rage. Paul felt that leaving her would cause her immense hardship. He feared her jealousy could lead to delusional and dangerous actions, potentially harming herself or even him. Despite his love and compassion for her, Paul often felt trapped. He remembered the night she accused him of flirting with a fan. She had been drinking all day, waiting, and watching as the band and staff prepared the stage. After their concert, she approached him with her eyes wild with jealousy, she smashed a beer bottle against the wall, shards flying like her fragmented trust. The memory sent a shiver down his spine.

Due to this behavior as well as others before, the group manager had asked spouses and significant others not to attend some of the promotional events. He used the excuse, "It's better for marketing and publicity if the band doesn't have the perception of being married men." Paul had reluctantly agreed, knowing it would be another point of contention with Dani.

Paul's heart ached at the thought of leaving Dani, but his mind was a storm of frustration and fear. He often found himself staring out the window, wishing for an escape. The excitement of the long-awaited record deal was tainted by the constant anxiety over Dani's next outburst. Success was within his grasp, but peace seemed more elusive than ever.

The memory of her tearful outbursts when he broke the news still haunted him. Her eyes had brimmed with hurt, and her voice had cracked as she pleaded, "Why can't I be there to support you?" Her sobs echoed in his ears, and the sight of her tear-streaked face was etched in his mind.

Paul often found himself torn between his dreams and his loyalty to her. His heart wrenched every time he saw her hurt, yet he couldn't ignore the thrill of his band's success. Each triumph felt bittersweet, a constant reminder of the sacrifices he had to make.

As he looked at the calendar filled with upcoming events, a knot of anxiety tightened in his chest. How much longer could he stretch himself between his two worlds before something broke? His excitement for the future was shadowed by the dread of inevitable conflict, and he wondered if he would ever find a way to reconcile his ambitions with his love for Dani. Dani was devastated. She believed everyone was conspiring to keep Paul from her, wanting him to leave her. Despite his efforts to explain that it was just business, Paul's words only seemed to deepen her suspicion.

You'll only get in the way, Dani," Paul said gently. "There are things I need to manage on my own. The budget doesn't allow for the expense of anyone other than band members. There are flights, lunches, dinners, photo shoots with photographers, meetings with attorneys, and promotional events. There's no room for anyone else, and it's not good for publicity." Paul remembered how Dani's hands shook as she clutched the edge of the table, her eyes filling with tears. "You always have an excuse, Paul. Why can't you see that I just want to be there for you?" Dani cried. Paul sighed, feeling the weight of their relationship pressing down on him. He wasn't sure how much longer he could juggle his career and his commitment to Dani. His heart ached as he watched the tears roll down her cheeks, but he couldn't let his emotions cloud his judgment. This was his chance, and he had to take it.

3 - All About Me

Jackie picked up her phone to hear her guest say, "It's Ron and Jennifer. Are you going to open the gate to this fortress or just let us peasants sit out here and stare at your gorgeous home?" Jackie laughed while pushing the button on her phone to open the gate remotely.

"Honey, they're here," she shouted down the stairs to Richard, her husband. "Can you greet them at the door? I'll be right down."

Richard opened the front door, stepping out onto the expansively covered entryway. The sun was setting, casting a warm glow over the manicured lawn and the cobblestone driveway. He adjusted his tie, then walked down the steps toward the driveway, where he knew Jennifer would soon arrive.

He waited patiently, listening to the faint rustle of leaves in the gentle evening breeze. Moments later, Ron's sleek black sedan pulled up smoothly. The car stopped with perfect precision, aligning just right so that Richard could open the door for Jennifer.

Richard stepped forward as Ron cut the engine, the car's lights dimming. He reached for the door handle, offering a warm smile as he opened it.

"Welcome, glad you could make it," he said, his voice sincere and inviting. Jennifer looked up, her eyes sparkling under the soft glow of the setting sun. She accepted Richard's hand, stepping gracefully out of the car.

"Thank you, Richard," she replied, her tone filled with warmth. "It's great to be here." As she stood up, Richard couldn't help but comment on the elegance of her dress and how beautiful she looked. He gently closed the door behind her, nodding a silent thank you to Ron, who acknowledged him with a brief nod and a smile before driving off to park the car.

Jackie married Richard Valentine, a highly successful entrepreneur fifteen years her senior. She was the type of woman who would not let anything, or anyone stand in the way of her desires. Her ambitions were not always about money; often, she craved attention and control over the people around her. Richard adored her, showering her with gifts and indulging her whims. But Jackie was happiest seeking the next thrill, the next conquest. Jackie and Richard often hosted dinner parties at their luxurious home, inviting clients crucial to his next big deal. Although these gatherings were meant for business, Jackie had a knack for making herself the center of attention. With a charming smile, she would deftly steer the conversation toward herself, her anecdotes sparkling with wit and intrigue. The guests couldn't help but be drawn in, their business concerns momentarily forgotten as Jackie knew how to work a room. As the evening progressed and the wine flowed, her influence over their company grew. She had an uncanny ability to sense when the spotlight might shift and would interject smoothly whenever one of the wives tried to join the discussion. Her voice, poised and confident, would rise above the others, effectively silencing what could be competition. She spoke over the women as if they were invisible, dismissing them as if they had no importance in the dealings.

The men, captivated by her stories and presence, often missed the subtle power plays happening before them. Jackie's eyes sparkled with a mix of charm and determination, ensuring that every eye remained on her. Richard watched with a mixture of admiration and mild concern, knowing that while Jackie's tactics were effective, they also walked a fine line.

The wives were all too familiar with Jackie's routine but felt powerless to counter it without causing a scene. They sipped their drinks and waited for moments when they could engage in quieter, more genuine conversations away from Jackie's dominating presence.

Jackie relished control, using her role as host to maintain the upper hand. She moved through the room with practiced ease, ensuring that every interaction reaffirmed her position. For her, these dinner parties were not just about securing business deals—they were a stage, and she intended to be the star of every performance.

Richard knew what he was getting into when he married Jackie. Her high need for attention, which sometimes raged out of control, occasionally even made him uncomfortable. At parties, when Jackie's behavior grew too bold, he would find himself tugging at his collar, his face flushing with embarrassment. Despite warnings from family and friends that she was a gold digger, Richard had been captivated by her charm and allure.

His adult children were furious, unable to understand how their father could be so careless. Their voices rose in heated arguments. "She's only after your money, Dad!" they would shout. "If you stay with her, don't expect to see us anymore."

Richard felt torn, the love for his children clashing with his desire for the excitement Jackie brought into his life. Each day there was a battle between reason, passion, family, and love. He felt the strain, caught between his wife and his family, but he couldn't deny the magnetic pull Jackie had on him.

As Richard, Ron, and Jennifer entered the house, their eyes were immediately drawn to the grand staircase where Jackie was descending with her usual grace. She looked elegant as always, dressed in a silky plum dress that was off the shoulder on one side, the fabric clinging to her body and accentuating her stunning figure.

The dress shimmered under the soft lighting, casting a subtle glow that made Jackie appear almost ethereal. Her hair was styled in loose waves, cascading over her bare shoulder, and her makeup was flawless, highlighting her striking features. She moved with a natural poise, measured every step and confident.

Richard felt a swell of pride mixed with the usual twinge of unease whenever Jackie made such a striking entrance. He knew the effect she had on people, how her presence could command a room and shift the dynamics of any gathering.

Ron, ever the bold one, let out a low whistle. "Wow, Jackie, you look absolutely stunning," he said, his eyes lingering a moment longer than necessary.

Jennifer, standing next to Ron, smiled politely but couldn't help feeling overshadowed by Jackie's commanding presence. "You look beautiful, Jackie," she added, her tone sincere but tinged with a hint of envy.

Jackie reached the bottom of the stairs and flashed them a dazzling smile. "Thank you, Ron. Jennifer, you look lovely as well," she replied, her voice smooth and warm. After greeting them with a warm hug and kiss on the cheek, she walked over to Richard, placing a light hand on his arm. "Darling, shall we head to the lounge for drinks?"

Richard nodded, still slightly mesmerized by Jackie's entrance. "Yes, let's," he said, guiding the group toward the elegantly decorated lounge where the evening's festivities would continue.

As they moved to the lounge, Richard couldn't shake the feeling of walking a tightrope. The combination of Jackie's allure, Ron's provocations, and the business at hand made for a delicate balance he was constantly trying to maintain. He took a deep breath, hoping the evening would unfold without any more of Ron's inappropriate jokes or unexpected complications.

Ron had been to the home multiple times; however, it had been a while since Jennifer had been able to make it. As they chatted, Richard was explaining the recent improvements they made to the home.

"Oh, Richard, you have to show me," Jennifer said. "I am excited to see them." Richard excused himself and led Jennifer away from the lounge area. Meanwhile, Ron stayed behind with Jackie, asking if he could see the wine cellar.

The elegant corridors were adorned with modern art pieces and sleek furniture, showcasing Richard's taste for luxury.

As they walked, Jennifer excused herself to use the restroom. Richard nodded and stepped away to give her some privacy, his eyes wandering around the hallway. A large, ornate mirror hung on the wall, reflecting the wine cellar's open door. To his shock, he saw the reflection of Ron and Jackie. Their bodies were close, their heads bowed together in what seemed like an intimate conversation. Richard's heart began to pound as he realized what he was seeing. He strained to hear their conversation but could only see their bodies leaning close together, their gestures too familiar.

He could see Jackie lean into Ron, pressing her breast against him while she reached for a bottle of wine from a shelf. Her eyes locked onto Ron's, conveying a message: "It's yours for the taking." She moved her face close to his, almost kissing him. Ron had admired her beauty all night and was intrigued by her flirtatious behavior. Staring into his eyes, Jackie sensed his arousal. She placed her hand on his chest, slowly rubbing it downward, which excited Ron even more.

Still looking into his eyes, she leaned forward and kissed him passionately but gently on the lips. Ron's breath quickened, his mind racing, torn between the thrill of the moment and the nagging sense of crossing a line. Against his better judgment, he responded by embracing her, pulling her closer. He pushed her back slightly, enough to admire her curves, kissing her exposed cleavage. His hand began to move downward, but they both stopped abruptly when they heard the bathroom door open and Jennifer's voice. Looking at each other they giggled like children and went on to enjoy the variety of wines in the collection.

"Sorry about that interruption. Can we continue with our tour?" Jennifer asked.

"Absolutely," Richard said, moving his position to hide the image in the mirror from her.

A wave of disbelief and anger washed over Richard's face. He clenched his fists, unsure whether to confront them or pretend he hadn't seen anything. The reflection in the mirror became a painful reminder of the delicate balance he struggled to maintain between his professional and personal life.

Richard held his composure to protect Jennifer, knowing she was an innocent victim of Ron and Jackie's devious ways. His hands clenched into fists at his sides, his jaw tightening as he forced a smile and guided Jennifer through the house. Throughout the evening, Richard hid his anger behind polite exchanges of words with Ron and Jennifer. However, he had a hard time looking at his wife or even speaking to her. Jackie, ever perceptive, picked up on his anger and found herself almost without words for the rest of the evening.

Richard's mind raced, struggling to maintain the facade of calm. He engaged in small talk, his responses measured and courteous, but there was an edge to his demeanor that did not go unnoticed by those close to him. Jennifer, sensing the tension, tried to lighten the mood with cheerful conversation, but Richard's strained smiles and curt nods betrayed his inner turmoil.

Ron, oblivious or perhaps indifferent to the tension he had caused, continued to be his usual boisterous self, making jokes and dominating conversations. His laughter rang out across the room, a stark contrast to the simmering anger Richard fought to suppress. Every now and then, Ron would glance at Richard, a mischievous glint in his eye, as if daring him to react.

Jackie, on the other hand, was uncharacteristically subdued. She moved through the room with less of her usual confidence, her sparkling anecdotes and charming smiles replaced with a quiet, almost tentative demeanor. She knew she had crossed a line, and Richard's silent fury was a palpable presence between them.

As the evening wore on, Richard's resolve to maintain his composure was tested repeatedly. When Jennifer, with her innocent curiosity, asked about the latest business ventures, Richard answered with a forced enthusiasm, all the while avoiding Jackie's gaze. The moments they did lock eyes, it was like a silent battle—her look of contrition meeting his unyielding anger. Eventually, the evening began to wind down. Ron and Jennifer started to make their polite farewells, and Richard saw them to the door, ensuring she left with a genuine smile despite the tension.

"Thank you for a lovely evening, Richard," Jennifer said softly, her eyes reflecting gratitude.

Thank you for coming, Jennifer," he replied, his tone gentle for her benefit.

Ron, still in high spirits, slapped Richard on the back "Another great night, eh, Rich?" he boomed.

Richard's smile was tight. "Yes, Ron. Another great night," he said, his voice betraying none of the anger that churned within him. When the taillights of their car reached far enough away, the house fell into an uneasy silence. Richard finally turned to Jackie, his composure slipping.

"What were you thinking?" he asked, his voice low but charged with emotion. Jackie looked at him, her eyes wide and remorseful. "Richard, I", "Save it," he cut her off, shaking his head. "I don't even know what to say to you right now."

He walked away, leaving Jackie standing alone in the dimly lit entryway, the weight of her actions pressing down on her. The evening had been a facade, a delicate dance of polite exchanges masking deep-seated frustrations and unresolved conflicts. And now, as the night came to an end, the reality of their fractured relationship loomed large, demanding to be addressed.

4 - You're Out-a-here

Jackie followed Richard throughout the house, crying out to him "I am so sorry Richard." Richard stopped suddenly and turned to Jackie angrily. "I want a divorce. I am tired of having a wife who disrespects me in my own house! I am so sick of seeing you throw yourself at men without any consideration of whether they're married or not. And what about me? You don't give a dam about me. After everything I have done for you!

Richard's fists clenched at his sides as he paced back and forth, his voice trembling with fury and pain. "Am I that unattractive to you that you must look elsewhere? Do I not give you the satisfaction that you need in bed? You need to get the hell out of my house," he shouted, his voice echoing through the hall. "I am done!"

Tears of frustration and hurt welled up in Richard's eyes, though he fought to keep them from falling. This was the breaking point; the moment he realized he could no longer endure the betrayal and disrespect.

"No! No! Richard," Jackie cried frantically. "Please don't talk that way. I don't want a divorce! I love you and only you! I don't know why I act the way I do. I don't know why I can't stop. Please forgive me, I beg of you, please, Richard, please!"

Jackie fell to her knees, her hands clasped in front of her as tears streamed down her face. But her pleads fell on deaf ears. Richard had heard her lies before and was tired of them. His face was set in stone, his eyes cold and unyielding.

Before turning away from her and heading upstairs to their bedroom, he shouted "I want you gone! Tomorrow, by the time I come home from work, you need to get your stuff and get the hell out of my house!" he demanded.

Jackie continued to cry frantically, her heart pounding in her chest as she realized the full impact of Richard's words. She knew that the prenuptial agreement she had signed meant she would leave with nothing. This would leave her without a car, a home, or any of the luxuries she had grown accustomed to.

"And for now, sleep in the guest room. I don't want you in my bed" he shouted as he turned and walked away, leaving Jackie stunned.

Jackie followed Richard up the stairs to their bedroom, crying, only to have the door slammed in her face.

"Can I get my clothes to sleep in, at least?" she begged. The door opened slowly. Jackie walked in, still crying, and wiping her tears. She went into the master bath, which led to the closet where she kept all her clothes, including her lingerie. She removed her clothing and walked over to the shower, turning on the water. Her hands shook as she adjusted the temperature, her sobs echoing in the bathroom.

"I thought you were just going to get your clothes," Richard said sternly, standing in the doorway with narrowed eyes.

In her teary voice, Jackie replied, "Well, I have makeup all over my face, all my supplies are in here and I just want to clean up before I go to bed."

"Fine," Richard yelled, his voice filled with frustration and resignation.

Jackie felt a pang of despair. This was the man she loved, the life she had built, crumbling before her eyes. She stepped into the shower, letting the water wash away her tears, but it couldn't cleanse the overwhelming sorrow she felt.

Richard could hear Jackie crying as she showered. He lay on top of his bed, his fists clenching and unclenching in frustration. The woman he loved seemed to have a problem he couldn't fix.

As Jackie finished her shower, Richard watched, still furious, as his beautiful wife dried off her naked body. He wondered how many men had touched her since they had been married. His heart was broken, and he felt both hurt and disappointed as he pondered what would become of his jewel. He no longer trusted her.

When Jackie finished her shower, she went back into the closet, slipping into one of her more elegant pieces of lingerie. She pulled her hair up into a messy bun and put on her slippers. When she walked out, the soft light of the bedside lamp cast a golden hue over her, accentuating the elegance of her lingerie and the sadness in her eyes. She looked like a supermodel from a centerfold magazine, yet there was a vulnerability about her that was impossible to ignore. Tears still in her eyes, she looked at Richard and said,

"I am sorry," her voice barely above a whisper. She slowly walked out of the room, hoping against hope that he would stop her.

Richard could say nothing. He got up, removed his clothes, pulled back the covers on his bed, and crawled in. All night, he tossed and turned, his mind racing with thoughts of betrayal and anger. He wondered if he would ever get the sleep, he needed for work the next day and how he would deal with Ron, knowing he had crossed the line with his wife.

In the morning, Richard went downstairs to get his coffee and make some toast. Surprisingly, Jackie was already at the table, with her coffee in hand, crying softly. She looked like she had been awake all night, her eyes red and puffy, her hands trembling as she held her coffee cup. The morning sun cast a pale light through the kitchen window, highlighting the stark tension between them. He glanced at her but said nothing.

"I'm sorry," Jackie said softly.

"I don't want to hear about it," he said sternly. Taking his coffee, he went back upstairs and closed the door behind him.

Richard continued to get ready for work, following his routine as he did every day. When he was ready to leave the house, Jackie was nowhere in sight. He walked out to the garage, feeling a mix of sadness and anger, knowing she would be gone by the time he came home. The weight of the previous night's events hung heavily on him, a reminder of broken trust and shattered dreams.

Jackie spent the morning pushing herself to pack her belongings. She walked through the house, tears streaming down her face as she lingered on the photographs that were sitting on tables or hung on walls, each one a painful reminder of the love and memories she had created with Richard. Each step felt heavier than the last, her heart weighed down by the imminent farewell. Richard's smile seemed to mock her now, a stark contrast to the turmoil churning inside her.

Jackie knew the roots of her troubles ran deep. As a child, she had been abandoned by her parents, shuttled from one foster home to another. She learned early on that playing the role of a promiscuous young girl around her foster fathers and brothers could get her what she wanted, or at least what she needed to survive. Even though she knew these men were wrong for their actions, she played along, a puppet in a cruel game. As she got older and navigated life on her own, Jackie discovered how easy it was to manipulate men. Her striking beauty only made it easier to attract them, turning her into a master at getting what she wanted with minimal effort. There were plenty of times she tried to forge genuine relationships, but someone or something always came around. She remembered the look of betrayal on a few men's faces when she was found with another man, a look she had seen too many times. Jackie knew the pattern well: a promising start, followed by her wandering eyes, and then the inevitable end. These failed relationships left her feeling hollow. She would lie awake at night, questioning if she was capable of change, or if her past had irrevocably shaped her present. The familiar sting of loneliness was her only constant companion. Now, standing in the home she shared with Richard, those old survival tactics felt like chains, binding her to a past she longed to escape.

5 - Ho-Tell-Lies

Later in the day, Jackie checked into a nearby hotel. She wore dark sunglasses to hide her red, swollen, tearful eyes. Once inside her room, she tore off her clothes and threw herself onto the bed, her body wracked with hysterical sobs.

A sharp, quick knock interrupted her breakdown. "Room service." It was Bellman. Jackie scrambled to put on a robe, hastily wiping her eyes before opening the door. The bellman stood there with a polite smile. "Ma'am, I have your bags. Can I bring them in?"

"Yes, please, just over there," she gestured to the luggage holder in the corner. She followed him, murmuring a soft "thank you" as she grabbed her purse, fumbling through her wallet for a tip. Her heart sank when she found she had no cash.

"Sir, I am so embarrassed to say I have no cash to tip you. Can I catch you later?" Jackie asked.

"Sure, no problem," the bellman replied, though his eyes lingered on her tear-streaked face. "Are you okay?" he asked.

Jackie forced a smile. "Yes, I'm just going through some hard times."

"Is there anything I can do for you?" he asked, his voice gentle with concern.

"No, not right now. If you could just come back later, I'd appreciate it."

"No problem," he said as he left, closing the door softly behind him.

Jackie returned to the bed; her hand pressed against her forehead in disbelief. Tears welled up again as she whispered to herself, "What have I done?" Jackie found herself alone, her heart pounding with fear and uncertainty. The hotel room felt cold and impersonal, a stark contrast to the warmth she had thrown away the night before. She glanced at the phone sitting on the table next to the bed. Its presence seemed to taunt her.

"Should I call him?" she thought, her fingers hovering hesitantly over the receiver. "No, he won't want to talk to me." The thought brought a fresh wave of despair. The guilt and shame weighed heavily on her, making it hard to breathe. She buried her head into the pillow and began to sob again. The sound of her cries filled the empty room, each sob echoing the depth of her sadness and remorse.

Jackie fell asleep, not waking until she heard another knock on her door. She got up, looked at herself in the mirror, adjusting her hair and makeup, and walked to the door. Through the peephole, she saw it was the young bellman from earlier. She opened the door slowly and asked, "Can I help you?"

"Yes, ma'am," he said, raising a long raincoat. "I believe this was part of your baggage, but somehow it got left behind."

"Oh, yes," Jackie replied. "Come in. What is your name, young man?" she asked, her curiosity piqued.

"Michael," said the bellman.

"Well, Michael, can you please hang it for me in the closet?" she asked.

"Yes, ma'am," said Michael.

As he walked to the closet to hang her coat, Jackie couldn't help but notice his athletic build. His broad shoulders and strong arms were evident even beneath his crisp uniform, and the way his pants fit perfectly around his firm bottom caught her eye for more than a moment. She found herself momentarily distracted, appreciating the way his muscles moved as he reached up to hang the coat.

Jackie's thoughts wandered for a moment, admiring the physicality of the young man before her. It was a fleeting distraction, a small indulgence amidst the evening's tension. She quickly composed herself, flashing a polite smile as Michael turned back toward her, his professional demeanor unwavering.

"Thank you, Michael," she said, her voice smooth and controlled. She knew how to mask her thoughts behind a veneer of charm, a skill she had perfected over years of navigating social and business circles.

"You're welcome, ma'am," he replied, his face expressionless but respectful. A flicker of desire sparked within her, momentarily distracting her from her sorrow.

"Can you sit with me for a moment?" Jackie asked, her voice taking on a softer, almost vulnerable tone.

Michael hesitated, glancing at his watch. "Well, ma'am, my shift is over, and I've signed out already, so I suppose I could stay for a few minutes," he said shyly, a hint of a smile playing at the corners of his mouth.

"Good," Jackie responded, her voice warm and inviting. "Can I get you a beer or wine?" she offered.

"Sure," said Michael, despite knowing the potential risk to his job. The temptation of her company was too strong to resist.

Jackie walked over to the small fridge, where she gracefully poured a glass of red wine for herself and grabbed a beer for Michael. She handed him the cold bottle, their fingers briefly touching, sending a small thrill through her.

"Thanks," he said, taking a sip to steady his nerves. He was well aware of the inappropriateness of the situation, but Jackie's presence was captivating, making it hard to think clearly.

As Jackie sat on the sofa, the room was too quiet, so she reached over to the coffee table next to her and turned on the radio. She lowered the sound and put the station on classical jazz.

"Please, call me Jane," she insisted, her tone gentle. "Tell me about yourself, Michael. How did you end up working here?"

He hesitated, then decided to share a bit. "Well, I've always been good with my hands and needed a job to support myself while I figure out my next steps. This seemed like a good fit."

Jackie listened intently, her eyes never leaving his. She found herself drawn to his sincerity and the quiet strength he exuded. "I admire your work ethic," she said softly. "It's not easy finding people who take pride in what they do."

Michael felt a flush rise to his cheeks. "Thank you, Jane. That means a lot coming from you."

They continued to talk, the conversation flowing more easily as the minutes passed. Jackie shared anecdotes about her own life, carefully curated to keep the focus on her successes and charm. Michael listened, fascinated by her stories and the way she seemed to effortlessly command the room, even in a one-on-one setting.

As the evening grew later, the wine and beer had done their job, loosening them up and easing the tension. Jackie's laughter rang out softly, a seductive melody that seemed to fill the space around them.

Michael knew he should leave, that staying longer could lead to complications, but he found it increasingly difficult to tear himself away from her magnetic presence. For Jackie, this was a welcome distraction, a chance to feel desired and in control amidst the chaos of her life.

Finally, sensing the moment was right, Jackie leaned in slightly, her eyes locking onto his. "Thank you for staying with me, Michael. It's been a pleasure talking with you."

"The pleasure's all mine, Jane," he replied, his voice barely above a whisper. They sat in silence for a moment, the air thick with unspoken possibilities. Then, with a reluctant sigh, Michael stood up. "I should go," he said, his tone regretful. "But thank you for the drink and the company."

Jackie stood as well, her eyes lingering on him. "You're welcome anytime, Michael," she said softly, her voice filled with promise.

He nodded, unable to find the words to express the mix of emotions he felt. With a final, lingering glance, he turned and walked to the door. Jackie followed him, wishing he could stay longer. When they got to the door, Michael turned toward Jackie. He brushed her hair off her face with his long, slender fingers. To his surprise, Jackie looked up and asked, "Can I get a hug?" Michael leaned in, wrapping his arms around her, but wanting to keep his distance respectfully. Jackie, however, clung to him, feeling the softness of his hair against her face. After a moment, she pulled back and whispered, "Thank you, I really needed that."

"Well, if you need me again, you know where to find me," Michael said seriously. He turned away slowly, grabbing the doorknob when he heard Jane's voice. "Wait."

Michael turned, curiosity in his eyes. "What's up?"

She held his gaze as she began to untie the belt on her robe. Slowly, the robe slipped off her naked body, revealing her vulnerability and desire. Michael's eyes widened in shock?. "Is this really happening"?" he thought.

Jackie reached up and wrapped her arms around his neck. "I really need someone right now," she whispered, her voice trembling with emotion. Without hesitation, Michael leaned in, capturing her lips in a passionate kiss. Their embrace deepened, fueled by the raw intensity of the moment. Jackie's fingers fumbled with his clothes, tearing them off as they maneuvered toward the bed. Michael scooped Jackie into his arms, laying her gently on the bed while continuing to kiss her fervently. Their passion ignited, and they made love with an urgency and intensity that reflected their desperate need for connection and solace.

Hours melted away as they lost themselves in each other, their bodies entwined in a dance of shared longing and unspoken emotions. After lying in bed without moving for several moments, Michael finally broke the silence. "Wow, I can't believe this happened. I really need to get going," he said, his voice tinged with disbelief.

"Yes, I understand, you should," Jackie replied, her voice a mix of resignation and lingering emotion. Michael got up from the bed, gathering his clothes scattered on the floor. He walked into the bathroom, closing the door softly behind him. The sound of the door clicking shut echoed in the stillness of the room.

Jackie lay back on the bed, staring at the ceiling. The reality of what had just happened began to sink in. "What is wrong with me?" she thought, the weight of her actions pressing down on her chest. Her husband's words echoed in her mind, a harsh reminder of her uncontrollable impulses. "I have a problem that I can't seem to control." She hugged the sheets closer, feeling the cool fabric against her skin, contrasting sharply with the warmth of the moment that had just passed. The room felt emptier now, the earlier intimacy replaced by a gnawing sense of regret. Jackie's thoughts raced, each one amplifying her self-doubt. She closed her eyes, wanting herself to find some semblance of calm, but the turmoil within her refused to be silenced.

In the bathroom, the sound of running water was a distant reminder of Michael's presence. Jackie knew that once he left, she would be alone with her thoughts, forced to confront the choices she had made.

Michael came out of the bathroom, fully dressed as if nothing had happened. He walked over to Jackie, still lying in bed, and kissed her one last time. "Jane, you are one incredible and beautiful woman," he said with a smile. Jackie managed a half-smile in return, watching as he turned and walked out of her hotel room. The door closed with a final click, leaving her in silence.

She grabbed the pillow next to her and pressed it against her face, her screams muffled but intense. "What the hell is the matter with me?" she yelled into the pillow; her voice choked with anguish. Tears streamed down her cheeks as she pulled the pillow away, staring up at the ceiling. "My husband just kicked me out of our home, and here I am fucking a young man I never met before today! Why? God, I am so stupid! Shit!" Her chest heaved with each breath, her heart pounding in her ears. The room felt cold and empty, a stark contrast to the heated encounter that had just taken place. The reality of her actions hit her with full force, amplifying her sense of self-loathing.

Jackie curled into a ball, clutching the pillow tightly. The room around her seemed to close in, her thoughts a relentless barrage of guilt and regret. She felt trapped in a cycle she could not break, each impulsive decision leading to more pain.

In a fit of rage, Jackie threw the pillow across the room. Breathing heavily, she yanked open the drawer in the nightstand next to her bed and pulled out the phone book. Her hands trembled as she frantically flipped through the pages, searching for "Therapists."

When she found the section, her eyes scanned the ads until she landed on the biggest one. Without hesitation, she began dialing the number.

"You have reached Alma Counseling. No one is available to take your call now. Please leave your name and number, and someone will get back to you within 24 hours. If this is a medical or psychiatric emergency, please hang up and dial 911 Thank you."

"Damn it!" she yelled, slamming the receiver down. Her frustration bubbled over, but she forced herself to calm down and dialed the next number on the list. Each call brought a similar response: voicemail after voicemail. Her desperation grew with each unanswered call. Finally, on what felt like the hundredth try, she heard a human voice on the other end. "

Hello, this is Dr. Gifford's office. How can I help you?"

Jackie burst into tears of relief. "I need to see a therapist. It's urgent. Please, can I make an appointment as soon as possible?

The receptionist responded, "I'm sorry but I must first ask if you're in danger of hurting yourself.

"No," said Jackie frantically. "I just need to see someone as soon as I can."

"Let me check our schedule," the receptionist said, the sound of keyboard clicks filling the silence. "We have an opening tomorrow at 2 PM. Will that work for you?"

"Yes, yes, that is perfect. Thank you," Jackie replied with enthusiasm

After hanging up, she let out a long breath, feeling a small flicker of hope amidst her turmoil. She knew she had taken a crucial first step towards addressing her issues.

6 - Tragic Exhaustion

Several days had passed while Kathy was recovering from major injuries to her right leg and minor ones to her head and neck, not to mention the bruises and lacerations scattered across her body. She had been moved from the ICU into her own room, but sleep eluded her. As Kathy woke, she could see her best friend, Nancy, standing over her bed, looking at her with a sweet smile and compassion. Nancy pointed at the doctor in a white coat on the other side of the bed.

"Hello, Kathy. My name is Dr. Harris. I am your neurologist. How are you feeling?" he asked. "Do you know where you are and how you got here?" Dr. Harris waited for some sort of reaction or words before he continued.

Kathy tried to sit up but was shocked to see the cast that covered her right leg and the other bandages on her arms. She had a neck brace that kept her from moving her head, as well as a bandage on her face that she could see out of the corner of her eye.

"This was a horrific accident you were in. You are one lucky lady," said Dr. Harris compassionately. "Do you remember the accident?" he asked.

Kathy's eyes were unfocused as she tried to make sense of his words. Who is he? What does he mean? Her eyes filled with tears as she tried to make out what had happened to her. She looked to Nancy for support in what she was experiencing.

Kathy took a couple of moments to gather her thoughts, as it was the first time she had opened her eyes and woken up since the accident. When she was awake enough, Dr. Harris explained the injuries that she had sustained which had brought her to the hospital. A deep concern came over her face as Kathy continued to try, with no success, to sit more upright. "Just relax," said Dr. Harris as he positioned the head of the bed a bit higher.

"Prior to the accident, do you remember having trouble sleeping or staying awake?" Dr. Harris asked, softly and directly.

"I can't seem to remember anything," Kathy slowly replied in a raspy whisper.

"While you've been asleep, I've done some extensive tests on your brain to check for injuries. Fortunately, you only have a bit of a concussion along with some bruises and cuts that will heal overtime," Dr. Harris continued, his tone serious yet kind. "I don't want to alarm you; however, along with the injuries, I've seen some unusual activity going on in your brain while you slept. Over the next several days, I will be running some further tests."

Nancy spoke up, "Kathy recently told me she was tired a lot and having trouble staying awake in the middle of the day."

Dr. Harris looked at Nancy, then back at Kathy. "I believe there is a chance that you have a sleep disorder" he continued to explain.

"There is a disorder called Narcolepsy; I want to check you for. This is a chronic neurological disorder caused by the brain's inability to regulate sleep-wake cycles. Normally, at various times throughout the day, people with narcolepsy experience a fleeting urge to sleep. If the urge becomes overwhelming, they fall asleep for periods lasting from a few seconds to several minutes. In rare cases, some people may remain asleep for an hour or longer."

Kathy looked on in deep thought and disbelief. "Wow," she murmured. "I can relate to that."

Nancy spoke up again, "That does make sense. I mean, Kathy told me about some of these symptoms."

"Really?" Dr. Harris leaned in, curiously. "How long have you been experiencing these symptoms, he asked Kathy?"

Kathy hesitated before answering, as she looked to Nancy for support again. Kathy began slowly, "A few years ago, I was at an intersection in my car, and suddenly the people behind me were honking their horns. It startled me because I felt lost, like I had just woken up, but I could not have because I was driving. Since then, there have been several occasions where this same loss of time freaked me out. I never said anything to anyone because I didn't know how to explain it, and I thought people would think I was crazy."

"This may explain the time lapses you've noticed," said Dr. Harris. He looked at Kathy with compassion. Like I said earlier, I'd like to run some more test on your brain.

Kathy nodded slowly, still processing the information. "Okay, Dr. Harris. I'll do whatever you think is necessary."

"Great," he replied reassuringly. "We'll start with some additional scans and a sleep study. Try to rest as much as you can, and we'll take good care of you."

Nancy squeezed Kathy's hand. "You're going to be okay.

We'll get through this together." Kathy offered a faint smile, grateful for her friend's unwavering support. She closed her eyes, trying to find some comfort in the midst of her confusion and fear.

7 - A Decision

Paul got out of his car after sitting, reminiscing for several moments, the good and the bad. He ran into the emergency room heading straight to the counter."

My girlfriend was brought here by ambulance," he said frantically to the receptionist.

"What is her name?" the receptionist asked.

"Dani. Dani Gregory. She overdosed on prescription drugs and alcohol," Paul replied, his voice trembling.

"Yes, I see her name here. Follow me, and I will take you to her," said the receptionist. She stood up and led him through the double doors into the emergency room.

As they walked in, Paul's eyes darted around, taking in the different beds—some occupied, some empty. His heart pounded in his chest as they moved down the hallway. The receptionist stopped in front of bed 23. She opened the curtains, revealing Dani lying with her eyes closed, an IV in her left arm and monitors attached to her right hand, along with an oxygen tube going into her nose.

Paul rushed to her side, grabbing her left hand gently. "Dani," he whispered. Dani opened her eyes, looking up at Paul with a mixture of fear and regret, like a scared child who had done something wrong.

"I'm sorry," said Dani, her voice trembling.

"Shh," Paul replied, his voice gentle.

"I didn't mean for this to happen," cried Dani, tears welling up in her eyes.

Paul looked at her with deep compassion. He did not know whether to be angry or to feel guilty for not being there for her. He squeezed her hand gently, trying to convey his support without words. Dani closed her eyes while Paul sat by her bedside, watching as she fell back to sleep.

As he sat there, Paul's mind wandered to the bumper sticker on the car in the garage: "LIVE YOUR DREAM OR YOU'LL LEAVE YOUR DREAM BEHIND."

He pondered the message, feeling a mix of sadness and determination. He knew that he needed to be there for Dani, to help her find her way back from this terrible place she had put herself in.

After about an hour of sitting by her bedside while she slept, a nurse came into the room to check on Dani. "Hello, I'm Nurse Kristy," she said to Paul.

"Hi," Paul replied softly, careful not to wake Dani.

"How are you handling this?" she asked, her voice gentle.

Paul sighed. "I do not really know how to handle this. I am not sure what to do or say. I feel lost."

"I understand," Nurse Kristy said, her eyes full of empathy. "We have a chaplain on premise. Would you like to speak to him?"

"No," Paul said, shaking his head. "I think I'll be okay for now."

"Alright," Kristy nodded. "Let me know if you change your mind."

"You got it," Paul replied.

Nurse Kristy checked Dani's vitals; her movements efficient yet caring. "She looks like she is doing fine," she said with a reassuring smile.

"Great," Paul said, feeling a slight sense of relief.

As Nurse Kristy left the room, Paul looked back at Dani, feeling a mixture of hope and uncertainty. He knew the road ahead would be challenging, but in the heat of the battle, he was determined to support her through it all.

Paul remained by Dani's bedside throughout the night. He would often doze off until one of the nurses made her rounds to check on her.

In the early morning, Kristy came back to the bedside and said, "The doctor will be in to check on Dani soon. Most likely, she will be released from the hospital, but she will probably have to go to the psychiatric center across the street."

Paul looked amazed. "What do you mean?" he asked, his voice filled with concern.

"When there is an attempted suicide, the patient is always put on a 72-hour watch to make sure they get the help they need and to prevent further attempts," explained Kristy.

"Oh my God!" Paul exclaimed. "You've got to be kidding, right?"

"No, unfortunately I'm not," said Kristy gently.

Paul placed his hands over his face, moving them upward and then downward in a gesture of frustration and despair. "I just don't know what I'm going to do," he said, his voice trembling.

Nurse Kristy looked at Paul with compassion. "I'm sorry, sir," she said softly.

The ER doctor walked in. "Hello, I'm Dr. Bender. You must be Dani's husband?"

"No sir," said Paul, shaking his head. "I'm her boyfriend. We live together."

Dr. Bender nodded and looked at Dani, then grabbed her medical chart. "Alright, let's see how she's doing." "From what I can see from all the tests we've run; it looks like she's going to be fine. However, we need to get to the bottom of this," said Dr. Bender, his tone serious. "Has Dani ever tried to hurt herself or commit suicide before?"

"No! No!" Paul exclaimed, shaking his head vehemently. "I've been with her for over five years, and she has never done anything like this before."

Dr. Bender frowned, looking thoughtful. "What is going on in Dani's life right now that makes her feel so depressed that she would want to take her own life?"

"Nothing!" Paul said, almost shouting. His voice was strained, and he could feel a lump forming in his throat. "I mean, we have our ups and downs like any couple, but nothing that would make her do this."

Dr. Bender glanced at Dani, her face peacefully sleeping, and then back at Paul. "Sometimes, people hide their struggles very well" Dr. Bender said with curiosity. Paul ran his hand through his hair, feeling helpless.

"She has been a little bit crazy from time to time due to the bipolar, but she never showed signs of being this desperate." Paul said with passion.

Dr. Bender nodded, making notes on Dani's chart. "We need to make sure she gets the support she needs."

Paul swallowed hard, the reality of the situation sinking in. "What do I do?" he asked, his voice barely a whisper.

"We will start with the 72-hour watch at the psychiatric center. After that, she will need ongoing therapy and support. I would like to see her check into a rehab program for at least 30 days. You can help by being there for her, listening, and encouraging her to stick with her treatment plan." Paul nodded slowly, trying to absorb everything he was hearing.

Paul took a deep breath and sighed. "Dani was diagnosed with bipolar disorder several years ago. I didn't know this about her until recently because she hid it from me. I was not familiar with this. She's always shown signs of ups and downs since I have been with her, but about six months ago, she finally confessed it to me," Paul explained.

"Does she take medication for this?" asked Dr. Bender.

"Yes, as far as I know. She's supposed to," Paul replied. "Sometimes she runs out, sometimes she forgets, and sometimes she's stubborn and doesn't want to take her medication."

Dr. Bender sighed, shaking his head. "People with Bipolar disorder cannot go off their medicine." So, from here she will be admitted to the Psychiatric Center across the street?" Dr. Bender explained.

"Yes, your nurse informed me of that right before you came in," Paul said showing deep frustration.

"How do you feel about that?" Dr. Bender asked.

Paul looked up at the ceiling wanting to think before he spoke. "How do I feel?" he repeated. Shaking his head in amazement, he looked at the doctor. "Can we step outside her room for a moment" Paul asked as he continued to talk? Once out of the room, Paul said,

"I am not sure I am capable of dealing with this." Paul continued slowly. "I have recently reached what I have been working for my whole life. This could not have happened at a worse time. And Dani knew this! How do you think I feel?" he asked sharply.

"I understand," said Dr. Bender. "I can make a referral for you as well for a therapy session with one of our counselors if you like."

Paul hesitated for a moment, with a thoughtful look on his face. "No!" Changing his tone to anger. "I am not the one who needs help here! Nor am I qualified to deal with this! This is her problem. I am tired of her trying to control me and holding me back from what I love doing. I am done! I am done trying to save her. I am done! She wants to kill herself. I am sorry, but I am not going to stay around and watch!"

Paul went back into the room, picked up his jacket from the chair's back, and said to the doctor and nurse, in a low but firm voice, "I know this seems cruel, but you have no idea what I have been through with this woman. I am not going to throw away any more of my life or the opportunity of a lifetime. I am done! She is yours to deal with!"

Dr. Bender tried to interrupt Paul, but Paul would not listen. He walked out of Dani's room and out the emergency room doors. He got into his car and drove off, feeling a mix of guilt and relief washing over him.

Back in the hospital, Dr. Bender and the nurse were surprised to see the reaction from Paul. "Please go ahead and make arrangements for Dani to be transferred to the Psychiatric Center across the street." Dr. Bender asked.

"Do you want her to stay sedated until after she gets over there?" Kristy asked.

"Yes, I think that would be the best thing for her right now," Dr. Bender replied. Kristy nodded and began packing up Dani's few belongings. She carefully placed Dani's clothing in a bag and then checked her purse for any information about a next of kin. As she opened the wallet, she found a picture of Dani and Paul together. They looked like a happy couple, Kristy thought sadly. Knowing Paul would not be around when Dani woke up, she felt a pang of empathy for her patient. "How is Dani going to deal with this?" she wondered. Finding no other useful information, Kristy placed the purse in the bag with Dani's clothing and put them on the chair by her bed. She checked the IV and monitors one last time before leaving the room, ensuring everything was in order.

At the nurse's station, Kristy called the Psychiatric Center. "This is Nurse Kristy from the emergency room. We need to prepare a room and arrange transport for a patient named Dani Gregory." The person on the other end confirmed the arrangements, and Kristy hung up, feeling a mixture of relief and concern. She hoped Dani would find the help she needed, despite the difficult road ahead.

Paul went back to the house he shared with Dani. Inside, the reminders of what Dani had done were left for him to clean up. He picked up the half-empty bottle of vodka and the prescription bottle with a few pills still in it, then walked to the kitchen. He poured the vodka into the sink, the smell of alcohol stinging his nose, and put the pills down the garbage disposal. Standing over the sink, he looked out the window, reminiscing about the good times they had shared. After a few moments, he sighed deeply, grabbed the empty vodka bottle, and threw it in the trash. Determined to move forward, Paul went to the bedroom and began gathering his clothing and belongings, tossing everything onto the bed. He grabbed a suitcase from the hall closet and started packing. In the bathroom, he pulled his toiletries out of the mirrored cabinet, glancing around for anything he might need. He grabbed his razor from the shower and threw everything into a travel pouch. While he packed, memories of Dani flooded his mind—her laugh, the way she looked at him with love in her eyes. He shook his head, trying to focus. This was not the life he had envisioned. Once his suitcase was packed, Paul stood in the bedroom, looking around one last time. The room felt empty, lacking the warmth it once had. He knew leaving was the right decision, but it did not make it any easier. With a final glance, he closed the suitcase, carried it out of the room knowing that would be the last of his memories of that room.

As he walked towards the living room, Paul stopped and grabbed a beer from the refrigerator. He twisted off the cap and took a long drink, the cold liquid momentarily soothing his nerves. He walked over to the couch and sank into it, feeling the weight of everything pressing down on him. For a few moments, he sat in silence, staring at the beer bottle in his hand. The house felt eerily quiet without Dani's presence. He took another sip, letting his mind wander realizing Dani wouldn't be coming home for a few days.

Paul realized he was jumping the gun, packing up and planning to leave right away as he still had a couple of days before he had to decide where he was going to go. He sighed, leaning back against the couch. His mind was a whirlwind of thoughts and emotions—anger, guilt, sadness, and a sense of relief all mixed together. He closed his eyes, trying to clear his head. He realized he needed to take a step back and think things through. Rushing to a decision would not help anyone, least of all himself. For now, he would take it one day at a time, figuring out his next steps as he went. "I should call John back," Paul thought. He pulled out his cell phone and dialed John's number.

"Hello, this is John."

"John, it's Paul."

"Hey Paul, how is Dani?" John asked.

"She's going to be alright, but she gave us a big scare," said Paul, his voice heavy with emotion.

"That is great to hear. I am sorry to hear that she did this," said John sympathetically.

"Yeah, well, me too," Paul replied, sighing. Paul hesitated for a moment before he began to rant. "John, I just cannot do this anymore. I know now might not be the best time to do this, but I don't know if there will ever be a good time. I am really done with this relationship. I need to move on. I have so much that I have worked for, and having Dani do this just shows me that she is not going to stop until she gets help. I just do not have it in me anymore to put my life on hold for her. I cannot do that anymore. Do you understand, John?"

John was silent for a moment while gathering his thoughts. "So, what are you saying? You are leaving her?" he asked.

"Yes," said Paul firmly. "I need a place to stay for a while. Can you spare the extra room in your house?

"Paul, you're always welcome at my house. I would do anything for you, you know that" said John.
"Thanks," said Paul, feeling a mixture of relief and sadness.

Paul and John had been friends since high school. John played bass in the band and wrote most of the lyrics for their songs while Paul was lead guitarist and lead singer. They had spent years trying to make a band that would someday hit it big. Paul reminisced about the countless nights they spent in John's garage, practicing until their fingers bled and their voices were hoarse. They went through years of trying to find the right drummer and keyboard player, as well as backup singers and managers. It never failed that when they thought they had the right team, something or someone would create chaos, causing them to regroup. If it were not a marriage of one of their band members, it was a death or a drug addict who could not stay clean. Paul remembered the time their previous drummer, Rick, got married and moved away, leaving them scrambling for a replacement before a show. And then there was the heartbreaking night they found out their keyboard player had overdosed. Despite all the setbacks, they were both extremely excited about the talent they had developed. They had a shared dream, and it had kept them going through all the difficulties. Neither one was willing to let it slip by without a fight.

8 - Untold Secrets

It was 10:45 a.m. when Jackie walked into the Psychiatric Center for her first appointment with the therapist. She felt very nervous, but you would never have known it by looking at her. She wore a tight-knit red sweater that exposed just enough of her oversized breasts to grab the attention she so desperately needed. Her black pants were silky and clung to her skin, accentuated by a thick black belt adorned with rhinestones and a large glittering buckle. She had open-toed 4-inch black sandals, revealing her freshly done pedicure. Her bleached blonde hair was long, layered, and tapered around her face, teased at the top for fullness

As she entered the reception area, the receptionist glanced up, momentarily caught off guard by Jackie's striking appearance. "Good morning," the receptionist said, regaining her professional composure. "You must be Jackie. Please have a seat. Dr. Gifford will be with you shortly."

Jackie nodded, offering a polite smile, and made her way to the waiting area. She could feel the eyes of others on her, exactly as she had intended. Settling into a plush chair, she crossed her legs, her foot bobbing slightly in nervous anticipation.

The minutes ticked by each one stretching her anxiety thinner. She took a deep breath, reminding herself of the necessity of this visit. Jackie's thoughts were a whirlpool of doubts and fears, but she maintained her poised exterior, knowing that appearing in control was half the battle.

"Jackie?" a soft, calm voice called out. Jackie looked up to see a nurse standing in the doorway, her expression welcoming.

"Yes, that's me," Jackie replied, standing up and smoothing her pants as she walked toward her.

"Come on back," the nurse said, gesturing toward the doctor's office.

Jackie followed her, her heels clicking softly against the polished floor. Dr. Gifford's office was decorated in soothing tones, with comfortable furniture and soft lighting that created a serene atmosphere. Jackie took a seat on the plush sofa, feeling a slight but comforting sense of calm washing over her as she read the certificates on the wall that were dated 30-plus years. "The doctor will be with you shortly," the nurse said as she walked out of the room.

There was a light knock on the door. "Hello, Jackie. I'm Dr. Gifford," she said with a kind smile as she walked in.

Jackie's nerves were still fluttering but slightly soothed by Dr. Gifford's gentle demeanor. She found herself drawn to the contrast between the doctor's old-fashioned appearance and the modern, inviting atmosphere of the office.

Dr. Gifford sat down opposite Jackie, opening a leather-bound notebook. "I understand this is your first session with us. How are you feeling today?" she asked, her tone inviting and patient.

Jackie hesitated for a moment, then responded, "A little nervous, but I'm here and ready to talk."

"That's perfectly normal," Dr. Gifford reassured her. "It's a big step to come here and open up about your feelings. I want you to know that this is a safe space where you can share anything that's on your mind."

Jackie nodded, taking a deep breath. "Thank you. I guess I'm here because I've been feeling really out of control lately, and it's affected my relationship with my husband and my life in general."

Dr. Gifford listened attentively; her expression thoughtful. "Can you tell me more about these feelings? When did they start, and how do they manifest in your daily life?"

Jackie began to recount her recent experiences, the moments when she felt overwhelmed by the need for attention, and how it often led her to act in ways she wasn't proud of. She spoke about her marriage to Richard, the lavish parties they hosted, and how she always felt the need to be the center of attention.

"Sometimes, I feel like I'm not even in control of myself," Jackie admitted, her voice tinged with frustration. "It's like I'm watching myself from the outside, doing things just to get noticed."

Dr. Gifford nodded understandingly. "It sounds like you're dealing with some deeply rooted issues that are manifesting as a need for attention. It's important to explore where these feelings are coming from and why they have such a strong hold on you.

Jackie looked down at her hands, her fingers nervously tapping against each other. "I don't know why I'm like this," she said softly. "I just know that it's hurting my marriage.

Gifford leaned forward slightly; her voice was gentle but firm. "The fact that you recognize this and are seeking help is a crucial first step. We will work together to uncover the underlying causes and develop strategies to help you manage these feelings in a healthier way."

For the rest of the session, Jackie and Dr. Gifford delved deeper into her past, discussing her childhood and significant events that may have contributed to her current struggles. Dr. Gifford's probing questions and insightful comments helped Jackie begin to see patterns and connections she hadn't noticed before. As the session ended, Dr. Gifford offered some parting advice.

"Jackie, I want you to take some time this week to reflect on what we've discussed. Keep a journal of your thoughts and feelings, especially during moments when you feel the strongest need for attention. This will help us in our future sessions. "Jackie nodded, feeling a mix of exhaustion and hope. "I will do that, thank you, Dr. Gifford.

"You're wecome, Jackie. I feel like we've made some pro gress today. I look forward to our next session," Dr. Gifford replied with a reassuring smile.

As Jackie left the office, she felt a sense of relief. For the first time in a long while, she felt that she was on a path to understanding herself and finding a way to control the chaos that had been dominating her life.

9 - Release Date

After six weeks in the hospital, Kathy was still in a lot of pain, and bruises were still visible; however, she was beginning to heal from the accident's wounds. Kathy felt ready to be checked out of the hospital and get back home to the life she had. Her leg was in a full cast, and unlike most patients, the nurses did not need to push her to walk around the hospital floors; she was eager to do it. Kathy was a "Make It Happen" kind of person, often referred to as a "Type-A personality." She always needed to be in control of her surroundings. At work, she was goal-oriented and a top achiever, sometimes misunderstood as pushy and abrasive.

The nurse who had been caring for her for most of her stay came into the room. "Good morning! I have good news for you Kathy. You get to go home today."

"That's Great!" said Kathy.

"Do you have someone who can pick you up?" asked the nurse.

"Yes, of course," said Kathy.

"Good, it will take about an hour to check you out, so if you can make arrangements, that will be great. In the meantime, the doctor will be making his rounds and will come to see you before you leave" said the nurse.

Kathy made a call to her best friend, Nancy, who lived a few houses down from her. She made the arrangements to be picked up just as Dr. Harris walked into her room. "I've got to go. See you when you get here," Kathy said as she hung up the phone.

"Good morning, Kathy, how are you feeling today?" asked Dr. Harris.

"I'm feeling good enough to go home," Kathy said, with a big smile on her face.

"Well, that is good to hear. I know the nurse is getting the process started. When you leave here, will you have someone at home to help you?" Dr. Harris asked.

"Oh sure, my neighbor and best friend will be at my beck and call," Kathy said with a chuckle.

Dr. Harris handed Kathy a list of papers with instructions and prescriptions to take home. "There are some things I want to discuss with you as well, and I hate to bring this up now," he continued after a pause. "You had an elevated blood alcohol level when you came in. Do you drink often?" he asked tenderly.

Kathy looked at him with disbelief. "Yes, I do drink. I have a couple of glasses of wine in the evening and sometimes more on the weekends."

Dr. Harris asked the dreadful question, "Do you remember drinking the night of your accident?"

Kathy lay in shock as she tried to remember thoughts of her evening before the accident. "I can't remember," she said with confusion.

"I believe the mix of alcohol and narcolepsy caused you to fall asleep at the wheel, leading to the accident," Dr. Harris said gently. Kathy's expression was one of shock and disbelief. Unable to say a word, she continued to listen.

"I am recommending you see a therapist," said Dr. Harris.

"A therapist?" Kathy asked, surprised. "Why do I need to see a therapist?"

"Two reasons," Dr. Harris replied. "First, it is likely that narcolepsy involves multiple factors interacting to cause neurological dysfunction and sleep disturbances. A psychotherapist can help identify underlying issues or conditions that may be affecting you. Second, if you have a drinking problem, we need to get you some help. Alcohol and narcolepsy do not work well together."

Kathy could not believe what she was hearing. "So, you're saying I am an alcoholic?" She stared off into the distance, cringing as she tried to deny the label in her mind.

"I am sorry, Kathy, but by law, it is mandated that I must report the blood alcohol level the night of your accident. Unfortunately, your driving privileges will be suspended by the state."

Kathy became furious. "What! That's ridiculous!" she shouted, her face cringing with anger and frustration. "How long do I have to wait to get it back?" she asked.

"I am not sure how that works, Kathy. The other thing is that you will have to attend group meetings with a therapist here at the hospital. I believe they are Monday, Wednesday and Friday nights. I truly am sorry," said Dr. Harris. He then handed another piece of paper to Kathy with the psychotherapist's name and phone number. "I need you to call and make an appointment with Dr. Sheila Gifford. She's been a doctor for three decades and is highly recommended by the board of psychiatry at Rossville Medical Center. She will do her own evaluation and assist you in going forward. It will be her call if and when you get your driver's license back. Do you have any questions?" he asked gently.

"No," Kathy cried, her voice breaking.

I will follow up with you by phone in a day to see how things are going at home," said Dr. Harris. With great compassion, he reached out, grabbed her hand, and squeezed it gently. He then proceeded to leave the room.

Kathy was still stunned when Nancy arrived to take her home. Nancy walked into the room, happy to see Kathy, only to find her in a state of disappointment and with tears in her eyes. Kathy explained what she had just gone through while Nancy looked on with disbelief.

The nurse came back in once again and handed Kathy a stack of papers. With a smile, she said, "I know you love this part." Kathy read the documents and signed them. When she was finished, she began to get out of bed and gather her belongings.

"You really should let us do that for you." said the nurse.

No, I need to be able to do it for myself once I get home. There's no reason not to start practicing now," Kathy replied with a half-smile.

An orderly showed up with a wheelchair to escort Kathy out.

"What is that for?" she asked with resistance.

"I will be giving you a ride down to your car," he said.

"I don't think so," replied Kathy.

Nancy spoke up, "Now, Kathy, you know they have to wheel your ass out of here as part of your exit procedure."

"Like hell they will! They made me get out of bed when I was sleeping, just to make me walk around the floors of this hospital so that I could build up my tolerance, and now they want to carry me out. No, I will be fine. You go help someone who really needs your help," she said sternly to the orderly.

The nurse could see that Kathy was going to be a challenge. "Kathy, hospital policy requires us to wheel our patients out. We realize and appreciate that you can walk, but if you could just cooperate, we will have you on your merry little way in no time."

Kathy fussed a bit but agreed and sat in the wheelchair.

"Damn, girl, if you're going to be that stubborn with me, once we get to your house, I'm just going to leave your ass to do everything on your own," Nancy chuckled.

As they got downstairs, Nancy had her car parked conveniently to make it easy to load Kathy and her belongings. When they reached Kathy's house, Kathy commented on how good her house looked. "I can't wait to get inside and sleep in my own bed," she said, a hint of relief in her voice.

"Now you wait here while I get your stuff and open the house," Nancy said sternly.

"Nonsense," said Kathy, as she began to open the car door and maneuver her way out.

"Damn, girl, you're stubborn," Nancy said, shaking her head.

Nancy took Kathy's belongings and walked up to the house. She opened the door and walked inside, turned on a couple of lights, and put a small suitcase down on the floor in the living room. As she turned to walk back outside to help Kathy, she noticed that Kathy was already out of the car, struggling with her crutches as she made her way into the house.

"Let me help you," said Nancy, rushing to help her.

Kathy sat down on the couch, exhausted from the effort.

"What can I do for you?" asked Nancy.

"I'll be fine," Kathy said, catching her breath. "Just check on me from time to time."

"What are you, crazy? I am not going to leave you here to fend for yourself in your condition," Nancy said. "At least let me get you comfortable and make you something to eat."

Nancy walked into the kitchen and looked around at the food supply. The refrigerator was empty, and the cupboards were bare.

"Looks like you could use a good supply of groceries. Let's get you comfortable, and I will run to the store and pick up a few items," said Nancy.

"No, I'll be fine, really," said Kathy. "I have an account to have my food delivered from the market around the corner. They will bring me anything I want. I just need my laptop if you would not mind getting it for me. I can also order prepared food too, just about anything I want."

"Are you sure?" asked Nancy.

"Yes, absolutely. I just need a spot on the couch with my laptop handy, my medication, a glass of water, my cell phone, and the remote control."

"I'll get you a blanket and a pillow as well," Nancy said eagerly.

"Okay, I'm just a few doors down, so you better call me if you need anything," Nancy said, while arranging the items for Kathy.

"I really appreciate everything you have done for me, Nancy. Really, if I need anything, I'll call you. I promise," Kathy said, giving Nancy a grateful smile. Nancy left, knowing that Kathy would be fine and trusting that she would call her if needed.

Kathy leaned back on the couch, looking around her familiar living room. Despite her pain, she felt a sense of comfort being back home. She opened her laptop, ready to regain a bit of control in her life, one small step at a time.

After several hours of resting on the sofa, Kathy became tired and ready for bed. She made her way into her long-awaited bedroom to sleep for the night. This is going to be interesting, she thought, as she mentally walked through all she had to do just to get into bed. Her friend Nancy had made some things easier for her, but she still had to maneuver to the bathroom to brush her teeth, figure out how to put on her pajamas, and position herself in bed. Somehow, she made it through the night.

When Kathy woke, she felt a mix of nervousness and frustration. She was happy to be home but uncomfortable knowing she had to attend a meeting with a bunch of people she considered crazy. She knew these were not people she would associate with by choice, and she was not in control of the situation. As the day progressed, it was all she could think about. Kathy was not one to wait until the last minute to decide what to do or how to do it. Her attitude was to just get it done. "I better figure out how I am going to get there, she thought. I better start looking for a ride. She picked up the phone and called Nancy. Nancy agreed to pick her up at 6:30 and take her to the meeting but would not be able to pick her up afterward due to another obligation. "Oh well, if I must, I'll grab a cab," she thought.

10 - Psychiatric Ward

Dani arrived at Roseville Psychiatric Center unconscious. The staff put her into her room and handed her chart to the head nurse. Shortly after her arrival, she began to wake up. She realized she was somewhere unfamiliar; she was in a hospital. Panic set in as she looked down and saw an IV attached to her arm. She sat up in her bed, finding herself restrained by the IV and other monitors.

"Hello?" she yelled, her voice trembling with panic. Her room was right next to the nurse's station, so all the nurses heard her. Nurse Bianca hurried in and introduced herself. "Hello, Dani. I'm Nurse Bianca. You are okay; calm down, you are in the hospital."

"What am I doing here?" Dani asked frantically.

"You were brought in unconscious, to our department" Nurse Bianca replied softly.

"What department?" Dani asked, frightened.

"Well, Dani, you were brought in as an overdose patient.

Dani did not respond immediately, her eyes darting back and forth as if trying to piece together what happened. Nurse Bianca continued, "The hospital did an amazing job taking care of you."

Still looking confused and panicked, Dani asked, "Where is Paul?"

"Who is Paul?" asked Nurse Bianca.

"Paul, my boyfriend," said Dani frantically.

"I'm not sure where Paul is right now, but I'm sure he will show up soon," Nurse Bianca said while charting in the computer.

"I need to call Paul," said Dani frantically.

"First things first, Dani. We need to get you better," Nurse Bianca assured her.

"NO! I need to talk to Paul, now! Please!" Dani shouted, tears welling up in her eyes.

The nurse had no choice but to ignore Dani's request. She continued to adjust the IV and tried to make Dani more comfortable by fluffing her pillows and adjusting the bed. "Excuse me for a moment," she asked. "I need to check on a few things, and I will be right back." She quickly left the room and went back to the nurse's station to call the assigned doctor.

"Dr. Gifford, you have a patient that just arrived from Rossville Medical Center," she said into the phone. "She just woke up, and she is a bit frantic."

"Thank you. I will be right there," said Dr. Gifford.

Nurse Bianca hung up and grabbed a glass of water on her way back to Dani's room. When she arrived, Dani was trying to pull out the IV from her arm.

"What are you doing?" shouted Nurse Bianca! "You cannot take that off. You need it right now."

Dani was very agitated, crying out, "Why don't you let me call Paul?"

Dr. Gifford walked into Dani's room. "What seems to be the problem here?" she asked calmly.

"She is trying to remove her IV and monitors, doctor," Nurse Bianca replied firmly.

Dani looked at the doctor with anger. "I do not want to be here. I want to talk to my boyfriend Paul," she yelled.

"Settle down now," said Dr. Gifford. "You are a sick lady, and we need to make you better."

"No, I am not sick!" screamed Dani. "I want out of here. Do you understand? Get me the fuck out of here!"

"Unfortunately, we cannot do that, Dani. But we do need you to calm down," Dr. Gifford said.

Dani yelled out again, "No! I don't want to calm down! I want out of here, and I want out now!" She began to scream and continued trying to remove the devices from her arm.

"Call for assistance," said Dr. Gifford to Nurse Bianca.

The nurse grabbed the phone and paged for an orderly to come to room 315 stat. Dani continued to scream and struggle against the hold of the doctor and nurse. Another nurse, passing by, checked into the room, and realized she needed a restraining device. She grabbed one from the hall closet and rushed back to the room. A male orderly came running to aid as well. The two nurses and Dr. Gifford held Dani down while the orderly placed the jacket on her, tying her arms down and securing her to the bed rails.

"Stop!" yelled Dani. "Why are you doing this to me? Stop! Somebody help me!" she screamed.

When they finished restraining Dani, the doctor ordered the nurse to give her a shot to calm her down. As things settled, the orderly asked if there was anything else needed.

"No, thank you. You may be excused," said Dr. Gifford.

Dani lay on the bed, her chest heaving, tears streaming down her face. The room seemed to close in around her as she struggled against the restraints, her mind and emotions slowly beginning to succumb to the sedative. Dr. Gifford watched the monitors as Dani's heart rate began to slow to a normal range, along with her blood pressure. Dani was now calm and ready to be talked to. "Good," said the doctor.

Dr. Gifford looked at Dani. She introduced herself and her position. "As your doctor, I want you to be comfortable and healthy. Unfortunately, I will have to keep the restraint on you until you are calm enough to be without it. Do you understand?"

With tear-filled eyes, Dani nodded gently. The doctor adjusted Dani's bed to a more upright position and pulled up a chair to talk to her. "Can you give us a minute?" she asked Nurse Bianca.

"Of course," said the nurse, leaving the room and closing the door behind her.

Dr. Gifford looked at Dani with a serious expression. "Dani, you have been through a lot. Your body has been through a lot. Do you remember taking pills and drinking alcohol?" she asked softly.

Dani looked at her like a little girl caught in trouble. Through her tears, Dani replied, "Yes."

"It appears as if you tried to take your own life, Dani," said the doctor gently.

Dani cried frantically, to the point of having to catch her breath. Dr. Gifford handed Dani a box of tissue to wipe her tears.

"I know this is hard to talk about, but we have to," said the doctor.

"I didn't mean to try and kill myself," said Dani. "I was lonely and depressed. My boyfriend was away, and I was feeling like I was losing him. I just wanted to go to sleep."

"No," said the doctor, shaking her head gently. "You do not just want to go to sleep with a whole bottle of prescription medication and a bottle of vodka. It is more than just wanting to go to sleep."

Dani began to cry hysterically again. "I don't want to live without Paul," she said through her tears.

Dr. Gifford knew of Dani. Diagnosed with bipolar disorder, she had been her patient a time or two over many years. Dani often went off her medication and skipped therapy sessions until she could no longer function. After hitting bottom, she was usually prompted to get help by desperate measures from her mother or someone else.

Dr. Gifford could see that Dani was beginning to tire as the medication took effect. "We are going to keep you here for a couple more days to watch over you, Dani," said Dr. Gifford. "I will have the nurses get you something to eat if you're hungry."

"That would be great," said Dani in a whisper.
The doctor reached over the bed and pressed the nurse button. "Nurses' station, how can I help you?" asked Nurse Bianca.

"Can you order some food for Dani? She is starting to get hungry," asked Dr. Gifford.

"Yes, certainly," said the nurse, hanging up the call. Dr. Gifford assured Dani that the food would come shortly and that everything was going to be okay. "I will be back later to check on you, Dani. Until then, try to stay calm and cooperate with the nurses. I cannot remove the restraints until I am sure you will not react the way you did before. Do you understand?" the doctor asked firmly.

"Yes," whispered Dani as she fought to keep her eyes opened. Gifford got up from the chair and left Dani's room. As she walked past the nurse's station, she told them she would be in her office if they needed her. Dani lay back, feeling the weight of her situation pressing down on her. The room was quiet, except for the hum of the medical equipment. She closed her eyes, trying to find peace amidst the turmoil.

11 - Group Therapy

Dr. Gifford sat at her desk, looking over her schedule for the week. She realized she would be taking on new clients in the group therapy sessions and needed to schedule one-on-one sessions with a couple of them. She began reading the file on Kathy Jones, whom she had not met yet but had a referral from her neurologist, Dr. Harris. "Ah, a calm one," she thought. Dealing with narcolepsy was nothing new for Dr. Gifford.

She picked up the phone and called her assistant. "Katie, can you please call Kathy Jones for a first appointment and confirm that she will be at the next group meeting here Monday night?"

"Yes, ma'am, I will do that right away," said Katie.

"Thank you," said Dr. Gifford. She put the file aside and began to look over Jackie Valentine's file. Since Jackie's visit, she knew it would take months of scheduling one-on-one sessions if Jackie followed through with the treatment. She had told Jackie to attend the group meetings for her own good. Though Jackie seemed motivated to change, the meetings would provide self-motivation and accountability. Dr. Gifford knew that patients with Histrionic Personality Disorder often struggled in group settings due to their desire to be the center of attention. Yet, she felt it was Jackie's best chance to get the help she needed, even if it only lasted a few sessions.

After reviewing the files, Dr. Gifford looked over the agenda for next Monday's group meeting. She kept the meeting format the same, although the attendees changed often. One constant attendee over the years was a sweet young lady named Tammy.

Tammy was a shy, soft-spoken woman in her mid-30s who still lived at home, where she had become the caregiver for her elderly parents. She was an only child raised by a demanding, manipulative, and jealous mother and a father who thought the world of her. She could do no wrong in her daddy's eyes.

Tammy had been diagnosed with Tourette's syndrome during her teens, a condition more common in males. Since Tammy struggled with shyness, finding Dr. Gifford, and attending the group sessions had provided Tammy with a safe place where she felt comfortable and accepted. Plus, it got her out of the house, away from her aging mother and father. Tammy always got there early, helping to set up chairs, making coffee, and setting out cookies for the meetings. Although she never spoke about herself or offered input, she was a reliable presence.

Dr. Gifford looked at the clock and realized it was getting late. She needed to make her rounds once more before leaving. When she arrived at Dani's room, she checked the medical chart on the computer to see any updates. The nurses had documented their checks and services, noting that Dani had slept most of the day. Dr. Gifford walked in and saw Dani sleeping. She gently whispered, "Dani, Dani," trying to awaken her.

Dani opened her eyes, disoriented, trying to make out where she was and who was speaking. "Hello, Dani," said Dr. Gifford. Dani squirmed, trying to adjust herself in bed with the restraints still on.

"How are you doing, Dani?" asked Dr. Gifford.

"I guess I'm doing okay," Dani whispered as she sat up a bit in the bed.

"Good," said Dr. Gifford. "Your body has been through a lot over the last 24 hours. I'm glad to see you're getting some rest."

"How long do I have to be here?" Dani asked, her voice filled with frustration.

"Today is day one so maybe two more days at the most," Dr. Gifford replied.

Dani closed her eyes in frustration and lay back as if trying to sleep.

"Dani, I must watch you until you are stable enough not to hurt yourself. When we believe a patient is at risk, we need to ensure their safety and arrange for longer-term therapy," said Dr. Gifford.

"Why can't I call my boyfriend?" asked Dani.

Dr. Gifford sighed, knowing this would be difficult. "He was here at the hospital when you arrived and stayed with you until the morning. Then he left once he knew you were safe. I did not meet him, but the nurse noted his presence in your file."

"Can I please get this harness off me?" Dani asked.

"Yes, but first I want to make sure you're not going to fight with the medical staff or try to escape," said Dr. Gifford.

"I have instructed the nurse that as you become more coherent and she feels it is safe, she can arrange to remove it. For now, I want you to continue resting with it on."

Dani took a deep breath and sighed.

"I will come to see you first thing in the morning," said Dr. Gifford as she turned to leave. "If the harness is not removed by then, we will reconsider based on your behavior overnight."

The next morning, Dr. Gifford arrived to make her rounds with her patients. She checked in with Nurse Bianca for an update. "Kathy Jones went home last night but confirmed she will be at the meeting at 6:00 on Monday night. Dani was irritable but tolerable, so I removed the harness with the supervision of an orderly. She is doing well and was sleeping when I last checked on her," reported Nurse Bianca.

"Great," said Dr. Gifford. "I'll go check on Dani and a couple of other patients, then I'll be available by cell phone."

Dani was sitting upright, eating breakfast, and watching the news when Dr. Gifford entered her room.

"Good morning, Dani," said Dr. Gifford. Are you doing alright"

Dani without a smile said, "Good morning." in a whisper.

"How are you feeling?" asked Dr. Gifford.

"I feel very rested," Dani replied without too much enthusiasm.

"That's good to hear," said Dr. Gifford. "My nurse tells me you did well enough to have the harness removed. I am pleased to hear that."

Dani barely smiled. "I just want to go home," she said softly.

"All in good time, Dani," replied Dr. Gifford.

Dr. Gifford knew she needed to find out if Paul was truly done with the relationship, and she needed to know who was the next of kin, or a friend that could be called.

"Can you excuse me for a moment, Dani? I will be back shortly." I need to make a phone call.

She pulled up Dani's file at the nurse's station and called the number listed as Dani's home. The phone rang several times before Paul answered. "Hello?" said Paul, his voice groggy.

"Is this Paul?" asked Dr. Gifford.

"Yes, who is this?"

"Paul, I am Dr. Gifford from Rossville Psychiatric Medical Center. I am working with Dani."

"Excuse me, I told the doctor at the emergency room that I'm done with her," Paul said, with frustration in his voice.

"Yes, I saw that note in her file, but it's been a few days, and I wanted to hear from you directly about your thoughts and feelings so I can help Dani through this crisis," said Dr. Gifford.

"Crisis?" Paul said, sounding irritated. "She created this crisis."

"I understand," said Dr. Gifford, keeping a calm tone. "I just need a few moments of your time to determine how to approach Dani about this. I need to find a support system for her as well."

"Just tell her I am sick and tired of her games, and I am moving on. I will be out of the house by the end of today, and she can have everything that is left. I am done with this relationship. I don't want to be bothered with her anymore," Paul said bluntly.

"I understand," said Dr. Gifford. "Can I ask you a few questions about Dani's health? I need to know who else might be a family or friend that we could contact."

"Sure," Paul said reluctantly. "Dani doesn't have friends," Paul muttered. "Her family is very dysfunctional as well. She has a sister, Patti, who lives about an hour away, but she does not stay in contact with her. I know they haven't gotten along in years. Her phone number is 555-823-8849."

"I know Dani a little from working with her in the past. Do you know if she has been taking her meds lately?" asked Dr. Gifford.

"No, she probably hasn't. That's one of the problems I have with her," Paul said angerly.

"Do you know when she last took her meds?" asked Dr. Gifford.

"No, I never know when she stopped taking her meds until she becomes intolerable, like now!" Paul said.

"Do you know why she stopped?" asked Dr. Gifford.

"She thinks she is fine without them, or she just forgets. I'm not sure. It's always something with her," Paul said, exasperated.

"Thank you for your honesty, Paul. I'll do my best to help Dani through this. If you think of anything else or need to discuss further, please do not hesitate to contact me," said Dr. Gifford.

"Sure, whatever," Paul replied. "I will not be around to watch what happens next. So please do not contact me again."

"Okay, but please let me ask you one more question. Have you and Dani broken up in the past?"

"Yes, said Paul. But what does that have to do with anything"?

"How long did that last?" asked Dr. Gifford.

Paul took a deep breath, frustration etched in his voice. "Look, Dr. Gifford, I know where you're going with this. I am absolutely done with this relationship. It's very dysfunctional. I do not love her anymore, and I have stayed with her because I was afraid she would do something stupid if I left. And she did, even though I stayed. This tells me that whether I'm with her or not, she's sick and needs help I cannot give her. Like I said earlier, I'll be out of our house by tonight. I'm not married to her, and I'm done. Do you have any further questions?"

"No," said Dr. Gifford, closing her notebook. "Thank you for your time."

"No problem. Please do not contact me in the future regarding her. I will not be available, and I am changing my phone number. Goodbye, Doctor."

Dr. Gifford sighed, knowing she had to return to Dani's room. She had to brace herself for the difficult conversation she was going to have with Dani. Dr. Gifford knew it was not going to be easy to break the news to Dani. She made notes of the conversation in Dani's file and then picked up the phone to call Dani's sister, Patti.

"Hello," said a pleasant voice on the other end.

"Hello, this is Dr. Gifford from Rossville Psychiatric Center. Is this Patti?"

"Yes, how may I help you?" Patti asked, her tone becoming reserved.

"Patti, I have your sister Dani here at the hospital," Dr. Gifford said not knowing what to expect the reaction to be on the other end.

"What did she do now, try to kill herself?" Patti asked with biting sarcasm.

"Well, as a matter of fact, she did," said Dr. Gifford.

"Damn," said Patti with a frustrated tone.

"I have a bit of a problem," said Dr. Gifford. "You are listed as her next of kin, and I was told by her ex-boyfriend, Paul that your parents are both deceased."

"Yes, that is true," said Patti. "What do you want from me?" she said defensively.

"Dani will have to stay in the hospital until Tuesday by law, but after that, she will be free to be released. Will you be able to come to the hospital and either visit her or at least be here when she gets released?" asked Dr. Gifford.

There was a long pause on the line, followed by a deep breath. "Dani and I are not on friendly terms," said Patti. "She has burned her bridges on quite a few occasions, and I have quite frankly disowned her."

"I understand," said Dr. Gifford. "Is there anyone else that you can think of who could be here for her?"

Patti paused, her voice changing to defensive. "We do have an aunt, but... ah shit, okay, I will come there on Tuesday, but I am warning you now, I may not be the best person for her, and things could get ugly."

"Great. When you get here, will you come and ask for me first? I can discuss a few things with you regarding Dani," asked Dr. Gifford.

"Yes, I will," replied Patti. "I will see you on Tuesday afternoon."

They both hung up the phone, feeling frustrated. Dr. Gifford had no choice but to be the one to tell Dani that her boyfriend was gone and that her sister would be there to pick her up on Tuesday. She walked back to Dani's room, knowing that Dani wanted to talk to Paul and could not.

As she entered the room, Dani asked her again, "Can I call Paul, please? I need to talk to him," she pleaded.

Dr. Gifford pulled up a chair next to Dani's bedside and sat down. "I have some news for you, and you're not going to be happy about it."

Dani sat up in bed. "There is no Paul anymore," Dr. Gifford said in a somber but caring way.

With a shocked look on her face, Dani said, "What are you talking about?" "What do you mean?" Dani said frantically, her face expressing horror.

"I am sorry, Dani. I just got off the phone with Paul a few minutes ago; he confirmed to me that he was moving out of your house as of tonight. He told me he was done with your relationship. There is no chance of him coming back," Dr. Gifford said slowly and compassionately.

Dani began to cry hysterically. "No, that isn't true," she cried. "He loves me, and he wouldn't leave me" she shouted.

Dr. Gifford looked at Dani with deep compassion. "Yes, dear, unfortunately, it is," Dr. Gifford said, reaching over to the table to grab a box of tissues and placing it on Dani's bed.

"I don't believe this," shouted Dani frantically. "What am I going to do? I need to go home before he leaves me. I have to get out of here! Please, doctor, I need to go home."

Dr. Gifford knew there was no way she could let Dani leave. It had not been 72 hours since her arrival at the emergency room. She also knew that this type of trauma could cause a relapse, and that Dani could be in grave danger.

"No, Dani, unfortunately, you cannot leave," said Dr. Gifford firmly but softly.

Dani began to get agitated, throwing the box of tissues across the room and looking for other items to throw.

"Dani, calm down. I know you are upset, but you need to get a hold of yourself," said Dr. Gifford.

Dani continued to cry hysterically and denied what Dr. Gifford was telling her. "No, no, this can't be true," Dani said while crying. She lay back in her bed, tucked her body into a fetal position, and sobbed hysterically. Dr. Gifford rubbed her back to comfort her. She knew that relationship breakups were not easy for anyone, sick or healthy.

Nurse Bianca walked into the room. She looked at the doctor and asked in a whisper, "Is everything okay?"

Dr. Gifford shook her head no. Nurse Bianca made a sympathetic facial gesture. She looked at the monitors that Dani still had attached to her. Everything looked okay, so she left the room.

Dr. Gifford comforted Dani for a while, staying by her side and consoling her. Eventually, Dani cried herself to sleep.

Dr. Gifford left the room and went over to the nurse's station to find Nurse Bianca sitting in a chair. Nurse Bianca looked up at the doctor and asked, "What happened?"

Dr. Gifford explained to Nurse Bianca what she had just gone through with Dani. Nurse Bianca shook her head in disbelief.

"You will have to watch her closely tonight. She may be traumatized and try to do something crazy. She may try to escape, or she may even try to hurt herself again," said Dr. Gifford. "You have my number in case things get crazy."

"Yes," said Nurse Bianca.

"Just try to keep her calm, and if you must sedate her, go ahead with the amount you used before or, in the worst case, put the restraint back on."

"Yes, Doctor," said Nurse Bianca.

Dr. Gifford left the nurse's station and went to make her rounds with other patients.

Nurse Bianca and the rest of the staff remained vigilant, keeping a close eye on Dani throughout the rest of the evening. When the staff checked on her, Dani stirred a few times during the night, but each time, she settled back into sleep.

Monday morning, Dr. Gifford returned to the hospital for her rounds. It was going to be a long day, with her usual schedule and group therapy session. After 25 years on this schedule, it was routine for her. Upon stopping at the nurse's station, she was pleased to hear they did not need to put a harness on Dani. She went to Dani's room first, "Good morning, Dani," said Dr. Gifford, entering the room.

Dani looked up and gave her a weak smile. "Good morning, Doctor Gifford."

"It looks like you are doing well. How are you feeling?" asked Dr. Gifford.

"I'm very heartbroken, but I'm trying to survive," said Dani with a soft-spoken voice.

"That's a great attitude, Dani," Dr. Gifford replied with a reassuring smile. "We'll get through this together." "I would like you to attend a meeting with me this evening here at the clinic. There will be about 10 to 15 people I would like to introduce you to." Dani nodded yes.

"Great," said Dr. Gifford. "I'll have one of the nurses escort you down to my office around 6:45." As Dr. Gifford left Dani's room, she felt a sense of cautious optimism. She knew that while the road to recovery would be challenging, Dani had taken a crucial step by agreeing to take part in the group meeting.

12 - Deception

Jackie, on the other hand, was eager to get out of the hotel and do something livelier than she had in the last couple of days. She put on a velour jogging suit with a sparkling sports bra underneath the jacket. She pulled her hair up into a ponytail and put on her clean white tennis shoes. As she applied her makeup, she looked in the mirror and thought the zipper of her jacket was too high. She pulled the zipper down, adjusting her breasts to expose her cleavage. She fluffed her hair in the ponytail to make it look a little messy. She smiled at herself in the mirror, then blew herself a kiss as she walked out of the bathroom.

Feeling a rush of excitement, Jackie grabbed her phone and purse, ready to embrace the day. She exited the hotel room with a confident stride, the sparkles on her sports bra catching the light with each step. She headed down the hall, her thoughts buzzing with anticipation about what the day might bring.

As she made her way to the lobby, she noticed several heads turning to watch her pass. Jackie reveled in the attention, her smile growing wider with each glance. The hotel staff greeted her politely, but she barely noticed, as she was focused on herself and the attention she was getting.

To keep things simple, she decided to start her day with a visit to the trendy café in the hotel. She had read reviews about the food; however, it was also known for its vibrant atmosphere and excellent people-watching opportunities.

The café was bustling with patrons when she arrived. She pushed open the door, immediately drawing the eyes of several customers. Jackie walked confidently to the counter, her presence commanding attention. She ordered a cappuccino and a croissant, her bright demeanor winning over the barista, who couldn't help but smile back.

With her coffee and pastry in hand, Jackie found a seat at a breakfast bar, by the window. She took a sip of her cappuccino, savoring the rich, creamy flavor, and glanced around the café, enjoying the lively ambiance. People were chatting, laughing, and typing away on their laptops, and she felt a thrilling sense of being part of the city's vibrant pulse.

Jackie noticed a booth near her with a group of young women getting ready to leave. They had been laughing and carrying on since Jackie came in. Jackie couldn't help but notice their admiring glances from time to time. She smiled to herself, wishing she could be part of a group of women enjoying time together.

One of the women, a redhead with a friendly face, caught Jackie's eye and smiled. As she got out of the booth, she said to Jackie, "Nice outfit," her tone warm and genuine.

"Thank you," Jackie replied, her smile widening. "I love your hair." They exchanged a few pleasantries, and before long, Jackie found herself included in their conversation.

The women were locals, full of recommendations for things to do and places to see. Jackie listened eagerly, her excitement growing with each suggestion. Jackie thought maybe they would invite her to join them, but the women left the café, leaving Jackie to go about her day by herself.

As she nibbled on her croissant, Jackie's mind wandered. She thought about the therapeutic session she had with Dr. Gifford and how it had felt to finally start addressing her issues. She wanted so badly to call Richard and let him know about her meeting and the feelings she was experiencing.

She got her cell phone out of her purse and dialed Richard's number. After four rings, voicemail picked up. "Hello, baby, it's Jackie. I want to let you know that I miss you, and I have been working on improving myself. I saw a doctor, and I am... well if you want, call me. I want to tell you some exciting news. I love you. Please call me. Please." Jackie hung up the phone and reminisced about the life she had with Richard.

Jackie was about to put her phone back in her purse and prepare to leave when she noticed two men sitting at the booth the young ladies had occupied.

As they made eye contact with her, they smiled. Jackie returned the smile as she always did, her charm effortlessly drawing people in. One of the men, a tall, well-dressed gentleman with an easy grin, asked, "How is the food?"

Jackie smiled and said, "It seems to be pretty good, especially since I've been trapped alone in my hotel room with room service for a couple of days." She was using her usual learned skill to lure them in, her voice light and inviting.

The man's eyebrows raised in surprise. "How could a beautiful woman like you get trapped in a hotel room all alone?" he asked, a note of genuine curiosity in his voice.

Jackie leaned back slightly, feigning a mix of exasperation and amusement. "Business meetings," she said with a dramatic sigh. "Sometimes they just never end, and all you get is a room service menu and a lonely evening."

The men laughed, and the one who had asked the question shook his head sympathetically. "That's a shame. No one should have to endure that, especially not someone as charming as you."

Jackie's eyes sparkled with mischief. "Well, I'm free now and looking for a bit of fun. Do you know of any good places around here?"

"We're actually from out of town as well. We need to go to a job site that we designed and make sure things are going as planned."

"Oh, so you're architects?" asked Jackie.

"Yes," said Jack. "We are architects and contractors."

"Afterward, we thought of heading to a place we were told about called The Blue Lounge. It's a few blocks away. Fantastic atmosphere, good drinks. You should join us."

Jackie tilted her head, considering the offer with a playful smile. "I do have to catch a plane later," she said.

Jackie pretended to mull it over for a moment, then nodded. "Why not? I could use a drink later." She stood up, gathering her purse, and walked over to their booth.

"My name is Jackie, by the way. And yours?" she asked.

The men introduced themselves as Jack and Bob. While shaking their hands, Jackie noticed both men were wearing wedding rings. "You both have wedding rings on. How long have you been married?"

Bob and Jack looked at each other. "I've been married for 15 years," said Jack.

Jackie looked at Bob. "And you?" she asked.

"I have been married for a couple of years," said Bob.

"How about you?" Bob asked, looking at the ring she was wearing.

Jackie smiled. After a moment's delay, Jackie said, "My husband passed away about two years ago." She looked at Bob in the eyes and said sadly, "I miss him so much." She began to speak in a soft, lower tone, as if saddened by the loss of her husband. Both men expressed their condolences. Jackie wrote down her cell number and handed it to Bob, whom she found to be more of a player than Jack. "I better get going," said Jackie. The men turned and watched her walk away from the table, then looked back at each other with amused grins.

13 - Recovery Begins

Dani was feeling a little restless. She phoned the nurse's station and asked if she could take a shower. Nurse Bianca was with another patient, so one of the other nurses said, "I'll be right there to assist you."

Dani began to get out of her bed and stand beside it. The nurse walked in and said, "Boy, you must really want to shower."

Dani replied, "Do I have to keep these monitors on while I take a shower?"

"No, we can remove the monitors. I'll unhook the IV as well," said the nurse.

This was Dani's first shower since she had been in the hospital. Her body froze as she enjoyed the warm water hitting her head and running down her back.

"The soap is in that dispenser on the wall," said the nurse as she handed her shampoo and conditioner for her hair.

"Ah," said Dani. "I am never coming out of here."

The nurse chuckled. "Sooner or later, all the hot water will be gone. Do you like cold showers too?"

After the shower, Dani asked the nurse if she could get dressed in her clothes since she would be going to a meeting with Dr. Gifford later.

"Sure," said the nurse. "Do you have clothes here?"

"Only the clothes that I came to the hospital in," said Dani.

The nurse went to the closet to see if someone had put Dani's clothes in it. Nothing was there. She checked the drawers. Nothing.

"I'm sorry, Dani; I don't know what happened to your clothes."

Dani began to softly cry, knowing she had to put a hospital gown back on. This nurse was not familiar with Dani and what she had been through. She didn't know that Paul, her boyfriend had left her at the hospital, never to return.

"I am sorry, Dani," said the nurse.

Dani lay down on the bed and buried her face in her pillow.

"Let's get you comfortable again," said the nurse.

Dani rolled over and put her feet under the blankets while the nurse pulled the IV rack closer to Dani's bed and hooked Dani back up to the monitors.

"I will be at the nurse's station seeing if I can figure out what could have happened to your cloths. If you need anything, just call," said the nurse as she left the room.

When she got back to the nurse's station, Nurse Bianca was sitting down, charting one of her other patients.

"How was Dani?" she asked.

The nurse told her what happened, and Nurse Bianca immediately got up to go check on Dani. As she walked into Dani's room, she could hear her crying.

"Dani, are you okay? The other nurse told me what happened with your clothes."

Dani sat up and looked at Nurse Bianca. "I don't have any clothes here," cried Dani. "I don't even know how I'm going to get some to go home in."

"Don't worry, Dani," said Nurse Bianca. "We have plenty of gowns and robes you can wear until someone brings something for you."

"But I am supposed to go to a meeting with Dr. Gifford at 7:00," said Dani. "There will be other people there, and I don't want to have to go in hospital clothing."

Nurse Bianca walked over to where Dani lay on her bed. "Dani, as long as you're a patient here, technically you should be wearing the hospital gowns. Do you know the meeting is held here at this facility? Most of the people who attend these meetings were once patients here. They, too, have gone to group therapy in their hospital clothing. It is no big deal, and you won't be the first to do it."

Dani looked at Nurse Bianca with eyes filled with tears and a sad, childlike frown. "Dani, the most important thing is that you attend the meeting. No one will care what you wear. They won't even remember that you wore a hospital gown," said Nurse Bianca. Dani seemed to get some relief from Nurse Bianca's words. She took a deep breath and wiped her eyes.

"I will be fine," she told Nurse Bianca.

"Good, that-a-girl," said Nurse Bianca. She looked at Dani for a few seconds and asked her if she wanted fresh water or anything. Dani shook her head no."

"Okay, call me if you need me," Nurse Bianca said as she turned and walked out of the room

14 - Double Dipping

Jackie had spent the day shopping alone, which was something she was used to. When she got back to her hotel room, she pulled her new items out of the bags. She went to the mirror and held up her new dress on her shoulders. She smiled and took it to the closet to hang.

Jackie knew it was time to start getting ready for the evening. She removed her clothing and went into the bathroom to shower. She was feeling a little aroused, not knowing what to expect from the evening. As she showered, she thought about how both men from the morning were interested in her, but she figured she would have more of a chance with Bob than with Jack. Bob seemed to have a hint of flirtation, while Jack seemed to be a family man, proud to be married for so long. The thrill of the challenge of Jack became her focus as she lathered her body with a soap-filled sponge.

While she was in the shower, she could hear her phone ring in the other room. She knew she would never reach the phone in time, so she did not make any attempt to try and answer it. When she finished her shower, she rinsed off, grabbed a towel, and began to dry off her body. She wrapped another towel around her hair.

There was a knock on the door, so she wrapped the towel around her body and went to the door, thinking it was Michael coming back.

As she looked through the peephole, she saw it was Jack, of all people. She quickly opened the door and said, "Jack, you're early! Come in." She ushered him in. "I am sorry that you caught me like this. I thought you would be here at 3:30 with Bob."

It was just a few minutes after 3:00. "Yes, I got off a little earlier than I expected, and I wasn't sure what to do with my time, so I headed here. I hope that's okay," he said, clearly out of his comfort zone.

"Oh, yes, of course," said Jackie, unashamed of her nakedness. "Where is Bob?" she asked.

"He got held up at the site and won't be off for another one or two hours. He told me to go on without him, and he'll catch up when he can."

"Oh, okay then, would you care for something to drink?" she asked. "I have beer and wine in this little fridge.

"Yes, sure, I'll have beer?" Jack said, as he watched her get it. "Great, let me grab one for you." She felt excited that Jack was there by himself. Though she was just wrapped in towels, she didn't seem to be modest about it. In fact, it turned her on.

As she handed Jack the beer, she asked him to sit down at the table. He agreed and sat in the same chair that Michael had sat in. She stood over him and asked if he liked drinking from a glass. Nervously, he said, "No, the bottle is fine." She pulled up a chair and placed it right in front of him. Still standing, she asked, "So, do you feel a little nervous being alone in a hotel with a strange naked woman, wrapped in a towel, in a strange town?"

Jack got a little embarrassed. "No, should I be?" he asked, obviously nervous.

She looked at him with a very sexy stare and said, "Yes," as she pulled the towel off her naked body and laughed.

Jack's eyes lit up with excitement, but he was also scared of what was happening.

Jackie reached out and softly touched the side of his face. "I am so lonely," she told him. She reached down and started to unbutton his shirt as she stared into his eyes. He grabbed her hand and looked at her intensely, not sure where he wanted this to go. He pulled her close to him and began to kiss and caress her body. She had him exactly where she wanted him. Jack fell into her trap, just as she had planned.

Jackie got dressed while Jack pulled himself together, fixing his hair and straightening his clothing. When she was ready to go, he looked at her in amazement at her beauty. "I have just had the most beautiful woman," he thought. "You look absolutely fantastic, Jackie," he said.

"Thank you, Jack," she replied, giving him a playful smile. He looked at her seriously, with a hint of fear in his eyes, and asked, "Can we keep this between you and me?"

She looked at him with a devious smile. "Of course, Jack. I never kiss and tell."

They arrived at the restaurant where they were to meet up with Bob. Bob hadn't arrived yet, so they decided to sit and have cocktails in the lounge until he got there. They both had martinis and talked as if nothing had happened between them. Finally, Bob showed up and sat with them long enough to catch up on the martinis. Bob had been interested in Jackie since the first time he saw her. Now that she was dressed for the evening, he couldn't take his eyes off her. Jackie noticed and played up to it. As they got up from the lounge and went to be seated in the restaurant, Jackie made sure she was noticed by everyone.

The host seated them at a booth with Jackie in the middle so she could communicate with both men. Bob flirted with Jackie throughout the evening, unaware of Jack's interest in her. The more they drank, the more Bob and Jackie laughed and carried on, leaving Jack feeling left out and uncomfortable. After dinner, Jack excused himself and went to the bathroom to collect his thoughts. When Jack returned, Bob was all over Jackie in the booth. She was clearly enjoying the attention. He cleared his throat as he returned to the table. Bob and Jackie looked up and started laughing. By this time, they all had a bit too much to drink.

"What time's your flight, Jackie?" asked Jack.

Jackie looked surprised. "What flight?" she laughed loudly. "I've decided to stay another day," she said, still giggling. She glanced at her watch. "Oops," she said. "I'm supposed to be somewhere." She scooted towards Bob to slide out from the booth.

"Where do you think you're going?" asked Bob.

"I'll be right back," she said, stumbling towards the restrooms.

Jack leaned in towards Bob. "Aren't you getting a little too close with Jackie?" he asked.

"Oh, I'm just having a little fun. What's wrong with that?" asked Bob. "She's pretty damn hot."

"Very true, even I have a hard time not wanting to hit on her," Jack admitted.

Bob laughed. "Yeah, right. You of all people? That'll be the day." Bob continued to laugh, and Jack reluctantly joined in as Jackie stumbled back from the restroom.

"Hey guys, I'd really like to stay, but I have to get going."

"Do you need a ride back to your room?" asked Jack.

"No, I've got a cab waiting outside," said Jackie.

"Wow, you're quick," said Bob.

Jackie leaned over to kiss Bob goodbye, almost falling over in the process. She pushed herself back up and went to Jack's side. She reached out to give him a hug, but he grabbed her and sat her on his lap. "You're not going anywhere baby," he said with a drunken laugh.

Jackie let out a loud "Woo Hoo! You want some more action?"

Bob looked at them with surprise. "More action?" he asked. "Do you guys have something going on that you didn't tell me?" Jackie laughed. "Wouldn't you like to know." She kissed Jack on the side of his face and embraced him. She stood up and said, "Really, you all are a lot of fun. Thank you for everything, but I really have to go." She left the two men, knowing she would never see them again.

15 - The Meeting

Meanwhile, Kathy spent her day preoccupied with thoughts about the meeting later in the evening. Despite her reservations, she resolved to attend.

At 6:30, Nancy arrived to pick her up. "Thanks for the ride, Nancy," said Kathy as she got into the car. "I'll just grab a cab or Uber back home when it's over."

"No problem, Kathy. Just let me know how it goes," Nancy replied with a supportive smile.

"I will," said Kathy, feeling a bit more at ease. They arrived at the clinic 15 minutes before 7:00. Kathy took a deep breath and stepped out of the car. Waving goodbye to Nancy, she said, "Wish me luck." Both women chuckled.

She walked into the clinic and made her way to Dr. Gifford's office, feeling the weight of her anxiety with each step.

When she entered the office, Dr. Gifford greeted her warmly. "You must be Kathy," she said, reaching out to shake her hand.

"Yes, I am," Kathy replied confidently, shaking Dr. Gifford's hand. "Very nice to meet you."

"How is your leg doing?" Dr. Gifford asked, glancing at Kathy's cast.

"It's healing slowly, but I'm managing," Kathy said.

"That's good to hear," Dr. Gifford said with a reassuring smile. "I'm just waiting for another patient of mine to arrive, then we will head down to the meeting."

Kathy nodded, feeling a bit more at ease. She took a seat, looking around the office and trying to calm her nerves. The room was filled with soft lighting and calming colors, designed to make patients feel comfortable.

A few moments later, the door opened, and another woman walked in, chaperoned by a nurse. Dr. Gifford stood up to greet her. "Ah, Dani, you're here. Come in and meet Kathy."

Dani was a bit embarrassed by her clothing. "I am sorry for my attire," she said as she spoke to Kathy. "Somehow my clothes came up missing."

"No worries," replied Kathy. "At least you're not dragging around 10 lbs. of cast and carrying crutches," she chuckled.

As they walked to the meeting room, both ladies were quiet and barely spoke a word to each other.

The meeting room was set up in a circle of chairs, creating an intimate and welcoming environment. Most of the participants were seated already, chatting quietly among themselves. Dr. Gifford gestured for Kathy and Dani to take their seats, then took her place at the front of the group.

A young lady came from the back of the room, introduced herself as Tammy, and sat down in a chair next to the two ladies.

"Welcome, everyone," Dr. Gifford began. "I'm glad you all could make it. Tonight, we have two new patients joining us,

Kathy and Dani. Would you ladies like to introduce yourselves and tell us a little about you?"

Dani stood up, looking at Kathy. Unsure who should go first, Kathy spoke up. "Hello, I'm Kathy. Sorry, I cannot stand up." Dani introduced herself as well, apologizing for the way she was dressed. She quickly sat back down; her face flushed with embarrassment. "Thank you, Kathy and Dani."

Dr. Gifford asked one of the regular members to introduce themselves and read the rules of the meeting to the rest of the group. A scruffy-looking man volunteered as he picked up the laminated rules flyer.

"Hello, my name is David," he said, beginning to read the rules of the meeting. "Welcome to our group session. We ask that you feel free to share your thoughts and experiences as you feel comfortable. However, we ask that there is no crosstalk during the session, and we ask that there are no negative comments made towards anyone or anything said. Each week, we meet here three times: Monday, Wednesday, and Friday nights, starting sharply at 7:00 p.m. and ending at 8:30 sharp. If you can't make it to a meeting, please make sure to call Dr. Gifford's office prior to 4:00 p.m. to explain why you will not be attending. Thank you."

David returned to his chair and sat down while the attendees clapped for him. Dr. Gifford said, "Thank you, David," as she shuffled through her papers.

"Okay, as we begin today, is there anyone experiencing something they would like to share?" The room fell silent as Dr. Gifford scanned the circle, looking into the eyes of each person to see if anyone would speak up. A man sitting across from Kathy squirmed in his chair as Dr. Gifford's gaze met his.

"Blake is there something you would like to talk about?" she asked curiously.

Blake stumbled over his words. "Uh, well, it's not that big of a deal, uh, but uh, I haven't been doing so well," he said.

"What do you mean by that, Blake?" Dr. Gifford prompted gently.

Blake, a long-term patient plagued with schizophrenia, began to share with the group, "My dog Buddy died, and I am having a hard time dealing with it." The room was quiet as they listened to his sad story until a loud noise from the hallway interrupted him.

Dr. Gifford was annoyed by the noise. She turned towards the door to see what the ruckus was. She saw a woman peeking through the small glass window of the door. The woman then opened the door and peeked in, realizing everyone was looking at her.

"Oh, hi, is this where the meeting is with Dr. Gifford?" she asked loudly, not caring if she interrupted anything important. "I'm trying to find Dr. Gifford's meeting," she repeated.

Dr. Gifford stood up. "Yes, this is where you need to be Jackie."

"Oh, hi, Dr. Gifford. I thought I would never find it," the woman continued loudly as she walked in. "I have been walking all over this place trying to find this meeting! Finally!" she said loudly.

"Come in and have a seat." Dr. Gifford introduced Jackie as she came closer to the group.

"I'm so glad I found this place. I was ready to give up and go home," Jackie said, rifling through her purse obnoxiously as if looking for something important.

Tammy got up from her seat, went to the closet where they kept the folding chairs, and grabbed one for Jackie. She placed it in the circle as Dr. Gifford said, "Thank you, Tammy."

"Oh, thank you," said Jackie. As she looked around the room at the people in the group, she loudly said hello to a couple of people who made eye contact with her.

Dani watched Jackie intently, showing a mix of curiosity and apprehension with her facial expressions. Jackie's confident demeanor was both intriguing and intimidating. Kathy, on the other hand, showed she was annoyed by the rude, self-centered behavior.

Dr. Gifford resumed the session. "Blake, you were sharing something important. Would you like to continue?"

Blake nodded, though he seemed a bit shaken by the interruption. "As I was saying, I've been struggling since my dog Buddy died. He was my best friend, and now I feel lost without him."

The room was silent, allowing Blake the space to express his grief. Dani glanced at Jackie, who seemed to be settling into her seat, her initial loudness replaced by a thoughtful expression.

Jackie looked around the circle, taking in the faces of the group. She felt a pang of vulnerability, realizing she was among strangers who might soon know her deepest secrets. Yet, she also felt a strange sense of belonging, hoping that maybe, just maybe, this group could help her find some peace.

Dr. Gifford offered Blake a sympathetic nod. "Thank you for sharing, Blake. Losing a pet can be incredibly difficult. We are very sorry for your loss of Buddy. We're here for you."

"We were just listening to Blake talk about dealing with losing his dog," said Dr. Gifford. She pointed at Blake as she explained so that Jackie would know who she was talking about.

"You lost your dog? Oh, I am so sorry to hear about that," said Jackie. "I had a dog, Truffle, but he stayed with my husband," Jackie continued. "I am hoping that I can see him again soon."

Dr. Gifford interjected, "Jackie, we try to listen and be here for each other without cross talk.

Jackie's smile fell, and she shifted uncomfortably in her seat. "Oh, I'm sorry. I get it," she muttered.

"Please continue, Blake," said Dr. Gifford.

Blake rubbed his hands together nervously before speaking again. "I feel so lost without my dog. He has always been with me during my good times and bad. I feel I have lost my best friend."

"And you probably did," Dr. Gifford replied softly. "Our dogs have a way of filling the voids in our lives and giving us a way to feel needed and loved."

"Maybe you can get a new dog from the pound," Jackie suggested.

Dr. Gifford looked at Jackie sternly. "That might be one answer, but the reality is that we first need to deal with the loss. We can't just get another dog to replace the one we had. It's like losing a family member."

Dr. Gifford took a deep breath before asking, "Is there anyone else struggling with something?" Again, no one replied.

"Well, I am," said Jackie.

Dr. Gifford hesitated before asking, "What are you struggling with?"

"I am trying hard to do the right thing, but my actions overcome logic," Jackie said.

Dr. Gifford was relieved that Jackie worded her challenge in a way that didn't disclose her true problem. But then Jackie continued, "I have been with other men since leaving my husband a week ago. I met two guys today, as a matter of fact."

Dr. Gifford interrupted, "Jackie, when we ask if anyone is struggling, we mean things that are group therapy appropriate. Some issues are better discussed one-on-one in my office, and it sounds like this is something for your next session with me."

Jackie looked a little surprised but agreed. Kathy and Dani exchanged glances, Kathy rolling her eyes. Kathy whispered to Dani, "I think we have a live one here."

Dr. Gifford sternly reminded the group, "No cross talk, please."

As the meeting continued, a few more people shared their experiences. Dr. Gifford offered advice on handling different situations. When the meeting ended, Dr. Gifford reminded everyone of their appointments during the week. "Feel free to stick around and socialize with each other for a few moments. We have coffee, juice, and cookies at the back of the room."

Kathy realized her cell phone died, so she wasn't able to pull up the Uber app. She asked Dr. Gifford if there was a phone she could use to call a cab. Overhearing this, Jackie asked, "What area do you live in?"

Thinking Jackie might offer a ride, Kathy replied, "I live in Midtown."

Jackie's hotel was on the way, so she asked, "Do you mind if I share a taxi with you?"

Kathy hesitated, not caring for Jackie's personality. "That is a great idea," said Dr. Gifford. Kathy, not wanting to be rude, agreed reluctantly.

"Sure, I guess that would be fine," Kathy said with a forced smile.

"Great!" Jackie replied, her tone cheerful.

Jackie walked over to the table where the cookies were while Kathy used the phone to call for a cab. A couple of people were socializing and eating cookies, including Dani.

Jackie extended her hand and introduced herself to Dani. "So, why are you here?" asked Jackie. Dani didn't know how to answer the blunt question and felt annoyed.

Tammy approached the two women, sensing the tension. "Hi, I'm Tammy," she said, shaking Jackie's hand. Tammy's arrival provided Dani with a chance to slip away so she could say goodbye to Dr. Gifford.

Seeing that Dr. Gifford was busy, Dani decided to leave quietly.

"Excuse me just a moment," said Dr. Gifford. "Dani, I need to escort you back to your room. Do you mind waiting a few more minutes until the room clears?"

Dani walked back to the circle of chairs and sat in one of them. When Kathy finished using the phone, she looked around for Jackie. Seeing her across the room, Kathy decided to sit next to Dani.

"My taxi should be here soon," Kathy said. "Yeah, I guess I have to wait for Dr. Gifford to take me back to my room," Dani replied. "Would you mind telling Jackie that the cab will be here shortly?" asked Kathy. "Not at all," said Dani.

Dani walked up to Jackie, who was still talking to Tammy. "Jackie, the cab will be downstairs any moment." "Oh, thank you," Jackie replied, turning back to her conversation with Tammy.

Kathy knew she was in for a journey home, sharing a cab with this woman.

As people left the room, Dr. Gifford saw that Kathy was sitting by herself. She walked over and discussed the meeting and what to expect at future ones.

Jackie saw Dr. Gifford with Kathy and walked over to the two women. "I hear you got a hold of a cab?" Jackie interrupted rudely. Both women looked at Jackie, surprised by her lack of manners.

Kathy decided to keep her cool. "Yes, he should be waiting for us downstairs," she said. "Oh good," said Jackie. "Let's not keep him waiting, shall we?" She turned and walked out of the room, not bothering to see if Kathy needed any help.

Kathy was about to unleash her frustration, but Dr.

Gifford intervened. "It is getting late, and I must be going too. Dani has been patiently waiting for me to escort her back to her room." Kathy grabbed her crutches to help her stand up. "I will see you Wednesday, if not before," she said to Dr. Gifford.

When Kathy got downstairs to the cab, Jackie was already sitting on the passenger side, which was the closest to the curb. Kathy had to walk around the cab to get in on the driver's side. As she opened the door, she dropped one of the crutches on the ground. She struggled to get into the cab without either Jackie or the cab driver offering any help. "I'll never do this again," she thought. Kathy told the driver the address; however, Jackie quickly interjected, "But we're taking me to my hotel first." Kathy shook her head in disbelief and remained silent, looking out the window for the rest of the ride. When they reached Jackie's hotel, Jackie got out and said, "Thanks for the ride," before closing the door and walking away. Kathy had no time to say, "This was supposed to be a shared ride." By this time, Kathy was just happy to see Jackie leave.

16 - Another Disappointment

When Dani got back to her room, she noticed a clear plastic bag on her bed. Inside were her clothes and shoes from the hospital. She immediately called the nurse's station. "Who brought these clothes to me?" she demanded.

The nurse sounded puzzled. "I'm not sure," she said.

Just then, Nurse Bianca walked up. "Oh, I see you got your clothes," she said.

"Did I miss Paul?" asked Dani excitedly.

"No, the hospital staff brought your clothes over from the ER. They were left behind at the nurse's station," Nurse Bianca explained.

Dani was disappointed to hear this. She had hoped Paul had brought her clothes and wanted to see her. She thought for a moment that maybe he had a change of heart.

Seeing the look on Dani's face, Nurse Bianca softened her tone. "I know it is hard but try not to let it get you down. Sometimes things do not happen the way we hope, but that doesn't mean you're alone."

Dani forced a smile and nodded. "I guess I was just hoping he'd come around."

Nurse Bianca offered a sympathetic smile. "It's understandable. Focus on getting better and let the rest work itself out."

Dani sighed, feeling a mix of disappointment and determination. She thanked Nurse Bianca and sat down on her bed, staring at the bag of clothes. She could not help but feel a pang of sadness, but she knew she had to focus on her recovery.

She opened the bag and took out her clothes, the familiar fabric feeling strange after days in hospital gowns. She decided to change into them, hoping it would make her feel a bit more like herself. As she dressed, she thought about the last conversation she had with Paul before his trip and the frustration in his voice.

"He's just overwhelmed," she told herself, trying to find some comfort in the thought. "Maybe he just needs some time."

Dani sat down on the edge of the bed, sadly looking out the window at the hospital grounds below.

After helping return Dani to her room, Dr. Gifford went back to the meeting room to clean up. Most everyone had left, except Tammy, who was putting chairs away. "Thanks so much for helping out, as usual, Tammy," said Dr. Gifford.

"My pleasure," said Tammy. "I like to help, as you well know."

Tammy's curiosity couldn't hold back. "So, is that one gal, Jackie, going to be coming here now?" asked Tammy.

"We shall see," said Dr. Gifford. "You know how some people come and go."

"Yes," said Tammy. "I just personally thought she was a project."

"A project?" asked Dr. Gifford. "What do you mean by that?"

Dr. Gifford knew exactly what Tammy meant but liked to get feedback on how others saw her clients.

"Well, you know, she has to have attention," said Tammy. "The kind of questions she asked someone she doesn't even know makes me cringe!"

"Oh really? Like what kind of questions?" asked Dr. Gifford.

"She had the nerve to ask one of the new ladies why she was here. I could tell the lady was uncomfortable, so I butted in and changed the subject."

"Really?" said Dr. Gifford in a concerned tone. "Who was this person?"

"The gal that wore her hospital clothes to the meeting," said Tammy.

"You're right, Tammy," said Dr. Gifford. "Some people just don't know when to keep their mouth shut."

"I wonder how her ride home with the other gal went," asked Tammy.

Dr. Gifford smiled and let out a little chuckle. "I guess we'll just have to see."

When Jackie got to her hotel room, she got undressed and lay on the bed, staring at the phone. She wanted so badly to call her husband, Richard, and let him know she was taking steps to improve. After several minutes, she mustered up enough courage and dialed the number. After four rings, the answering machine picked up. "Hello, you have reached the home of Richard Valentine. No one is available to take your call. Please leave a message, and I will return your call as soon as possible." Jackie felt her heart sink. He had changed the message, excluding her. After the beep, Jackie stumbled over her words. "Ugh, hey, Richard, I wanted to tell you, ugh... Could you please call me? I really need to talk to you." She hung up, shocked and disappointed that Richard had changed the greeting.

17 - Dani Goes Home

In the morning, Dani was woken up by her nurse saying, "Wake up, you get to go home today."

Dani slowly opened her eyes, in disbelief. She sat up. "What? When?" she asked.

"We are working on the release documents, but I would think no later than noon," said the nurse.

"I guess I better take a shower," she said softly. After showering, she put on the clothes from the bag. Her breakfast had been delivered while she was in the shower. She sat in the chair by her bedside and enjoyed her breakfast.

Meanwhile, Gloria arrived at the hospital, her steps heavy as she approached the front desk. She asked to meet Dr. Gifford, who was waiting for her in her office. Gloria's shoulders slumped, and she avoided eye contact as she walked, clearly reluctant to be there. After the introductions, Dr. Gifford gestured to a chair.

"Please sit down," Dr. Gifford said. "Can you tell me a little about your relationship with your sister, Dani?"

Gloria sighed deeply; frustration etched on her face. "If you had any idea," she began, her voice taut. "I've been dealing with my sister's crazy behavior my whole life, and quite frankly, I'm tired of it."

"Really, what kind of things have you experienced?" Dr. Gifford asked, leaning forward slightly.

"A typical bipolar personality," Gloria said with a huge attitude. "Dani is either ridiculously high on enthusiasm, driving everyone around her crazy, wanting to do everything at once, or she's down in the dumps, convinced the world is out to get her," Gloria explained.

"When our mother died, Dani was on vacation with her boyfriend. She promised to come home immediately but didn't show up for two weeks. By then, we'd already had the funeral. She had the nerve to complain about the arrangements and didn't contribute a cent towards the expenses. That was the last straw, but there have been so many incidents."

Dr. Gifford nodded; her expression sympathetic. "I understand. I don't expect you to change your opinion overnight, but I appreciate you coming to get her from the hospital."

"Tell me about your father," Dr. Gifford asked after a pause.

Gloria rolled her eyes. "Another disaster. If being bipolar is hereditary, she gets it from him. He was in and out of our lives so many times I've lost count."

Dr. Gifford's face fell slightly. "Yes, unfortunately, it can run in families. Do Dani and your dad have any relationship today?"

"Yes, and it's terrible," Gloria replied bitterly. "I honestly believe they would kill each other if they could."

Dr. Gifford sighed. "Well, I hope Dani continues with group therapy, and ideally, I'd like her to come to one-on-one counseling and stay on her medication."

"Please don't think I'll be bringing her. I'm only here today because my aunt can't deal with her problems. I have my own life, with a husband and children. I don't need or want to babysit my sister."

"Can I use you as a contact in case we need to get in touch with you?" asked Dr. Gifford.

"Really, I would rather you didn't," Gloria replied, exasperated. "Dani will just have to figure things out on her own. I'll take her home today, but that's it."

Dr. Gifford felt a pang of disappointment but was glad Gloria kept her commitment. "Let's go to her room and see if she's ready to be released," she said.

They walked to Dani's room, where she was eating breakfast. Dani looked up, her face twisting in anger. "What the fuck is she doing here?" she snapped.

"I'm here to take you home, Dani, so you need to be nice for once," Gloria retorted.

"Nice my ass. I'm not leaving here with that bitch," Dani spat, glaring at Dr. Gifford.

"Dani, this is your only chance to leave. We can't let you go on your own, and your sister was kind enough to help," Dr. Gifford pleaded.

"Kind? Fuck her. I hate that bitch," Dani screamed. Gloria turned to leave. "Maybe I made a mistake. Let her rot here; I don't care."

"Gloria, stop," Dr. Gifford called out. Turning to Dani, she said, "Your alternative is to be taken home in a straitjacket in an ambulance. The neighbors will see, and the fees will be in the thousands. Is that what you want?"

Dani sat quietly for a moment; her head bowed. "Fine," she muttered. "I'll go with her." She gathered her belongings while Dr. Gifford fetched a wheelchair. The ride home was silent. When they arrived, Dani got out, murmured a quiet "thank you" without looking at Gloria, gathered her belongings, and walked away, not looking back.

18 - Fight or Flight

Wednesday night's meeting couldn't come soon enough for Dani. After being dropped off at a lonely house the night before, the opportunity to be around other people was exactly what she needed. Dr. Gifford had instructed Dani to call her between 8:00 and 10:00 a.m. each day until further notice, a way to keep her clients engaged and reaching out for help.

When Dani arrived at the group meeting, Tammy greeted her warmly. "Well, I see you made it back," Tammy said, walking over and giving her a hug. "I don't remember your name, but I remember you were a patient here Monday night."

"I'm Dani, and yes, I was a patient. I was released yesterday," Dani replied.

"Well, I'm glad to hear it," Tammy said.

Thanks for helping me out Monday night with that other nosy gal. You came at the right time and distracted her so I could leave.

Dani chuckled. "Yeah, thanks a lot," Tammy said sarcastically. "She hung out with me and annoyed me for a bit."

"What a bimbo," Dani said, rolling her eyes.

"Well, she is trying to turn her life around too," Tammy replied, a hint of skepticism in her voice.

Dani just shrugged. "Sure, whatever."

"My name is Tammy, but they call me the savior of the world." Both girls laughed. Dani helped Tammy set up for the meeting while the other attendees trickled in slowly.

As Kathy walked in, still using her crutches, Tammy helped her get seated and welcomed her back to the group. Dr. Gifford joined the circle and took her seat.

"Okay, let's get started, folks," Dr. Gifford said, as the clock struck 7:00 exactly. The people at the coffee and snack counter stopped what they were doing and joined the group.

The meeting began in its usual way, with Dr. Gifford speaking first. "Does anyone have any pressing problems they want to discuss?" she asked.

Kathy spoke up. "No, especially since a certain person isn't here." The group looked at her in amazement, some with knowing smiles.

Within minutes of Kathy's sarcasm, a noise began outside the room. A loud voice, either speaking to herself or to anyone who would listen, approached, accompanied by the clanging of items in a purse. As the door opened, Kathy rolled her eyes and whispered, "Speak of the devil." Dr. Gifford gave her a disapproving look, but Kathy just smirked back.

"Hello, everyone," Jackie said as she entered the room. "I'm so sorry I'm late. I had a taxi from hell, and he was being rude to me, and—"

"No problem, Jackie," Dr. Gifford interrupted. "Please take a seat so we can get on with our meeting."

Jackie sensed Dr. Gifford's annoyance and sat in the empty chair, which happened to be next to Kathy. "Oh, hi," Jackie said to Kathy.

Kathy gave her a half-phony smile and turned away.

Dr. Gifford continued, "Before we were interrupted, I asked if anyone was experiencing any problems they wanted to talk about. If not, I'd like to discuss dealing with stress."

"I have been going through a hard time," Jackie interjected.

"Would you like to talk about it?" asked Dr. Gifford.

"Well, I suppose," Jackie began hesitantly. "Some of you may know, but some don't. My husband and I have separated. I called his house, and he changed his message to not include me anymore. This really hurts. I can't seem to get myself going. I had to push myself to get here. I left messages, but he won't call me back."

Dr. Gifford asked, "What are you doing to work on the personal issues we discussed in my office?"

Jackie looked surprised. "Well, I have been trying to get out into the world a bit more independently."

"Good," said Dr. Gifford. "Anything else?"

Jackie knew she hadn't been doing what Dr. Gifford had suggested. She avoided eye contact with everyone in the room by putting her head down.

Dr. Gifford continued, "The only way things will change is if you start working on yourself and focusing on what makes you happy. You have years of mending to do before you can think of making someone else happy."

Turning to the group, Dr. Gifford said, "We've all been through challenging times. Some things are not our fault, and some are self-inflicted wounds. Most of us need to take a personal inventory of our lives and what has happened. Were we born into families that didn't look after us properly? Were we abused? Some of us have genetic dispositions we can't help—depression, anxiety, eating disorders, addiction.

We are here to accept our problems and learn to deal with them. If you aren't doing the exercises I suggested and are focusing your energy elsewhere, you're denying the depth of your problem and slowing down recovery."

Dr. Gifford looked at Tammy. "Could you please get paper and pens for everyone?"

"Yes," said Tammy, as she got up to retrieve them.

After the paper and pens were passed out, Dr. Gifford addressed the group. "Okay, now, you are each here for a reason. Do you know what that reason is? Write down on the piece of paper that Tammy just gave you the reason you're here."

The group began writing, glancing up as they finished.

"Great," Dr. Gifford said. "What you wrote down on your paper is why you are here. If you didn't have that problem, you wouldn't be here, right? So, now that we know the problem, what's the solution?"

She paused, allowing the group to consider her question.

"Combating some of your problems can be enhanced by the medications I've prescribed. But that's only one step towards wellness. What are some other steps? You are here right now, attending a group therapy class to get support and feedback. Write that down as part of the solution. So now we should have on our papers: 1. The problem. 2. Solutions: medication, group therapy. How about meeting with your doctor as prescribed to discuss your situation? Exercise regularly? Avoid alcohol and other drugs?"

She scanned the room, making eye contact with each member. "Nowhere on this paper does it say to contact ex-husbands or boyfriends, girlfriends, or anything else that you may have lost. It's time to focus on you, and only you," said Dr. Gifford. "Focus on this paper. Now, write down things that make you happy and healthy."

Dr. Gifford looked around the circle. "Does anyone want to share their condition and what they do to overcome it?"

The group exchanged glances, hesitantly. Finally, a woman stood up. "Sure, I will. My name is Jackie, and I have agoraphobia."

"And what does that mean?" asked Dr. Gifford.

Jackie took a deep breath. "It's like the opposite of claustrophobia. I have major anxiety about going outside my home. I would panic and need to get back to my safe space. I lost my job because I couldn't leave my house. My parents and siblings had to come to me if they wanted to see me. It got so bad that I couldn't leave my bedroom. I saw a television show that featured someone recovering from the same symptoms. I didn't even know I had a problem, let alone that there was a name for it. At the end of the show, they had an 800 number to call if you experienced any of the symptoms discussed. I called, and the rest is history."

"So, what do you do now to overcome it?" asked Dr. Gifford.

"Well, for starters, every day, I admit I have a problem. I know it's there, and I tell myself I have to be stronger than my problem.

I also tell myself I have a solution for my problems. I have become very routine-oriented. I take my prescribed meds first thing in the morning. I get up at a certain time, shower, and get dressed as if I were going to work. I don't turn on the TV or clean the house. I sit at a table and write out my day. I write out what needs to be done. Where do I have to go, and what do I have to do to accomplish my goals? I peek my head out of the back door. Then I go to the front door and peek my head outside. I try to plan on going for a walk to the park or the grocery store as my therapy."

"Great job, Jackie. Thank you for sharing with us," Dr. Gifford said, nodding. "You can sit down. Jackie is a patient I've been working with for about three years now. As you can see, if you put enough effort into yourself, you can live a better life."

"My goal for today was to talk about stress and how to overcome it," Dr. Gifford continued, looking around the group. "For those of you who haven't been working with me long, one of the things you will hear is 'Fight or Flight.' As we have evolved from our primitive ancestors, we deal with stress differently. Back then, we had to hide from predators or fight for survival. When we sensed danger, our bodies created a chemical reaction, diverting blood from our digestive system to our muscles and limbs as we ran or fought. Our heart rate and adrenaline spiked, and once the danger passed, things returned to normal."

Dr. Gifford smiled at the group as she continued, "In our modern world, the threats are different, but the response can be the same. Understanding this is the first step in learning to manage your stress. "Today, our bodies don't have to run and hide or fight the way they did back then. Yet, we still get anxious and stressed, placing the same strain on our bodies. Our minds go into overdrive, but our breathing doesn't increase unless we consciously take deep breaths. This mismatch leads to an overabundance of stress hormones, which are harmful to our health. Consequently, more people suffer from heart attacks, strokes, digestive trouble, concentration problems, depression, and other concerns. A lack of oxygen during stressful times worsens these issues. That's why doctors often recommend exercise and getting the heart rate up with at least 20 minutes of cardio per day. Dr. Gifford stood up, folding her chair. "Now, let's apply this advice and get our heart rates up by putting our chairs back in the racks. See you next Friday. Thank you for coming

As the room cleared, Kathy approached Dr. Gifford with a hesitant smile. "I'm really sorry for how I acted about Jackie," she said. "The cab situation just threw me off, and honestly, her personality doesn't sit right with me."

Dr. Gifford nodded, her expression softening. "I understand completely, Kathy. No need to worry about it." Both women shared a weary smile before gathering their things. The room, now empty, echoed with the quiet hum of the evening. They walked out together, both tired and eager to get home and into bed

19 - Same Pattern

As Dani opened the door to her empty house, she paused and looked around. "Quiet," she thought. She put her purse and keys on the table, then sat on the couch in the living room, thinking about the meeting she had just come from. She glanced over her notes. "I should really put these into a plan and follow it," she mused.

Rising, she went to the kitchen and poured herself a glass of wine, as she always did, forgetting that she was going to try not to drink. Grabbing a pen and a notepad, she returned to the couch. Her mind was racing. She sipped her wine as she wrote, and soon the glass was empty. She poured another and sat back down, but the wine's effects made it hard to focus.

Impulsively, she picked up her phone and dialed Paul's old cell number. Hearing the disconnect message, she sighed and hung up. She tried calling her old friends, but no one answered. Frustrated, she looked at her notes again. "Fuck this shit," she muttered. She finished her second glass, stumbled to her bedroom, and threw herself onto the bed, yelling, "Fuck all this shit!" before falling asleep in her clothes.

In the morning, Dani couldn't believe she had slept in her clothes. She stumbled to the bathroom, shedding her clothes before taking a shower. Despite sleeping through the night, she felt exhausted. After her shower, she wrapped herself in towels and, feeling drained, crawled back into bed. An hour later, the phone rang, waking her. "Hello?" said Dani, with her voice tired.

"Hello, Dani, this is Katie from Dr. Gifford's office. I'm calling to remind you of your appointment at 11:00 a.m."

"Oh, I forgot. Thanks for reminding me," she replied, surprised. Though she had slept, Dani still felt exhausted. She dressed and went to the kitchen, staring blankly into the refrigerator. "Nothing looks good," she thought. She repeated the same with the pantry. "There is nothing to fucking eat here," she said aloud. Seeing it was already 9:30, she thought, "Wow, I better get moving," and dragged herself to the bedroom to finish dressing and putting on makeup.

At 11:00, Dani arrived at Dr. Gifford's office. After being greeted and escorted in, Dr. Gifford asked, "How are you doing?"

Dani took a deep breath. "I could be doing better."

"Really? What seems to be the problem?" asked Dr. Gifford.

"I don't know. I just woke up this morning and felt like shit. I haven't been motivated to do anything except sit around watching movies and drinking wine for the last couple of days." Dani said with a sad unmotivated tone.

"Really?" Dr. Gifford glanced at her file. "Are you taking the medication I prescribed for you?"

"Yes, I've been taking it faithfully," Dani replied.

"I know you probably don't want to hear this, but you shouldn't drink alcohol. It's a depressant, which is likely why you've been feeling down." Dr. Gifford said sternly. Dani knew this but felt too frustrated to care.

"What are you doing to keep yourself busy?" Dr. Gifford asked curiously.

"Well, I went to the meeting last night, but other than that, I've just been at home."

"And what do you do when you're at home?"

"Not really a whole lot of anything."

"Can you see why it's important to have a plan for your day? There's a pattern here: you feel down, you drink, you feel more depressed, you drink more. It's a vicious circle."

Tears welled up in Dani's eyes. "It hurts so much."

"I know," Dr. Gifford said gently. "That's why we need to keep you busy. The busier, the better." "What would you do if you had the perfect job and unlimited money?" asked Dr. Gifford.

Dani looked at her with sad eyes. "That's just it. I don't know. I don't know what I want to be when I grow up," Dani said sarcastically with a hint of a smile. "I go through this shit in my head until I want to scream. I don't have any talent. I didn't go to college, hell, I didn't even graduate from high school. So how the fuck am I supposed to know what I want to do?" Dani said while crying.

Dr. Gifford listened patiently. When Dani calmed down, she asked, "Why don't you start slow? Have you thought of getting your GED?"

"Yes, but it's been so long. I wouldn't remember shit anymore, and I'd have to go back to school for who knows how long. And then what?"

"I know it feels overwhelming, but setting a small goal and achieving it can show you that you do have talent. Along the way, you might find something that interests you." Dani rolled her eyes and slumped in her chair.

"Okay, Dani, I want you to continue taking your meds regularly. You must do your best to avoid alcohol. Go to an AA meeting every day, no excuses. That will also give you something to do." Dr. Gifford paused with compassion. "And most importantly, call me every morning to check in. I'll see you at the group meeting tomorrow night." Sound good?" asked Dr. Gifford.

Both women stood and shook hands. Dani left the room feeling frustrated but knew she had no choice but to take small steps toward improving.

As she reached the elevator, the doors opened, revealing Kathy struggling with her crutches and purse. "Let me help you with that," Dani said.

"Oh, thanks. If you only knew what I went through to get this far," Kathy replied, sighing. They walked together to Dr. Gifford's office while Kathy recounted her bus trip.

"Why don't you call me in the future for a ride?" Dani suggested.

That would be wonderful, especially for our group therapy meetings," Kathy said, smiling.

Dani wrote her phone number on the back of one of Dr. Gifford's business cards and handed it to Kathy. "What are you doing after your appointment with Dr. Gifford?" she asked.

"I need to find the bus stop and figure out how to get home," Kathy chuckled, a hint of frustration in her voice.

"How about I give you a ride home?" Dani offered, her tone warm and friendly.

"Oh no, I couldn't ask you to do that," Kathy protested, shaking her head.

"It's not like I have anything else to do. What if we go for lunch after your appointment?" Dani suggested, her eyes sparkling with genuine interest.

"Okay, that would be nice. But I'd hate for you to wait around," Kathy replied, still hesitant.

"No problem at all. I need to run a small errand anyway. I'll be back to pick you up," Dani assured her.

"Great! I'm really looking forward to this," Kathy said with a smile, feeling her earlier worries start to dissipate.

"Me too," Dani replied as she turned and left the office, leaving Kathy with a newfound sense of anticipation and relief.

As Kathy settled into a chair at Dr. Gifford's office, she reflected on the support she was beginning to find in the people around her. It felt like a new chapter was starting, one where she wasn't alone in her struggles. This simple act of reaching out and connecting with someone was already making a difference.

Dani, on her way to run her errand, couldn't help but feel a sense of fulfillment. Offering Kathy a ride and planning to share a meal felt like the right thing to do. It was a small step, but it was part of her own journey of healing and helping others.

After her errand, Dani returned to the clinic just as Kathy's appointment was finishing up. She parked the car and waited outside, enjoying the fresh air.

Kathy emerged from the clinic, her face lighting up when she saw Dani waiting for her. "Ready to go?" Dani asked with a smile. "Absolutely," Kathy replied, feeling grateful.

Kathy got into the car, chatting easily with Dani as they drove to a nearby café. The atmosphere was cozy and inviting, perfect for a relaxing lunch. They found a table by the window and ordered their meals. When the server asked for their drinks, Kathy spoke up and said, "Just water for both of us." "Wow, that's different," said Dani. "Me drinking water. I haven't ordered water since I was a kid."

"Well, we are in a healing period of our lives. I'm your support and you can be mine," Kathy said with a smile.

Over lunch, they shared stories about their lives, their struggles, and their hopes for the future.

"So, do you think you'll go back to school and get your GED?" Kathy asked.

"I don't know. I just don't see what it will do for me," Dani replied.

"I think it's a great idea," Kathy said. "You're still young, and it will be the start of proving to yourself that you can achieve whatever you want."

"I think it's great that you're so strong, Kathy. It must be nice to have control and not rely on anyone," Dani said.

"Yes, but it can get you in trouble. Most men don't like a woman with a strong personality. I think I intimidate them, and some just don't know how to handle a woman as a boss. I've always been extremely independent and don't like taking shit from anyone."

Dani chuckled. "It must be hard for you now, not being able to drive or work."

"Yeah, and pretty soon I won't be able to pay my bills either," Kathy said with a sigh.

"I'm sure you'll figure it out. You're tough," Dani said with a chuckle.

The connection between them grew stronger with each passing moment, making both women realize how much they had in common despite their different journeys.

By the time they finished their meal, Kathy felt a deep sense of gratitude for Dani's kindness. "Thank you so much for this. It really means a lot to me," Kathy said sincerely.

"It was my pleasure, Kathy. I enjoyed it too," Dani replied, her eyes reflecting the warmth of her words.

As they left the café, both women felt a renewed sense of hope and companionship. They knew that this lunch was just the beginning of a supportive and understanding friendship, one that would help them navigate the challenges ahead with a little more confidence and a lot more care.

After lunch, Dani drove Kathy home and helped her inside. "Wow, what a nice place," Dani remarked. "You bought this on your own?" "I sure as hell don't have a knight in shining armor to buy it for me," Kathy chuckled.

Dani admired the cleanliness and the perfectly manicured yard with flowers in full bloom. "I can't see myself ever buying my own place," Dani said.

"That's because you haven't had someone kicking your ass to finish school," Kathy teased. Dani smiled.

"I'd best be running along. Please call me tomorrow to remind me to pick you up. I tend to be forgetful," Dani said as she headed toward her car.

"No problem, but could you come a little early? I don't like to be late," Kathy replied.

"Sure," Dani said. "See you tomorrow."

The following evening, Dani picked up Kathy, and they went to group therapy together. Tammy, as usual, was already there and noticed the two women entering together.

"Oh, I see you made a friend," Tammy said. Kathy ignored her, heading straight to her usual chair.

"Yes," Dani replied. "Kathy and I ran into each other at Dr. Gifford's office. We had lunch, and I offered to bring her to the meetings."

"How nice," Tammy said. "Anytime you want to invite me to lunch, I'd be happy to join."

"That's a great idea," Dani agreed. "Maybe we can all meet for lunch sometime."

"I'm game," Tammy said as she continued making coffee. Dani picked up the bag of cookies and began arranging them on a dish.

Once the meeting started, Dr. Gifford told the group she hadn't been feeling well and might have a fill-in for the next meeting or two.

"I have to have some tests run and might be down for a couple of days," she said. Tammy, her longtime patient, looked concerned. "I'll be fine and back on schedule in no time," Dr. Gifford assured the group.

"Now, does anyone have anything pressing that needs to be addressed?" Everyone seemed fine as no one commented.

"Okay then, at the last meeting, I wanted to discuss stress relief but ran out of time. If you remember, I asked you to write down things that make you feel a little happier. We talked about exercising and its benefits. Today, I want to talk about diet. Exercise and diet are often mentioned by doctors because they help significantly."

As Dr. Gifford continued, the warning alarm of Jackie's arrival became apparent. She was on her phone, laughing and talking. She opened the door and said, "Oops, I got to go," hanging up abruptly.

"Hello everyone, you're never going to believe what happened. My husband called me, and he wants to talk after our meeting. I'm so excited," she exclaimed.

"That's good news, Jackie," Dr. Gifford said sternly, "but we are trying to have a meeting here."

"Oh, okay," Jackie said as she grabbed a chair. Dr. Gifford resumed, "As I was saying, our diet plays a significant role in our behavior. Alcohol, for example, can lead to depression, anxiety, and mood changes."

Jackie piped up, "Yeah, a little tequila and—"

"Jackie," Dr. Gifford interrupted sternly, "please hold those comments." Jackie smiled, looking around for approval. Dani glanced at Kathy, who looked angry and disgusted.

Dr. Gifford continued her talk on diet and exercise. As the meeting ended, everyone put their chairs back and headed either for the cookies at the back of the room or the door to leave.

Dr. Gifford pulled Jackie aside. "I really need you to be a bit quieter and more considerate of the group when you come into the room. And if there's any way you could be on time, it would help avoid disruptions."

Jackie felt a bit put out by the reprimand but agreed to do better in the future.

Dani and Kathy were at the back of the room, sharing thoughts by the cookie table. As Tammy walked up, Dani said, "Hey, how about the three of us have lunch sometime and then catch a movie?"

Tammy's face lit up. "That's a great idea," Kathy agreed, just as Jackie approached.

"What's a great idea?" Jackie asked. Kathy looked away, clearly shunning her. Tammy explained, "We're planning to have lunch and see a movie."

"How wonderful," Jackie said. "Let me know when, and I'll join you."

"The more, the merrier," Dani said.

Becoming annoyed with the conversation, Kathy asked, "Can we go now?" Her eyebrows raised with frustration.

"Did you catch a ride with Dani?" Jackie asked Kathy.

Kathy rudely shunned her, grabbing her crutches and heading for the door.

Dani replied, "Yes, it turns out she lives on my way."

"How lovely," Jackie commented snootily. "Well, have a safe ride home."

"We will," Dani replied.

Tammy and Jackie exchanged phone numbers as they walked to their cars. Jackie shared how excited she was to visit her husband, and Tammy was thrilled to have friends for the first time since high school.

When Jackie arrived at her home, Richard was sitting on the porch with a glass of wine. She felt a mix of excitement and fear. Maybe he wants to talk about a divorce, she thought, or maybe he wants me to come back. Richard smiled and handed her a glass of wine.

"I've missed you," she said, tears in her eyes.

"Sit down, Jackie. I want to talk," Richard said. Jackie nervously talked about her improvements and how he'd be proud of her.

"It sounds like being apart has been good for you," Richard noted.

"No! Not really," Jackie cried. "I miss you. I don't like being away from you."

Richard smiled, extending his hand. She placed hers in his, tears streaming down her face. He pulled her closer, and she maneuvered onto his lap, both holding each other tightly.

"I missed you," Richard said. "I married you knowing what you were like, yet I turned you away for it. You're beautiful, and any man in his right mind would want you."

Jackie looked into his eyes. "I love you so much," Richard said. Jackie continued to cry.

"I'm so sorry I hurt you," she said. "I'm getting help. I started seeing a therapist and attending group therapy."

"Great," Richard said.

They continued to cuddle, drinking their wine, and catching up on the past weeks.

"Let's go inside," Richard said softly.

Holding hands, they walked into the house, their steps synchronized in a rhythm of shared anticipation. Richard lifted Jackie up effortlessly, carrying her upstairs with a look of devotion in his eyes. He gently laid her on the bed and began undressing her slowly, kissing her as he savored each moment. Their kisses were tender, their caresses filled with the joy of being together again after too long apart.

"You're not leaving me tonight," Richard whispered, his voice filled with a mixture of desire and affection.

"You're not getting rid of me tonight," Jackie replied with a giggle, her eyes sparkling with mischief and warmth.

Richard smiled, his heart swelling with love. "Good," he said softly, continuing to explore her body with gentle, loving touches. "Because I've missed you so much."

"I've missed you too," Jackie murmured, pulling him closer. Their connection was electric, each touch and kiss reaffirming their bond.

They moved together in a seamless dance of intimacy, their bodies and hearts entwined. The world outside faded away, leaving only the two of them in their private sanctuary. Every whispered word, every shared breath was a testament to their deep affection and mutual longing.

As the night wore on, their passion ebbed and flowed like a gentle tide, bringing them closer and closer. They talked in between their lovemaking, sharing their thoughts and dreams, reaffirming their commitment to each other.

Richard brushed a stray lock of hair from Jackie's face, his fingers lingering on her cheek. "I love you," he said, his voice a tender caress.

"I love you too," Jackie replied, her heart overflowing with emotion. She traced the lines of his face, memorizing every detail.

Eventually, they settled into a comfortable silence, their bodies wrapped around each other. Richard held Jackie close, feeling her heartbeat against his chest, a steady reminder of the love they shared.

"You're my everything," Richard whispered, pressing a kiss to her forehead.

"And you're mine," Jackie replied, her voice thick with emotion. They fell asleep in each other's arms, feeling content and at peace, knowing that they were exactly where they were meant to be.

The night was theirs, a precious gift, and they cherished every moment of it. Together, they faced whatever the future might hold, confident in their love and commitment to one another.

In the morning, Jackie's cell phone rang, waking her. As she looked around the room for it, she noticed Richard was gone, and his side of the bed was made. Her phone was on the dresser across the room. She got out of bed and rushed to reach the phone before it went to voicemail.

Too late. "Damn," Jackie said. She saw it was Tammy who had called and hit the call-back button.

"Hi, Jackie," Tammy answered. "I was wondering how your night went."

"I'm here, back home with my husband."

"Really?" Tammy exclaimed. "That's fantastic!"

"He missed me," Jackie said. "Why don't you come over for coffee, and I'll tell you all about it."

"Okay," Tammy said excitedly.

Jackie gave her the address and then went downstairs to make coffee, finding it already made. She looked around the kitchen for food to serve and found some Danish in the pantry and fruit in the fridge. She set the table and then went upstairs to shower. Most of her clothing and personal items were still in place. Jackie dressed and went downstairs, finishing the preparations for her guest.

The phone rang again. "Jackie, it's Tammy. Either I'm lost, or you live in a mansion. Damn, are you sure you want me to come in?"

"Don't be silly," Jackie said, pressing the button to open the gate that led to the long driveway up to the house on the knoll. Tammy got out of her car, looking around in amazement. "OMG!" she kept saying.

Jackie opened the door, seeing Tammy standing by her car. "Wow!" Tammy said. "This is incredible. Can I be your daughter and live with you?"

Jackie laughed. "Yes, it is beautiful, isn't it? Come in! I can't wait to tell you about my evening."

As Tammy walked into the house, she stood in awe. "OMG," she said, looking at the fine furniture and incredible design. "I can't believe my eyes," she said.

Jackie smiled. "Come on, I have coffee and some treats. Let's sit on the veranda by the pool." Tammy was speechless as she followed Jackie out to the pool and veranda. They sat at a table, sipping coffee while Jackie dominated the conversation about her evening with Richard. Tammy tried to listen but was in awe over the house. After a couple of hours visiting Tammy glanced at her watch.

"Wow, as much as I love being here, I really need to get going." she said.

"Sure, I understand," Jackie said. "I have some things to do as well." Jackie showed her to the door, and they embraced.

"I am so happy for you," Tammy said as she turned to leave.

"Thanks," Jackie replied with a huge smile. "And thanks for coming over." Tammy drove off, amazed that she had a friend who lived in such a place.

20– The New Therapist

At the next group therapy meeting, Dani and Kathy arrived to find Tammy happier than usual.

"What's up with you?" Dani asked.

"OMG, Jackie and her husband got back together, and she invited me over for coffee. You wouldn't believe the house she lives in! It's not just big; it's a mansion!"

"I'm sure he's lost his mind," Kathy said sarcastically.

Dani chuckled. "Come on, she isn't so bad."

Kathy raised her eyebrows and went to grab their seats, saving one for Dani.

Tammy explained how she befriended Jackie. "Well, maybe we can all go to her house for lunch," suggested Dani. "And she has an amazing pool too. Maybe we can all sit out by the pool and hang out." Dani said overjoyed with enthusiasm.

"Oh, that would be great," Tammy agreed.

Jackie showed up late as usual, but she wasn't the only one late. The group therapy attendees were snacking on cookies and coffee, socializing as they waited for the meeting to start. Kathy began to get upset with the lack of respect from the clinic for not having someone there. "Well, someone should come to take her place," she said.

"I agree," added Tammy. "This has never happened before."

Kathy walked to the wall phone and picked up the receiver. She asked the operator why the doctor was not at the meeting yet and if anyone was going to replace her. She added, "This is not a professional way of conducting business, especially with mental illness patients. These people can become agitated, and who knows what kind of mess you'll have on your hands. I'm thinking of filing a complaint." "Never mind, someone just showed up," Kathy said as she hung up the phone and returned to her chair.

The meeting room door opened, and a handsome, well-dressed man entered. "Hello everyone. My name is Dr. Peters. I am sorry I'm late," he said. The room went quiet as all eyes turned to him. "I took a wrong turn thanks to my navigation and ended up ten miles out of my way. Again, I'm sorry I'm late. Can we all take a seat and get started?"

He sat in Dr. Gifford's usual chair and addressed the group with a warm smile.

"I was asked to fill in for Dr. Gifford while she is on leave. I'd like to start by telling you a bit about myself, so you know who I am and that I'm qualified to work with you."

Dr. Peters shared his education, experience, and ongoing certifications. He also opened up about his personal challenges with ADHD, which required medication throughout his childhood and into adulthood. He spoke candidly about the difficulties he faced in his personal life due to his busy schedule and how his career meant everything to him.

"I'll do my best to fill in for Dr. Gifford," Dr. Peters continued, "though with her reputation, it will be hard to compete. I'm honored to step in for her, and I hope you all can benefit from my experience as well."

The group listened attentively, their initial skepticism about the new therapist beginning to dissipate. Dr. Peters' openness and willingness to share his own struggles created a sense of connection and trust.

"I understand change can be difficult," Dr. Peters said empathetically. "But I'm here to support you and help you through your challenges, just as Dr. Gifford has. Let's work together to make this a positive and productive time for all of us."

He looked around the room, making eye contact with each member of the group as he spoke. "My approach is collaborative and focused on finding practical strategies that work for you individually and as a group. I believe in creating a safe and open environment where you feel comfortable sharing and exploring your thoughts and feelings. Together, we'll work on developing skills and insights that can help you navigate your challenges more effectively."

"I have reviewed Dr. Gifford's notes and treatment plans. I aim to maintain continuity while also bringing in my own expertise and perspective. I'm here to ensure that the progress you've made continues and that we build on it together." The group seemed reassured by his words. Dr. Peters smiled again, feeling the room's tension ease. "Alright then, let's get started." With that, the session began, and Dr. Peters felt a sense of fulfillment as he saw the group members start to engage and open up. It was the beginning of a new chapter for all of them, and he was committed to making it a positive one.

"I'd like to go around the room and have you tell me your names," he said, opening his briefcase and searching for the attendance sheet and a pen. Finding what he needed, he began to write. "Let's start with you," he said, pointing to the first person on his right.

The first person was a man named Joseph. Joseph hardly ever spoke at the group meetings. Joseph was diagnosed with paranoid schizophrenia and would always attend but sit through the session without saying anything. Most of the time, Joseph looked down and rocked back and forth in his seat. If he made eye contact, it was only for a split second before he quickly looked down again.

"Joseph," he said in a very low voice as he rocked. Dr. Peters checked his name on the sheet of paper, giving him a moment to see if he would say anything more. When Joseph remained silent, Dr. Peters looked to the next person, signaling them to introduce themselves.

After everyone had briefly introduced themselves, Dr. Peters reached into his briefcase and pulled out more papers.

Standing up, he began passing them around. "This is a little assessment test," he explained. "It's a simple questionnaire to help me get more familiar with each of you. Do you all have something to write with?"

Tammy got up from her chair, grabbed some pencils, and handed them out. They began filling out the questionnaires, some taking longer than others.

Jackie spoke out loudly as she answered some of the questions, making sure everyone noticed her. "This isn't a group discussion," Kathy said sharply. "This is so Dr. Peters can get to know us better."

"We already know all about you," she added, her tone biting. Jackie looked surprised, while Dani, sitting next to Kathy, nudged her with her elbow. "Kathy," she said quietly, almost scolding her.

Dr. Peters noticed the animosity. "Yes, this is for my information to get to know you better individually," he reiterated, smiling at Jackie before scanning the room to see how everyone was progressing. When everyone was done, he collected the papers and put them back in his briefcase.

"Is anyone having any trouble or difficulties they'd like to discuss?" he asked, looking at his notes. No one, including Jackie, spoke up.

"Okay then," he continued. "Every therapist has their own style. I know Dr. Gifford personally, and she has given me the thumbs up to introduce my techniques. I am a hands-on person and like to work inside and outside of this circle."

Most of the patients were now paying full attention.

"I like to discover ways of helping people push through their weaknesses with little exercises that stretch them. However, we do it together, with support from each other."

Kathy spoke up, "What do you mean by going outside this circle? As in, outside this meeting room?"

"Yes," said Dr. Peters.

"I don't know if I'll be able to participate. I'm recovering from a major accident and can barely make it here."

"No worries," Dr. Peters reassured her. "We'll work around that. I don't mean to scare anyone off. My first goal is to get to know you all individually and as a group. I'll be meeting with each of you individually over the next week."

"If it's alright, I'd like to break up this circle and use the last 30 minutes to have some punch and cookies and talk more casually."

Tammy got up to make sure the punch and cookies were laid out nicely while everyone began to mingle.

After several minutes, Dr. Peters noticed Kathy sitting by herself and walked over to shake her hand.

"So, you're Kathy?"

"Yes, I am. Do I have a reputation?" she asked.

"No, nothing like that," he said. "Dr. Gifford told me about your accident. I can't imagine what that must have been like."

"Fortunately, I don't remember anything," replied Kathy. "But I'm a bit more impaired because of it. I can't drive and must rely on others, which doesn't go over well with someone like me."

"Well, you made it here, and that's what counts," he said.

"I don't really have a choice. My driver's license is suspended indefinitely," Kathy said.

Across the room, Dani noticed Kathy talking to Dr. Peters and walked over to introduce herself.

"So, are you going to be our new therapist?" she asked.

"For the time being," he replied.

"Well, I like a little change now and then. I can't imagine coming to the same meetings, seeing the same people, and listening to the same crap each week," Dani said sarcastically.

"I'm sure it's not that bad," Dr. Peters said.

"Okay, if you say so," Kathy responded with a smile.

Tammy walked up excitedly. "Jackie just confirmed we can have a day at her house. We can meet there, have lunch, and hang out by the pool. Are you both free on Thursday?" she asked.

"Don't include me," Kathy said. "I have no desire to be anywhere near that woman."

Dani chuckled. "Kathy doesn't care for her too much."

"It's more like I can't stand that woman," Kathy corrected. "You guys go and have a good time."

Tammy looked at Dani. "Will you come?"

"Yes, sure, I'll come," Dani replied. "It will be fun."

"Sounds like you all have a plan to do something fun together," Dr. Peters remarked. "Good for you. So, which one is Jackie?"

Tammy and Dani pointed towards Jackie by the cookie table.

Kathy piped up, "You can't miss her. She's the one with the big mouth."

Jackie noticed them pointing and walked over. "Why are you pointing at me?" she asked.

"We were just showing Dr. Peters who you are," Tammy explained.

"Oh, hello, Dr. Peters. I'm Jackie," she said, extending her hand.

"So, you're the one having the party?" he asked.

"Well, I wouldn't call it a party, just a couple of friends over for lunch. Would you like to join us?" she invited.

Tammy looked surprised, and Dani lit up. "Yeah, that's a great idea."

"Oh, no, you all go ahead. I have a lot of catching up to do with work," he replied.

"Well, maybe next time," Jackie said.

Jackie stayed around, dominating the conversation, and trying to flirt with Dr. Peters, who had been prewarned about her and did his best to ignore her overtones.

"Excuse me," he said, walking over to the punch and cookies table, where some other patients greeted him.

"Are you ready to go?" Kathy asked Dani.

"It's still early. What is your hurry?" Dani asked.

"Do you mind if I ride home with you?" Jackie asked. "My car is in the shop."

"That would be fine," said Dani.

"Let's stop and have a drink at the club on the way home," Jackie suggested.

"No thanks," Kathy replied. "I'm on medication that doesn't mix well with alcohol, looking at Dani as she spoke. I believe Dani is trying to quit drinking as well."

"How about just a soda or something?" Dani suggested.

"No, I'd rather go home. I'll take a cab, so you don't have to drive me," Kathy insisted showing a bit of frustration.

"I'll give you a ride home," Tammy offered.

"No, thanks. I'll take a cab," Kathy replied being stubborn.

"Would you like to come with us to the club, Tammy?" Dani asked.

"No, I have to get up early for work tomorrow," Tammy said.

"Alright then," said Dani. "Let's go," she said to Jackie.

Though Kathy agreed to take a cab home, she was fuming inside. She valued friends who kept their word and was frustrated by Dani's change of plans. As the people began to leave, Kathy found herself more frustrated trying to get a cab. Tammy asked again if she wanted a ride, but Kathy refused, as she was being stubborn.

Moments later, Dr. Peters walked over to where Kathy was sitting.

"Why are you still here? I thought you rode with Dani."

"I guess she had a better opportunity," Kathy replied curtly.

"How far do you live from here?" he asked.

"Not too far. I'll take a bus or catch a cab," Kathy said.

"I'll give you a ride home, and you can't argue with me," he insisted. "Just let me finish closing up shop, and we'll go."

When Dr. Peters was ready, he helped Kathy with her things and insisted on carrying her items. Kathy felt a bit embarrassed but appreciated his help. He opened the doors for her and helped her into his car. At her house, he insisted on making sure everything was okay inside.

"Nice place you have here," he commented.

"Thank you. I kind of like it," she responded, unsure how to act with the doctor in her home. She offered him a soda or coffee, but he declined. "I really must be getting on. I've got a little drive ahead of me," he said. Kathy showed him to the door, but he insisted on locking it behind him. Kathy sat in her home, amazed at how she felt. Was she interested in this doctor? she thought. No, she couldn't allow herself to be so weak. As she prepared for the night, thoughts of Dr. Peters raced in her head. She tossed and turned for hours before finally falling asleep

21 - A Night on The Town

Dani and Jackie went to a local place called "Player's." They were excited to sit, talk, and maybe meet some men and dance. Their new friendship was moving in the right direction for both of them. Dani had a couple of drinks while Jackie sipped her wine. They sat at a bar table, talking about their past. Dani enjoyed that more men were paying attention to them than she was used to.

"Wow," she said. "I've had a few guys hit on me from time to time, but damn, girl, you really know how to turn heads."

Jackie laughed. "Yes, it's amazing what a guy won't do for a little attention."

Both laughed, enjoying the moment of having a girlfriend. The server brought over a couple of drinks.

"We didn't order these," Dani said.

"Compliments of those guys over there," the server replied, pointing to a table with four men. The girls looked over and thanked the men. Jackie blew a kiss toward them.

"I could get used to this," Dani said.

Moments later, two of the men came over to introduce themselves.

"Ladies, how you doing? I'm Bill, and this is Derrick."

Jackie perked up, excited to see them. Dani finished her drink and began drinking the one the guys had sent over.

"I see you're enjoying your drinks," one of the men said.

"Yes, that was very nice of you," Jackie replied.

The men noticed Jackie's wedding ring and focused more on Dani. By now, Dani had had a couple of drinks and was feeling the effects. As the four talked and got to know each other, Jackie became uncomfortable with the lack of attention she was getting. She tried to dominate the conversation, drawing attention toward herself.

Derrick looked at Jackie's ring. "I'm sure your husband is a lucky man," he said.

Jackie played it down. "It's a trophy from my last victim," she joked. The guys laughed. "No worries, he isn't around anymore. The lawyers said he wasn't so lucky after all," she added with a devious grin. Dani looked on with wide eyes, knowing Jackie had just gotten back with her husband.

It became clear that Jackie was craving attention. Meanwhile, Dani and Bill were hitting it off. Sensing the shift, Jackie pulled a power move.

"Bill, would you care to dance with me?" she asked.

Surprised, Bill looked up. "You don't have to ask me twice."

Dani was shocked by Jackie's behavior. She didn't know Jackie well, but it was clear that Jackie had just pulled a power play.

"What the hell was that all about?" Dani asked Derrick.

"I don't know. I guess your friend wants to have a little fun. Do you want to dance?" Derrick asked.

"Okay, I guess," Dani replied.

They walked to the dance floor and began dancing to the music. Shortly thereafter, Jackie noticed them on the dance floor. She positioned herself between Derrick and Dani, pressing her body against Derrick provocatively. Bill danced with Dani, who was still in shock at Jackie's actions. She watched her new friend dirty dance with Derrick, feeling uncomfortable but rolling with it.

"Let's go have another drink," Bill said to Dani, pulling her from the dance floor and holding her hand as they returned to their table. They watched as Jackie and Derrick continued their erotic dance, Derrick's hands all over Jackie as she moved provocatively against him.

"I like your friend's dance style," Bill remarked.

"Yeah, I bet you do," Dani replied, downing her drink. She was becoming more intoxicated by the moment, the first time she had been near another man since her boyfriend, Paul, had left her.

Jackie and Derrick returned to the table, laughing, and carrying on. "Let's have another drink," Jackie said, signaling the cocktail server. While waiting, Dani finished off the accumulated drinks on the table. Derrick was all over Jackie, clearly wanting to take things further. When the drinks arrived, Dani, already tipsy, needed to go to the bathroom.

"Would you like me to walk you there?" Bill offered.

"No, I think I can make it," she said, stumbling off.

Bill watched as Jackie and Derrick made out at the bar table they had all been sitting at.

"Why don't you guys get a room?" he asked.

Jackie smiled wickedly. "Why get a room when it's more fun in strange places with people watching?" She walked over to Bill, placing his hand on her breast and the other on her ass.

"Now, you see what I mean?" she teased. Derrick and Jackie laughed while Bill looked unsure and a bit embarrassed.

Dani stumbled back from the bathroom and saw Jackie making her move on Bill.

"What the fuck is your problem?" she demanded.

Jackie grinned deviously. "I'm just having a little fun."

Dani, drunk but aware, knew this behavior wasn't right. "I think I'm going to go home. I'll see you at the next meeting," she said, looking at the men with disgust before walking away from the table and out of the bar.

Bill followed her outside to the curb, trying to talk to her, but Dani ignored him, jumping into her car and driving away.

When he returned to the bar, Jackie and Derrick were gone. He rejoined his buddies, who had been observing from a distance, entertained by the spectacle.

"I guess you didn't get as lucky as Derrick tonight," one of them said. "That bitch took him behind the curtain over there and... Bill interrupted. "Whatever, guys. That bitch is fucking weird. He can have her."

Dani awoke the next day with a headache, still feeling the buzz from the night before. She lay in bed, trying to remember how she got home and into her house. She noticed her clothes were thrown on the floor, and she was in her underwear. Seeing the clock, she realized it was already 1:00 PM. Frustrated, she lay back down but couldn't stay in bed. She got up, went to the kitchen, made coffee, and had a bite to eat.

The phone rang a couple of times before she could reach it.

"Hello, Dani... this is Tammy."

"Hey, Tammy, what's up?"

"I was thinking of you and Jackie and wanted to see how your night on the town was."

"OMG, Tammy. That girl is wacked. You're so lucky you didn't come out with us."

"What do you mean?" Tammy asked.

"Jackie is fucking over the top. She got the attention of not just a few men, but the whole bar. We had drinks lined up. The more she drank, the sluttier she got."

Tammy was silent on the other end as Dani continued.

"You still there?" Dani asked.

"Yeah, I just can't believe what I'm hearing."

"You wouldn't believe your eyes either if you saw what I saw. I hate to cut you off, Tammy, but I have a horrible headache and I'm in the middle of eating."

"Oh, I'm sorry. I hope you feel better. Let me know if there's anything I can do."

"No, there's not, but I'll see you at the next group," said Dani.

Dani tried to reach Kathy before the next group meeting to arrange a pick-up time. She kept getting voicemail and figured Kathy must be busy. When it was time to leave, Dani went to Kathy's house but found nobody at home. Annoyed, she thought, "That bitch, she could have told me she didn't need a ride."

At the clinic, Dani saw Kathy getting out of a taxi. Furiously, she parked her car and went inside. Kathy ignored her, sitting in her usual place as others mingled.

Dani walked up to Kathy angerly, "Why didn't you answer your phone? I went by your house to pick you up, and you were already gone," Dani said sternly.

"I am capable of getting my own ride, thank you," Kathy replied.

"Are you mad at me for not giving you a ride home after the last meeting? I offered, but you were too stubborn. You wouldn't even let Tammy give you a ride," Dani pressed.

Kathy sat stiffly, avoiding further conversation. Dr. Peters noticed the tension. "Okay, let's get started. How was everyone's weekend?"

No one responded.

"I see I have a quiet group today. Dr. Peters began to say, when Jackie burst in through the door.

"Oh, so sorry I'm late." She saw a seat next to Dani and sat down, attempting a friendly hug, which Dani rebuffed. Jackie looked shocked but shrugged it off. "Whatever," she mumbled.

Dr. Peters continued, trying to elicit responses but sensing the friction. He looked to Tammy for support, but she offered none.

"Well then, this week's appointments will be about discussing some ideas to help you manage your life with tools that will help you individually." He glanced over at Kathy. "Kathy, I don't have you down for an appointment."

"When is Dr. Gifford coming back?" Kathy asked.

"She'll be out a few more weeks; no one knows for sure," Dr. Peters replied.

"Can we discuss it after the meeting?" she asked.

"Sure," he replied.

Dr. Peters used humor to lighten the mood, sharing stories of past patients overcoming fears. As the meeting ended, he reminded everyone of their appointments and asked them to call ahead if they couldn't make it.

When the room cleared, Dr. Peters approached Kathy. "Is everything okay?"

Kathy first tried to deny anything was wrong, then she finally admitted her frustration. "I don't have mental issues. I find it a waste of time to be around people like Jackie. I fell asleep at the wheel. How does that make me crazy?"

Dr. Peters listened compassionately. "As you know, this is a small town. We have no choice but to mix different conditions together. There's no specific group therapy for Narcolepsy or even AA meetings here."

"It's important to work on the exercises I plan to introduce. They can make a huge difference now that you know your condition. Can we book a time?" Reluctantly, Kathy agreed and gave him a suitable time. She stood up, trying to gather her belongings, but Dr. Peters grabbed them first.

"Let me help you," he said, unfazed by her controlling demeanor. They turned off the lights and locked the door behind them.

"I'll give you a ride tonight if you don't have one already," he offered firmly.

"I was going to grab a cab, but okay," Kathy agreed. In the car, Kathy lightened up a bit, making small talk before opening up about her frustration with losing her independence.

"I went from being independent to asking a stranger for help. Dani let me down as soon as a better opportunity came along. And for Jackie, of all people."

Dr. Peters laughed. "Welcome to my crazy world. Most people in therapy haven't had 'normal' lives. They've been tossed around, abused physically, sexually, and mentally. If you think you have problems…"

"Thank God I'm normal," Kathy replied, and they both laughed.

At Kathy's house, Dr. Peters insisted on opening the door for her. "Please let me do this for you," he said, touching her arm. Kathy, feeling uncomfortable but appreciative, agreed. He helped her out of the car and carried her belongings to the door. Inside, he put her things down and commented, "I'll see you this week at your appointment," as he made his way to the door. "Can I get you something to drink before you go?" Kathy asked.

"No, I must get on the road. I have a long drive. Thank you anyway," he said, heading for the door and closing it behind him. Dr. Peters was not showing any signals to Kathy of anything more than a caring person helping her out. Being that it was on his way home, he didn't mind.

22- What is Histrionic

The next day, Jackie arrived at her appointment with Dr. Peters ten minutes early. She wore a white leather skirt, a red silky blouse with ruffles around the V neckline that exposed her cleavage, and red and white stiletto heels that accentuated her legs. Her makeup was heavier than usual, and her hair was curled and backcombed to create a big hair look.

The nurse led Jackie to Dr. Peters' office. As they reached the door, Jackie fidgeted with her clothes until she made eye contact with Dr. Peters. "Hello, Jackie," Dr. Peters greeted. "Come in and have a seat." He pointed to the chair across from his desk. She sat on the edge, then scooted back. "So, how is everything going with you?" he asked.

Jackie began enthusiastically. "Everything is wonderful. My husband and I are getting along better than ever. He was so lost without me and begged me to come home." She went on, embellishing her story, but Dr. Peters kept his eyes on his computer, typing as they spoke. This lack of attention made Jackie uncomfortable.

"I wanted to speak with you personally, Jackie, to get to know you better," Dr. Peters said. Jackie took this as flirting and gave him a lustful smile. What I mean is," Dr. Peters continued, "I know Dr. Gifford's diagnosis, but I want to hear your perspective. What do you think about your diagnosis and how are you dealing with it?"

Jackie was taken back. Clearing her throat and squirming in her chair, she asked, "What do you mean?"

"What do you think of the term 'Histrionic' and what does it mean to you?" Dr. Peters asked. Realizing she wasn't getting the reaction she wanted, Jackie became more nervous.

"Dr. Gifford said that because of my childhood with different dads and being tossed around, I tend to need more attention and don't always pursue it properly," she admitted.

Dr. Peters nodded. "And do you agree with that?"

"Well, yes, I suppose at times," Jackie said, clearly uncomfortable.

"What do you notice about yourself when you feel insecure?" Dr. Peters asked.

"Insecure, I don't think I'm insecure. I'm not insecure at all," Jackie insisted.

Dr. Peters continued typing. The sound of a document being printed filled the room. He placed the printed document in front of him, waiting until Jackie finished speaking. "This is an overview of typical Histrionic symptoms. It doesn't mean you have all these symptoms, but many people with this disorder show strong signs of some or most. Be honest with yourself and me," Dr. Peters said. "As I read through this out loud, think about which ones might apply to you." Jackie watched and listened defensively as Dr. Peters began reading the list:

- Be uncomfortable unless he or she is the center of attention.

- Dress provocatively and/or exhibit inappropriately seductive or flirtatious behavior.

- Shift emotions rapidly.

- Act very dramatically, as though performing before an audience, with exaggerated emotions and expressions, yet appears to lack sincerity.

- Be overly concerned with physical appearance.

- Constantly seeking reassurance or approval

- Be gullible and easily influenced by others.

- Be excessively sensitive to criticism or disapproval.

- They have a low tolerance for frustration, and they become easily bored by routine, often beginning projects without finishing them or skipping from one event to another.

- Not think before acting

- Make rash decisions.

- Be self-centered and rarely show concern for others.

- Have difficulty maintaining relationships, often seeming fake or shallow in their dealings with others.

- Threaten or attempt suicide to get attention.

As he finished reading, Dr. Peters looked directly into Jackie's eyes. Neither spoke for a moment.

"I have never tried to kill myself," Jackie said. "And I like to dress nicely because it makes me feel good. Does that make me mentally ill?" Jackie said with an attitude.

Dr. Peters saw her becoming defensive. "I want you to circle anything on this list that you feel might apply to you," he asked, placing the paper in front of her. "Keep in mind, Jackie,

I'm here to help you." She grabbed the pen sharply and began reading. She circled:

- Not think before acting

- Be excessively sensitive to criticism or disapproval.

With an attitude, Jackie said, "I do not see myself in most of these categories. I like attention, but I do not need to be the center stage all the time."

Dr. Peters listened without commenting. "Yes, I agree I don't have many friends, but that's because I make other women feel uncomfortable because of my looks or what I might have. Especially people like Kathy and Dani. Most women would go through these items, circling items on the list. Does that make them crazy?"

"Crazy isn't what we're referring to," Dr. Peters explained. "If you knew others saw you exhibiting many of these traits, would you want to do something about it? Would it make you uncomfortable?"

"What are you trying to say?" Jackie asked, defensive again.

"I want you to take this list and share it with someone close to you, such as your husband or a close friend. Pay attention to their reactions. The goal is for you to see how others perceive you. Think about it for a week, and if you find yourself acting out any items on the list, journal about it. We'll discuss your journal next time we meet. Do you agree to try this exercise?"

"Sure," Jackie said. "What could it hurt?"

"Changing the subject, is there something going on with you and Dani or Kathy?" Dr. Peters asked.

Jackie smirked. "That's what I'm talking about. I went out with Dani, and Kathy got mad because her little schedule was interrupted. We asked her to come, but she refused. While Dani and I were out, guys bought us drinks, and Dani got jealous because they were hitting on me. She even commented on how she never gets that kind of attention. One guy asked me to dance with him, and I said yes. I guess that pissed her off, so she left."

"I knew there was something going on because no one was talking at the last group meeting," said Dr. Peters. "Now I understand." He began typing on his computer again. "Can we meet again same time next week?"

"Yeah, sure," Jackie replied. "I enjoy our little meeting."

Dr. Peters filled out an appointment card, stood up, and shook Jackie's hand while handing her the card. "Great, then we'll see you next week." Jackie grabbed her items and left the room feeling a bit confused as to what was on the list and did, she really act that way.

Dani was supposed to meet with Dr. Peters that day as well. When she did not show up, Dr. Peters called her house number and her cell phone, but there were no answers. He left her voice message asking her to please call him.

Dani was home but not in the mood to talk. She heard the phone ring and the messages but did not get up to answer. She had been drinking since the night before she and Jackie went out, which helped put her in a dark mental state. She had not showered, brushed her teeth or hair, or changed her clothes.

She made a comfort zone on the couch with pillows and blankets, watching TV and eating only popcorn.

The following day, Kathy went to her appointment with Dr. Peters. He was happy to see her and shook her hand as she entered his office.

"I'm glad you made it," he said.

"You think I'd no-show you?" Kathy chuckled.

"Well, I would hope not," he replied. "Have a seat." "I've met with some others from the group, and that has gone really well," he said. "I was able to find out a little more about why there are some hard feelings among the group."

"Oh, really?" Kathy said inquisitively. "And what did you find out?"

"It's confidential," Dr. Peters said with a smile. "What I hear or share here with you or anyone else is just for my ears only." Kathy smiled. "Okay, I get it."

"What I'm concerned about is that one of the gals didn't keep her appointment with me. I called her, but she didn't answer."

"If I were to guess, I'd say it was Jackie," Kathy said.

"No, actually, it wasn't," he replied. "But let's talk about you. How are you doing?"

"Is it Dani?" Kathy asked. Dr. Peters took a deep breath, showing concern. He changed the subject.

"Kathy, sometimes people can't help how they turn out. You can't always judge someone because they irritate you. If you look deeper, you might see that they are the way they are because of something or someone that hurt them." Kathy rolled her eyes.

"Yeah, I know, but damn, it's so obvious that Jackie is just out to get attention, and the way she goes about it is repulsive. Everything is about her! It's so irritating."

"Try to be a little more understanding," Dr. Peters said tenderly. "These people need help; they don't even realize they are so needy and self-absorbed."

"How can they not know?" Kathy replied with attitude.

"Trust me," Dr. Peters said. "So, what I would like to do is give you some exercises to work on that will make you more aware of your current condition with regards to the narcolepsy." He began typing into his computer, searching for the Fact Sheet on Narcolepsy. When he found it, he printed it out and placed it in front of him.

"It is Dani," Kathy said. "Do you think something is wrong with her?" Looking up at Kathy, he said, "Please, Kathy, I can't talk about it."

Kathy had a look of concern on her face. "I'm mad at her, but I wouldn't like to see anything happen to her," she said compassionately.

Dr. Peters held the document, going through all the titles briefly explaining: "This is a lot to read, but I believe if you know more about your condition, it will help you understand why you feel tired a lot of the time." He then handed it to Kathy. "So, Kathy, what I would like you to do is read this and follow any links to articles on the internet or get books at the library about narcolepsy. I would also like you to start journaling daily, several times a day. Keep a notepad by your bedside so you have it if you wake up during the night. Note how you feel from the time you wake up until you go to bed.

Are you waking up tired? Do you find yourself more tired at certain times of the day? After eating, do you get more tired than usual? Also, note any patterns at night that you may or may not be aware of. We can review your journal entries the next time we meet. How does that sound?"

"I can do that," Kathy said. "It will be interesting to find out more about Narcolepsy, and I don't really have anything else to do with my time these days" she chuckled.

"Great. So, how is your leg healing?" Dr. Peters asked.

"I go to the orthopedic doctor tomorrow, so I guess we'll see what he says," Kathy replied. "I'm sure I won't be going back to work anytime soon due to my other issues. I need to find something to do with myself, or I'll really be one of your crazy clients." They both laughed.

They continued chatting casually until her time was up. Dr. Peters stood up and walked over to Kathy. As she stood, he reached out his hand to assist her, then shook her hand. Placing his other hand on her shoulder. "You're going to be just fine Kathy" he said with a warm smile. "C'mon, I'll Walk you out," he said. They both could feel there was something more than just a doctor-patient relationship developing.

When Kathy got home, she dialed Dani's cell. No answer. She called her home number but only got her recorded message. "Dani, this is Kathy. I need to talk to you. Can you please call me? You know my number, call me, okay?"

The next day, Kathy called again, leaving another message. "Dani, this is Kathy. I am worried about you. You didn't call me back. I would like a ride with you to the group meeting if you wouldn't mind coming and getting me. Could you please call me? Okay, bye." Kathy knew she could take a cab if needed but wanted Dani to commit to picking her up.

That evening, Kathy entered the meeting room and spotted Tammy. "Tammy, have you heard from Dani?" she asked.

"No, I haven't," said Tammy, looking concerned. "Is something wrong?"

"I don't know. She won't answer her phone," Kathy replied, then walked over to the chairs.

Dr. Peters entered the room, scanning for Kathy. When he spotted her, his eyes lit up, as he smiled. Kathy smiled back. He then looked for Dani and noticed she was not in the room. Hse became concerned for her but kept it to himself. "Okay, let's get started," he said.

'I don't see Miss Dani here today." He said casually.

"I tried to call her a couple of times," Kathy said, "but she won't answer her phone." Dr. Peters took a deep breath.

"I hope she is okay."

Jackie walked in, late as usual, dressed provocatively. Kathy whispered to her as she sat down, "Have you seen Dani?"

"No, why?" Jackie asked. Kathy just shook her head and looked back at Dr. Peters. The meeting proceeded as usual, but Dr. Peters didn't show his concern for Dani throughout the rest of the session.

As the meeting ended, Jackie approached Kathy. "What's going on with Dani?" she asked.

"Nobody has heard from her since the last meeting," Kathy replied. "I'm thinking of going by her house on my way home."

"If it's okay, I'd like to go with you," Jackie said.

"Sure, if you want," Kathy agreed hesitantly.

"Do you have a ride home?" asked Jackie.

"I was planning on getting a cab," Kathy said.

"Why don't you let me pay you back for the cab ride and give you a lift home? On the way, we can stop by Dani's house," Jackie suggested.

"That works for me. Thanks," Kathy said humbly.

Dr. Peters and Tammy walked up to the two women. Kathy said, "We are going to go by Dani's place on our way home to check on her and make sure everything is okay."

"That's a great idea," Dr. Peters said. "I was planning on doing the same, but I'm not sure where she lives."

"Oh, just follow us," Jackie said. "I know right where she lives."

Tammy, with a concerned look on her face, said, "Do you mind if I follow you there as well? I'd really like to know that she is okay."

"Of course you can," Jackie said. "Let's all meet down in the parking lot."

The four of them left the clinic more concerned for Dani than they had been. It had been four days since anyone had heard from her. As they approached Dani's house, they saw faint lights inside. They got out of their cars and met on the sidewalk in front of the house.

"Let's peek in the window and see if we can see her," Kathy suggested. They walked up the walkway and the three steps to the porch. They peeked into the window and saw a dim light coming from the back of the house. There was no sign of Dani, but they saw the TV was on.

Dr. Peters knocked hard on the front door and rang the doorbell several times while checking to see if the door was unlocked. Dani didn't come to the door. "Can someone go around to the back and see if they can see something," Kathy asked. Jackie and Tammy left Dr. Peters and Kathy at the door as they circled the house, peeking through every window they came across. Frustrated, they returned to the front door.

"We didn't see anything," Jackie said. Dr. Peters twisted the doorknob again, and this time the door opened. "C'mon, the door is open," he called. They all walked in slowly, looking around at the mess Dani had created. As they approached the back part of the house where the TV was, they saw Dani lying on the couch, passed out cold. Empty beer bottles littered the coffee table and surrounded her on the couch. The ashtray was full of cigarette butts, and popcorn was scattered everywhere.

Dr. Peters immediately checked for a pulse. "Dani, wake up," he said softly, moving her hair out of her face and lifting her head. "Dani, it's me, Dr. Peters." Dani opened her eyes slowly, blinking repeatedly as she tried to make sense of what she was seeing.

"What the fuck are you doing here?" she asked. As her eyes roamed, she noticed the women from the group. She began to sit up, asking,

"Why are you guys here?"

"We were concerned for you," Dr. Peters said.

"Yeah, and we didn't want anything to be wrong with you," Kathy added.

"You gave us quite the scare," Jackie said. "I hope you didn't do this because you were mad at me."

Dani, still waking up, looked at them in shock. "How did you get in my house?" she mumbled.

"You left the door unlocked," Dr. Peters said. "We knocked several times, we could see your car in the driveway, the TV and lights on, then I tried to open it."

"How long have you been drinking Dani?" Dr. Peters asked with concern.

"I do not know. I have been sitting here watching TV on and off," Dani replied. "I haven't kept track of the time, she mumbled."

Dr. Peters looked at Tammy. "Can you go in the kitchen and find some coffee or tea to make? Grab some water too if you can."

"Yes, sure," Tammy said. She went into the kitchen, looking through the drawers and cabinets until she found the coffee. The kitchen was a complete mess, with dirty dishes piled in the sink. The coffee pot was half full of moldy coffee. Tammy cleaned it out and made a fresh pot, then began tidying up the kitchen while she waited.

"You missed your appointment with me," Dr. Peters said. "And when you didn't show up for the group meeting the next day, I figured it was time to check on you."

"I tried calling you for days," Kathy added. "I didn't know where you lived, or I would have been here sooner."

"I thought you were still mad at me from when we went out," Jackie said. "I drove Kathy here on my way to take her home."

Tammy returned with the coffee pot and cups. "Who wants coffee?" she asked.

"Give Dani some," Dr. Peters said, "and I'll have some too." As Dani sat up on the couch, she complained of a headache.

"Drink some coffee; it will help you wake up," Dr. Peters advised. "You will need to drink lots of water too," said Kathy. "I look like shit," Dani said in a raspy whisper as she fussed with her hair "

We don't care what you look like," Kathy replied. "We're just glad you're okay." The group huddled around the couch, talking, and sharing stories until midnight. The bond that took place that night was the beginning of a relationship that would eventually become a strong circle of friends. Dr. Peters reminded Dani of the dangers of alcohol, especially with her bipolar disorder and the medications she was on. Dani agreed that her behavior was not appropriate and promised it wouldn't happen again.

They all agreed it was getting late and they needed to leave. Dani showed signs she was going to be okay, and they felt it was safe to leave her. Jackie was the first to leave, but she showed personal growth by asking Kathy if she wanted a ride. Dr. Peters spoke up. "No worries, I will give her a ride home from here." Tammy was the last to leave. She stayed to ensure Dani was okay, even offering to spend the night so she

wouldn't be alone. Dani insisted she would be fine, so Tammy
left.

23 - The Sleep Over

As Dr. Peters pulled up to Kathy's house, he was exhausted. "This is a later than usual night. I am too tired to drive home. I am going to get a hotel." he said.

"Would you like to stay here?" she asked. "I have an extra room."

"Oh no, I couldn't do that." Dr. Peters said while rubbing his eyes to stay awake. "Besides, it's against the rules, but I don't think I'd have a problem driving to the hotel we saw on the way here," Dr. Peters admitted.

"Oh no, you come into my house. We will get you set up for the night," Kathy said not taking no for an answer.

"Okay, you've twisted my arm," he said with a smile. This must be just between us." He got out of the car and rushed to open the door for Kathy, helping her out. They walked to the front door together. Kathy flipped on the lights and Dr. Peters followed closely behind.

"Would you like coffee, or are you beat?" she asked.

"I am sorry, but honestly, I am beat. I have been up since 4:30 this morning. I think I will go into a coma once my head hits the pillow," Dr. Peters said with a chuckle.

"Follow me then," Kathy said, struggling with her crutches, leading him down the hall towards the bedrooms.

"I can sleep on your couch. Just give me a pillow, and I'll be fine," Dr. Peters offered.

"I wouldn't hear of it," Kathy said. "Besides, nobody puts their feet on my couch, let alone sleeps on it," she chuckled. "C'mon back here. That's why I have a guest room, so when people visit, they have a nice, comfortable place to sleep." He followed her down the hall to the guest room.

"Now, if you need to use the facilities, they're down the hall on the right. And if you happen to get scared, I'll be down the hall on the left," she teased.

"Oh yeah, I'll be knocking on your door within 30 minutes," Dr. Peters laughed.

Kathy started to walk away until Dr. Peters said, "Wait, I really appreciate you letting me stay here." Looking deep into her eyes, he said, "Really, thank you."

"You're very welcome. Now get some sleep," Kathy said, walking away from the room and down the hall towards her bedroom.

Dani awoke to quite a mess she had created during her drunken stupor. She immediately went to the bathroom, turning on the shower and climbing in. She stood frozen as the warm water splashed onto her head and down her body. "How can I let myself get like this?" she thought.

Dani could hear the phone ringing in the background, but she wasn't about to get out of the shower to answer it. At the other end of the line was Tammy. Listening to the phone ring with no answer made Tammy concerned. After the phone went to the recorder, she hung up and dialed again. Dani continued to ignore the call and stayed in the shower. Tammy put the phone down and began to worry. "Should I go over and make sure she is okay?" she thought. She picked up the phone again, this time calling Kathy.

"Hello," said Kathy in a half-asleep voice.

"Kathy, it is Tammy. I just called over to Dani's house two times, and she did not answer her phone. Do you think she is okay, or do you think I should go over there and check on her?"

"Hell, I don't know," said Kathy. "Why don't you wait a couple of minutes and try again? Maybe she is still sleeping, she did have a rough night after all."

"Okay, I am just worried about her," said Tammy.

"I know, but let's give her time to wake up from her hangover. If she does not answer in an hour or so, maybe then we can start to worry."

There was a knock-on Kathy's bedroom door. "I'm scared," said Dr. Peters, continuing to knock.

"Tammy, I must go. Call me back if you hear anything or if you go over there."

"Okay," said Tammy feeling frustrated.

Dr. Peters continued to knock lightly on the door. Kathy got up, grabbing her robe as she made her way to the door. Before opening it, she checked herself in the mirror on her dresser. Hesitantly, she opened the door to see Dr. Peters standing there with a cup of coffee in hand.

"I wondered how late you were going to sleep in," he said, handing her the cup.

"What is that smell?" asked Kathy as she walked down the hallway towards the kitchen.

"I don't know what you're talking about," Dr. Peters said. As Kathy got closer to the kitchen, she realized he had made breakfast for her and had everything ready and neatly served on the table.

"Wow," she said. "I don't know what to say."

"How about if you don't say anything and just sit down and eat?" he suggested with a smile.

"Okay," said Kathy, in a bit of a shock. "I don't remember the last time someone made me breakfast. This is a very special treat." Dr. Peters waited on her, making sure she had everything she needed.

"Please sit down with me, Dr. Peters. I want you to relax and eat too," said Kathy.

"How about you call me Steve?" asked Dr. Peters. "Okay," said Kathy with a bashful smile. "I like the name Steve."

Steve filled his plate with the food he had prepared and sat down at the table to enjoy Kathy's company for quite some time, until the phone began to ring again.

"Kathy, it's Tammy. I have been calling over to Dani's house since we last talked. She is not answering. I think I am going to go over there. Do you want to meet me?"

"No, I have a guest at my house right now, and I can't get away. Why don't you go over there and check on her? You can call me if you need me," said Kathy.

"Okay, I can do that," said Tammy. "I wish I knew how to get a hold of Dr. Peters. He should probably know what's going on, don't you think?"

"No," said Kathy abruptly. "There may be nothing going on, Tammy. You need to check her house first before you call anyone else. She could not be home, or she could have gone out for some reason. Let's not get into a panic."

"Okay," said Tammy. "I will call you after I find out where she is and what she is doing."

"Great," said Kathy as she hung up the phone.

"Everything okay?" asked Steve. "Yes, it's just Tammy getting nervous and overreacting about Dani again. I told her to go over to her house and check on her if she was so worried. She wanted to get a hold of you to let you know. That is crazy," said Kathy.

"Not really," said Dr. Peters. "People like Dani sometimes have trouble pulling themselves out of a deep depressed state. It takes a lot of time to get back on track after dealing with a loss. After leaving her last night, Dani could have done something stupid like trying to end her life. Then again," he paused, "she could be in a state of mania, and who knows what she is doing?" Kathy looked confused.

"What do you mean by mania?"

"People with Bipolar Disorder can go from one extreme to the other in a short period of time."

"Like how?" asked Kathy.

"Well, you saw her in a state of depression." "Yes, I sure did," said Kathy.

"So, imagine the opposite. Try to imagine someone super high on enthusiasm and wanting to do everything at once shop, spend money, have fun."

"That actually doesn't sound so bad," said Kathy.

"You don't understand," Dr. Peters said. "Imagine you just got a new credit card in the mail for $2,000. All your other bills are due, and the other credit cards you have are all tapped out."

"Ya, so?" said Kathy.

"People like Dani will take that credit card and go shopping until they're broke, buying things very compulsively. Things they don't even need. They will spend every dime and possibly even max out the new card." Kathy looked incredulous. "As much as I would like to stay and chat all day, I should go check on Dani as well then head to the office," said Dr. Peters.

"You do what you have to do, but I think it's crazy," said Kathy with a bit of sarcasm. They both got up from the table. Steve began picking up the plates. "No, no, just leave those there. I will tend to them myself. You have done far too much already," said Kathy, taking the plate from Steve's hands

"You sure? It's the least I could do since you saved me from making that terrible drive home last night," said Steve. "Okay then, how about I take you to dinner sometime to make up for it?" asked Dr. Peters.

"Wouldn't that be against the rules?" asked Kathy with a bit of sarcasm.

"What rules would those be?" asked Steve with a flirtatious grin.

"Well, you know, dating a client is probably off-limits for you," Kathy said.

"Yes, you're probably right, but when Dr. Gifford comes back, we can," he suggested.

"That might be fun," said Kathy. "I'll take you up on that." Kathy walked Steve to the front door and then just outside to the porch, making small talk all the way. He turned to her and reached out to give her a hug. He held her tight; a bit longer than she expected for a friendly hug. As they embraced, he pulled back slightly and kissed her on the forehead, saying "thanks again for everything."

Kathy wasn't sure what to think about this new friendship that was developing. She looked into Steve's eyes, feeling a mix of confusion and joy. "I hope you have a really nice day," she said.

Dr. Peters smiled at her as he pulled away and headed for his car. "You have a terrific day yourself," he said. Kathy watched him as he got into his car and drove off. Feeling stunned and confused about her feelings, she walked back into her house and shut the door.

24 - You've Got a Friend

Tammy arrived at Dani's house to find her worries were unfounded. Dani was outside in her front yard, mowing in her robe and slippers.

"Dani, Dani," Tammy called out. Dani could not hear her over the mower. Tammy got out of the car and walked up slowly to Dani as she looped around in her direction. "Oh, hi! What are you doing here?" Dani shouted.

"Well, you didn't answer your phone, so I got worried," said Tammy.

"Oh, you don't need to worry about me. I'm fine," Dani shouted back. "I'm just catching up on chores I've neglected for a few days." Tammy went and sat down on the front porch, watching Dani while she finished mowing the yard.

When Dani was done, Tammy expected her to sit and chat, but Dani kept working. She got a large trash can from the side of the house and dumped the grass clippings into it. Then she retrieved the hedge trimmer from the garage. She started the trimmer before reaching the front yard, making it too loud to talk. Tammy continued to watch patiently. A couple of times, Dani made eye contact with Tammy, smiled, and quickly looked away. Tammy thought maybe she wasn't wanted there and got up from the chair to leave. Dr. Peters' car pulled up in front of the house which Dani paid no attention to and kept working. Tammy walked over to Dr. Peters to greet him.

"So, is everything okay?" Dr. Peters asked.

"It appears to be," said Tammy. "Dani has been working in her yard since I got here. She hasn't stopped for a break, not even to talk to me."

"Hmm, well, let me say hi to her and see for myself," Dr. Peters said.

"Great," said Tammy. She returned to the front porch and sat down.

Dr. Peters approached Dani as she was trimming the bushes in front of her house. He had to wave his hands to catch her attention. She put down the trimmer and turned it off to talk to him.

"What brings you here, Dr. Peters?" Dani asked.

"You do," he replied. "I thought I would stop by and check on you to make sure you are alright before going into the office."

"Of course, I am alright," said Dani. "Why wouldn't I be?"

"Great," said Dr. Peters. "Do you have time to sit on the front porch and chat for a moment?"

"Of course," she said, leading him to the porch where Tammy was sitting.

Dr. Peters grabbed a chair and sat down. "Can I get you guys something to drink?" Dani asked, sweat dripping down her face.

"Water is fine," said Dr. Peters.

"That is good for me too," Tammy added. Dani went inside to get some water for them.

When Dani came back to the porch, she had a tray filled with 3 glasses, a container of lemonade, chips, raw vegetables with dip, grapes, and cheese. "I thought you might be a little hungry," she said.

"Oh, you shouldn't have gone through all the trouble," Dr. Peters said.

Dani poured the lemonade into the glasses and handed them to both Dr. Peters and Tammy. She poured herself a glass and drank it quickly. As she poured herself another glass, she commented on how thirsty she was and hadn't even realized it.

"I came by to make sure you were okay," Dr. Peters repeated. "Why wouldn't I be?" replied Dani.

"Dani, you haven't shown up to any meetings in the last few days, and you didn't call to let us know you were okay. Then we came to your house last night to find you, well... Let's just say you had been drinking heavy last night," said Dr. Peters.

Dani was in denial that she had done anything wrong. To her, everything seemed normal. She began to get agitated. "You know, sometimes I get sick and tired of all the bullshit I have to go through just to keep people like you happy," she said with feist. "I don't understand why you must keep harping on me. Why can't you all just leave me alone and let me be? If I want to get drunk and sleep for days, that should be my business!" The more she talked, the more riled up she became.

Dr. Peters could see she wasn't responding well to his concern. "Dani, I am not here to hassle you or make you feel bad," Dr. Peters said. "I want to make sure you are safe."

"I am fine," said Dani bluntly.

"I can see that you are, and I am pleased," said Dr. Peters. "Can we just sit here and be friends and enjoy each other's company as friends?" he asked. Dani looked at him, still defensive.

"Yeah, sure, but lay off the interrogation. I am fine!"

Dr. Peters knew it was best to change the subject.

"So, Tammy, how are you doing?" he asked, shifting the focus off Dani.

"I am doing okay," Tammy said in her quiet voice.

They continued to sit on the porch and conversed for a while before Dr. Peters had to leave.

"I must be getting to the office," he said. "I haven't been able to go by there today." Dr. Peters picked up his cell phone to see if he had any messages. "Looks like no one really needs me that bad," he chuckled. He stood up and gave the women a handshake.

"I will see you both at the next meeting, right?" he asked. They both agreed they would be there. He left the porch, walked to his car, and waved one last time before driving off.

Dani continued to sit and talk with Tammy, allowing the two of them to get to know each other better.

"I haven't had anyone care about my well-being like this ever," claimed Dani. It feels so strange and intrusive."

"Well, I haven't had anyone to worry about other than my parents in a long time," said Tammy. "So, I guess this is new for both of us." "Oh, I better call Kathy. She is also waiting for my call to make sure everything is okay," said Tammy.

"What?" exclaimed Dani.

"Yeah, she was here last night along with Jackie. I guess you better get used to the fact that other people care about you," Tammy chuckled.

Dani listened in on the call that Tammy placed to Kathy. When Tammy hung up, she said, "Kathy is happy to hear you're alright."

"So, what about Jackie?" asked Dani. "Are you supposed to call her and let her know as well?" she chuckled.

"Well, I only called Kathy this morning when I couldn't get in touch with you. I never even thought to call Jackie."

"Just as well, she doesn't need to be worrying about me right now," said Dani.

"So, why are you part of these crazy people meetings?" asked Dani. "You seem rather normal to me." Dani chuckled.

"Well, I don't know about that, but I guess you can say it is a safe place for me, and I have gotten used to it," said Tammy.

"But, do you have issues that need a therapist?" asked Dani.

"Doesn't everyone,"? asked Tammy. Tammy got a little quiet and put her head down.

"I am sorry, Tammy, you don't have to answer my stupid questions," said Dani.

No, it's okay," said Tammy. "Actually, besides being extremely shy and learning to deal with that, I have what is called Tourette's Syndrome. I have it under control through medication, but it is something that I have had to deal with since I was a young teenager." "What is Tourette Syndrome?" asked Dani.

"The best way for me to explain it is that Tourette syndrome (TS) is an inherited, neurological disorder characterized by multiple involuntary movements and uncontrollable vocalizations called tics that come and go over years. In a few cases, such tics can include inappropriate words and phrases."

"So, what's the big deal? I don't understand," said Dani.

"These movements called tics are uncontrollable. Some people twitch their noses, blink their eyes, or their body moves. My lips would move as if I was blowing kisses."

Dani laughed.

"OMG! That is so funny."

"Well, that is not all," Tammy continued. "I also blink my right eye as if I am winking at someone."

"No way," said Dani! "That is too cute."

"Cute? No, it is not cute to be winking and blowing kisses uncontrollably at male teachers or strange men that you don't know. Nor is it cute to be saying things like 'fucking cunt,' or 'shit' or 'asshole' or anything else that wanted to just blurt from my mouth at any time without any control whatsoever. No, that is not cute," Tammy said, sadly, putting her head down in shame.

Dani realized it really bothered Tammy to talk about it. "I am sorry, Tammy. I didn't mean to make light of something that bothers you so much," she said. "I have never heard about it and my ignorance thought you were kidding." Tammy lifted her head slowly, making eye contact with Dani.

"That's okay. The group is where I feel most comfortable around people. Anywhere else I go; I must worry about what people are going to think about me. Am I going to be laughed at? I just like helping at the clinic and being a part of something that makes me feel good."

"I understand," said Dani in a compassionate tone.

The conversation was interrupted by a call coming in on Dani's cell phone. "Hello, this is Dani."

"Hey, Dani, it's Jackie. I'm just calling to see if you're doing okay and if you need anything," replied Jackie.

"Wow, Jackie, yeah, I am doing just fine. Tammy is here visiting with me, and Dr. Peters just left."

"Do you want any more company?" asked Jackie. "I have to go out for a while and thought I would stop by just to chat for a bit."

"Why sure, I'm going to be here for a while. I don't plan on going anywhere," said Dani. "Great, I'll see you after a while," said Jackie.

Dani hung up the phone, raising her eyebrows. "That was just Jackie. She is going to come by after a while as well."

"See, people care about you," Tammy said with a smile. Tammy stayed with Dani for most of the afternoon, visiting and offering help whenever possible.

After several hours of visiting, Tammy said, "I should be getting on my way. I need to check on my parents."

Dani put her arm around Tammy as they headed toward her car. "Thank you so much for being there for me," she said. "I guess I need to pay more attention to how much I drink, especially when I am by myself."

"Well, maybe you shouldn't be drinking at all," suggested Tammy gently.

"Yeah, I've thought about that, but I do like to have a little fun once in a while," admitted Dani. "Okay, I'll talk to you later," said Dani as she reached out to Tammy giving her a hug. As Tammy turned to walk away, Jackie drove up in her Mercedes, pulling into the driveway. Jackie got out of the car, waving.

"Hello! Sorry I didn't make it sooner." She was dressed in a short magenta skirt that matched her high-heeled shoes. Her blouse was made of fine silk, adorned with a floral pattern in brilliant colors. One sleeve fell off her shoulder, and the front was open, revealing her cleavage. Her hair and nails were impeccably done.

"Wow, you look terrific," said Tammy." What's the occasion?"

"Oh, thank you, darling," replied Jackie, ignoring Tammy's question. "Are you heading out?"

"Yes, I have been here all day. It is about time I get something productive done," replied Tammy. The gals embraced, Tammy turning to walk away. "You guys behave yourselves," Tammy chuckled.

"You don't have to worry about that with me," said Dani. "I think I won't be drinking for a long time."

As Tammy walked away, Dani invited Jackie up onto the porch to sit for a while. Jackie began talking about all the things she had done during the day, never asking how Dani was doing. It was all about her. After some time, Jackie asked, "Do you have anything to drink in there?" pointing to the house.

"Well, yes, of course. Let's go inside and see what I have that would be suitable for you," Dani said. When they got to the kitchen, Dani opened the fridge. "Hmm, would you like water, orange juice, soda, or beer?" asked Dani.

"Well, what do you have to mix with soda?" asked Jackie.

Surprised that Jackie would want to drink around her, Dani replied, "well, if there's anything left, it's in that cupboard," pointing to the left of where Jackie was standing. Jackie walked over to the cupboard, opened it, and after a moment's hesitation, pulled out a bottle of rum.

"A little rum and coke are good anytime," said Jackie. "Do you have any lime? Where are your glasses?" she asked.

Dani reached into the cupboard to get Jackie a glass. She grabbed two glasses, put them on the counter, then fetched a two-liter bottle of coke from the fridge. Dani put ice in the two glasses and poured coke into them, stopping just before the top. She handed Jackie a glass and watched as she poured the rum into her own glass, setting down the bottle in front of her. Dani then reached over, grabbed the bottle of rum, and poured some into her glass of coke. "No limes, dammit," said Dani.

"I thought you would be done drinking for a while," said Jackie.

"Well, I was going to but, I can't have my company drinking alone," said Dani with a smile, followed by a chuckle. "Let's go back to the front porch," Dani suggested as she walked toward the door. The two women sat on the porch making small talk at first.

"So, when did you first know you had a problem?" asked Jackie.

"Problem? Are you referring to my drinking?" Dani asked defensively.

"Well, that and the other stuff," replied Jackie.

"Being bipolar or whatever it is that you are."

Dani hesitated before answering, "Bipolar, schizoid, and whatever else," Dani said sarcastically. "Yeah, that would be as a young teen." Dani picked up her glass and took a large drink. As she put down the glass, Jackie could see Dani's eyes beginning to gloss over. "My doctor says I should stay on my meds and not mix them with alcohol."

"Then why do you?" asked Jackie curiously.

Dani hesitated, "I don't fucking know. Hell, I want to stop, but I just end up like this." Dani began to get agitated. "It's bullshit," she said, "just a bunch of bullshit." Jackie sipped her drink slowly while Dani drank hers much faster.

"That night we went out together was pretty fucked up," said Dani. "You can pretty much get any fucking man you want."

Jackie chuckled. "Yeah, I don't know if it's a gift or a curse."

"Did you fuck that guy at the bar?" Dani asked bluntly.

Jackie laughed, "I never kiss and tell."

"You did! Why you little whore" said Dani as she laughed. "Wow! The other guys at the table were talking shit about it."

Jackie chuckled again.

Dani got up. "I'm going to get a refill. Do you want more?" she asked.

"Oh, no, I'm okay, but thanks," said Jackie.

Dani went inside the house and poured herself another drink, this time filling the glass halfway with coke and halfway with rum. She then took a swig of the rum right out of the bottle. She wiped her lips and went back outside with her drink in hand.

"That was quick," said Jackie. "So, are you okay?"

"Fuck, I don't know," said Dani. "I don't know why everyone makes such a big deal out of me drinking. I'm in my house, and no one is being bothered, so what the fuck?" Jackie laughed.

"Yeah, I guess," Jackie said.

"So why are you here?" asked Dani.

Jackie looked a little confused but replied, "I told you I was concerned for you. We all stopped by last night and found you pretty fucked up. I wanted to see if you needed a friend."

Dani was already almost finished with the second drink she had just made and was starting to show signs of intoxication. "You want to be my friend?" she asked. "Why do you want to be my friend?"

"Oh, come on, Dani," replied Jackie. "Everyone needs a friend now and then."

"Yeah, well, I don't," said Dani. "The only reason people want to be your friend is to take from you. It's more of a pain in the ass to have friends. I could never be friends with someone like you."

Jackie was shocked by her comment. "What is that supposed to mean?" she asked.

"I went out with you and saw how you are. The first time I had a guy hit on me, you couldn't handle the attention not being on you. I saw you throwing yourself at him to get noticed. You asked him to dance when he was talking to me" Dani said as her words began to slur from her drinking.

"That is not true," claimed Jackie.

"Yes, it is true," said Dani.

Jackie stood up. "I don't have to take this bullshit," she said. "What, you can't handle the truth?" Dani asked. "How many friends do you have? You don't have any friends because you try to fuck their husbands." And speaking of husbands, what about your husband? If he knew how you really are"! Dani said loudly.

"You know what? Fuck you," Jackie said loudly. "I do have friends. And if this is what you are really like, I do not want you for a friend. Fuck you!" Jackie grabbed her purse and headed for her car. "You are really one messed up woman," Jackie said as she walked down the steps.

"Yeah, well, fuck you too," shouted Dani. "You are pretty fucked up yourself. Look at how you dress all the time. Your boobs are falling out of your top, or your skirt is so short that if you bend over, your whole ass will show. Who are you trying to impress? Surely not your husband." Jackie turned and looked at Dani with the angriest face.
"You're a fucking disgraceful drunk bitch," Jackie shouted before she got into her car, peeling away as she left the driveway.

That evening, at the group meeting Kathy noticed that Dani was not there again. She felt a knot of worry tightened in her chest. She approached Steve, who was preparing for the session.

"What's up with Dani," Kathy asked quietly. I am surprised she's not here?"

Dr. Peters said, his brow furrowing. 'When I left, Tammy was still with her." Tammy, who was nearby, glanced up and walked over, her face thoughtful. "

When I left, Jackie was just pulling up," Tammy said softly. "If she comes, we can ask her how Dani was doing.'"

As the night progressed, Jackie never made it to the meeting either. Dr. Peters thought it was odd that neither she nor Dani was there. As soon as the meeting was over, he dialed Dani's number.

"Hello," said Dani.

"Dani, this is Dr. Peters. Are you doing alright?"

"Yes, I'm alright," she said in a slurred voice.

"Have you been drinking again?" asked Dr. Peters.

"Uh, just a little bit," she said.

"Dani, you shouldn't be drinking. Did you take any of your meds?"

"I don't remember," said Dani. "Why don't you leave me alone and just let me be?" she mumbled.

"It is my job to not leave you alone and to help keep you out of harm's way. I will be there as soon as I can. Meanwhile, I want you to stop drinking."

Steve looked over at Kathy, frustration and concern filled his face. "What's wrong," she asked.

"I'm sorry I am going to have to make a stop on my way home. You can go with me, or I can drop you off first or you can get a ride home with someone else." he said, frustration written on his face.

"I'll go with you. It's not like I haven't been through this already with you," said Kathy, with a hint of frustration in her voice.

Dr. Peters called Jackie to confirm her visit with Dani. "Hey Jackie, how are you doing?"

"I am fine, thank you. Is everything okay?" she asked.

"I am sorry to disrupt what you are doing, but I was told that you went by and saw Dani today. Did everything seem okay when you were there?" he asked her.

"Why? Is something wrong?' asked Jackie.

"Well, I don't know," said Dr. Peters. "I was concerned because you and Dani didn't make the group meeting tonight."

"Oh, I had some other things I had to do tonight. I know I should have called you," said Jackie.

"If you don't mind me asking, what was it like with Dani today?" asked Dr. Peters.

"That woman is messed up. It started out okay, but as soon as she started drinking, she turned into the Devil."

"She was drinking"?" asked Dr. Peters.

"Yes, she was friendly at first, but then she offered me a drink. She made herself one then a second. She started yelling at me like a crazy person," said Jackie. "I told her to fuck off and I left. That woman is a piece of work!"

"She didn't seem like she was going to hurt herself, did she?" asked Dr. Peters.

"No, if anything, it seemed like she could hurt someone else, like me if I didn't leave. She got really angry, and then it was like she was a different person," said Jackie. "Her eyes were like floating, and she was a different person all together."

"I am on my way over there right now to check on her. I am sure she is fine, but I wanted a heads-up on how she was when you were there," said Dr. Peters.

"Sure, I understand. I hope everything works out," said Jackie.

"I am sure it will. Thank you, Jackie. I will talk to you later."

Kathy anxiously asked, "So, what did she say?"

"She was drinking and got a little worked up. I guess we shall see when we get there," said Dr. Peters."

When they arrived at Dani's house, all the lights were on. They walked up to the porch and noticed the door was ajar, the screen door closed but unlocked. "Dani," Dr. Peters called out, "are you here?"

They opened the screen door and walked into the house. "Dani!" he shouted, heading to the back family room where they had found her before. Dani was slumped on the couch, clearly intoxicated. Her hair hung in stringy clumps around her face. As she looked up, her eyes struggled to focus.

"Oh, hi Kathy. What are you doing here?" Dani mumbled.

"Dani, you said you weren't going to drink anymore. What happened?" Dr. Peters asked, concern etched in his voice.

"I don't know," Dani muttered. "That other lady came here, and she pissed me off. That slut, she thinks she's so hot. She's just a slut, that's all she is."

Dani was highly intoxicated not making sense of what she was saying, slurring her words so bad, it was hard to make out what she was talking about.

Kathy exchanged a puzzled look with Dr. Peters. "This is crazy," she whispered.

Dr. Peters raised his eyebrows and said to Kathy, "Can you go make some coffee?" Kathy nodded and headed to the kitchen.

"Dani, this isn't good for you. I'm going to have you drink some coffee, and we'll hang out with you for a while," Dr. Peters said gently. Dani kept fading in and out, falling asleep for moments at a time.

Dani woke up a few times acting angry. "Why are you looking at me like that?" Dani snapped. "Don't try to analyze me. Leave me alone," she muttered angerly, sinking back into the couch.

In the kitchen, Kathy was making coffee while rummaging through the cupboards. "Oh my gosh"! She called Dr. Peters into the kitchen. "What on earth is this gal doing with this much alcohol in her house?"

"Pretty sad," Dr. Peters replied, surveying the bottles.

"What motivates you to work with people like this? Doesn't it get to you" Kathy asked?

"I'm really not sure," Dr. Peters admitted. "I grew up in an alcoholic home. Both my parents struggled with alcohol and drug abuse. I went through a lot of this type of behavior when I was a boy. I thought if I made it to adulthood, I'd never drink or use drugs because I didn't want to be anything like my parents. As I grew older, I believed I could help people like them and save some poor child from going through what I did."

"Have you been able to?" Kathy asked.

"Well, I'd like to think so," Dr. Peters said. "When you have parents constantly in a drunken, unconscious state, as a child you're at their mercy. If they drive drunk and you're in the car, your life is in the hands of someone who shouldn't be behind the wheel, let alone raising children."

Kathy shook her head in amazement. "Wow, I can't even imagine."

"Yeah, it was pretty radical. There were times I had to sit in the car alone for hours while my parents got shitfaced in a bar. They'd stumble out, only to pass out, throw up, or fight. I'd sleep in the car without blankets or food. If I got out of the car and my dad found out, he'd beat the tar out of me."

Kathy's eyes were beginning to open a bit more as she listened to the stories. "I had no Idea" she said sadly.

Dr. Peters filled a cup with coffee. "Let's see if we can revive Dani," he said. Kathy followed him back to the couch. "Dani, I have some coffee for you. Wake up," Dr. Peters said gently. Dani opened her eyes, confusion clouding her face.

"What the fuck do you want?" she mumbled. "Leave me alone." she tried to yell.

"Dani, drink this coffee," Dr. Peters coaxed. Dani's eyes rolled back in her head as well as from side to side as she tried to focus on him.

"Don't look at me!" she suddenly shouted at Kathy. "I see you judging me. What makes you so fucking perfect?"

Kathy looked to Dr. Peters for support. He gave her a reassuring smile.

"She'll never remember this," he told her quietly. Dani continued to glare at Kathy, her eyes glassy and unfocused, before drifting back into her stupor.

"What do you do with patients like this?" asked Kathy. "Not much," said Dr. Peters. "All we can do is wait and make sure they don't hurt themselves." "Come on, Dani, drink some coffee," ordered Dr. Peters.

Dani opened her eyes, fury flashing. "I don't want no fuckin' coffee! I said, leave me alone!" She glared in Dr. Peters direction, her eyes struggling to focus. "Leave me alone," Dani whispered, lying back down, and closing her eyes.

Dr. Peters gently took Kathy's hand. "C'mon," he said, leading her out to the front porch. He gestured to her to sit at the table. As he settled into a chair, he said, "I don't think I'm going to get anywhere with Dani tonight."

"Yeah, I think she's pretty much gone," Kathy agreed.

"All we can do now is wait," said Dr. Peters. "What I don't understand is how someone can be okay one moment and then turn into that within a short time," said Kathy.

"Alcohol brings out the beast in people," Dr. Peters explained. "It can worsen emotions and amplify personality traits, especially in those who are mentally ill. When you mix alcohol with any medication, they're on, you've got yourself a cocktail of anything can happen".

"I drink but I've never been drunk in my entire life," said Kathy. "Even the night of my accident I only had a glass of wine. I can't imagine not having control over my drinking or my life for that matter."

"I wish there were more people like you," said Dr. Peters.

Kathy continued, "The majority of my life has been spent trying to improve who I am." "Now that I know I have a sleep disorder, all I want to do is manage it. I do not understand why someone like Dani, who knows she has a problem and has had sober episodes, can't or won't choose to stay sober."

"It's an illness," said Dr. Peters. "The mind is a funny thing."

"I've always thought that was bullshit," said Kathy. "I think people hide behind a mask of alcoholism or mental illness. It's easier to take medication and say they're mentally ill rather than deal with their problems." Dr. Peters smiled as Kathy continued. "Dani just needs to stop drinking, take charge of her life, and learn that she can be strong."

"It's not that simple," Dr. Peters countered. "In Dani's case, she's an alcoholic. Even without alcohol, she must deal with an ever-changing imbalance of serotonin in the brain. Medication helps regulate serotonin, but only if the patient takes it. With bipolar disorder, getting the patient to take their meds regularly is like pulling teeth."

"That's what I don't understand," said Kathy. "The solution to most of their problems is right in their hands, yet they refuse to take responsibility. Why? Why wouldn't someone want more control over their lives? And why add to the problem by drinking?"

"Addiction is a chronic, relapsing brain disease," explained Steve. "Brain imaging shows that addiction severely alters brain areas critical to decision-making, learning, memory, and behavior control. This may explain the compulsive and destructive behaviors of addiction."

"Well, again, I have to hand it to you for having the patience and tolerance to deal with it," said Kathy. "So, what now? Do we have to sit here babysitting and wait for her to get sober?" asked Kathy.

"Well, I am enjoying sitting here on the porch, spending time with you," said Steve.

Kathy was surprised by his comment. She chuckled. "I can think of other, more enjoyable ways of getting to know someone," she said.

Dr. Peters smiled. "Yeah, I guess this isn't a very romantic way of showing interest in you." They both chuckled, keeping eye contact. There was a moment of silence as they gazed into each other's eyes, the attraction between them was undeniable.

"You know, I've been trying to hold back my feelings for you," said Steve. "I've never been in this situation before, and quite frankly, I'm not sure how to handle it." Kathy smiled. Steve took her hand. "You make me feel so alive," he said. "From the first time we met, and every time since, I've wanted to kiss you." Kathy chuckled; she was surprised by his honesty.

"I appreciate your honesty, really, I do. But... what about me being your patient?"

"That's what holds me back," said Steve.

Kathy was flattered by his words. She had grown an attraction to Steve as well, but she knew that for everyone's sake, the relationship had to stay professional.

"I am flattered," said Kathy, pulling back her hand. "I just don't know if this will work."

Grabbing her hand again, Steve said, "Kathy, you are not my typical patient. This is temporary until Dr. Gifford returns, which could be anytime. You and I both know that Narcolepsy is not your typical mental illness that a psychologist would treat. You're forced into attending group therapy based on the experience you had and the fact there was alcohol in your blood test the night of your accident. It's what the law requires you to do to get your driver's license back."

Kathy slowly sat back in her chair, still holding Steve's hand. "This complicates things, you know," she said, smiling. Steve pulled Kathy's hand towards him and kissed it softly. They both smiled, feeling the undeniable connection.

Kathy's cell phone began to ring from inside her purse. She reached for it, grabbing the phone from the outside pocket. Seeing Tammy's name on the caller ID, she answered quickly.

"Tammy, I'm sorry I forgot to call you," said Kathy. "Yes, she's fine now. We made her some coffee, and she's asleep on the couch. No, we don't need anything, but thanks for asking. Okay, alright, we'll talk tomorrow."

Steve and Kathy continued talking on the porch for another hour while Dani slept. Eventually, Kathy glanced at her watch. "Wow, it's getting late. Do you mind driving me home?"

"No, not at all," said Steve. They stood up and went into the house to check on Dani again. She hadn't moved since the last time they checked on her.

Whispering, Kathy asked, "so do we just leave her here by herself?"

"She'll be fine," said Dr. Peters. "Most likely, she won't wake up until morning. If she does, she'll probably just get up to go to the bathroom and then either come back to the couch or go to her bedroom."

"I guess you know your stuff," Kathy chuckled.

Dr. Peters searched around for a blanket and pillow, placing them next to Dani as she lay sleeping. He then walked over to the kitchen and turned off the lights. "Let's leave the bathroom light on for her in case she gets up," he said.

Kathy watched as Steve prepared the house so they could leave. He signaled for her to come as he maneuvered to the front of the house.

"I'll stop by first thing in the morning on my way to work to check on her," he said.

"What commitment," said Kathy.

As Dr Peters approached Kathy's house, he began talking about his long drive home.

"You know, you have a place to stay if you want it," Kathy said hoping he would stay the night again. He pulled into the driveway; leaving his car running, he got out and walked around to open the door for Kathy.

"I'd really love to take advantage of your generosity, but I don't have any clean clothes with me, and all my stuff is at home. But thank you so much." he said.

Steve helped her walk to the door, holding onto her arm as she struggled with her crutches. Kathy pulled out her keys and unlocked the door.

Turning to Steve, Kathy began to say 'thank you for the ride home" but Steve placed his finger over her lips. "Shh," he said. "It is my pleasure."

They looked into each other's eyes for a moment until Steve leaned in and kissed Kathy softly on the lips. He pulled back, still holding her gaze.

"I'll talk to you tomorrow."

Kathy, stunned but excited, watched as he turned and walked to his car. She kept the door open until he got in and drove away.

Dr. Peters called Dani first thing in the morning to make sure she was okay. He got a little nervous because she picked up on the fourth ring.

"Hello." "Dani, this is Dr. Peters. I came to your house last night. Do you remember?" he asked.

"Yeah, sure," Dani said in a groggy voice. "I'd really like you to come to my office today and sit with me for a few moments. Do you think you could arrange that?" he asked.

"I suppose," said Dani. "What time?"

"How about 11:30? Do you need a ride?" he asked.

"No, I have a car. I can drive there myself."

"Great," said Dr. Peters. "I'll see you then."

As the day progressed, Dr. Peters anxiously awaited Dani's visit. He really hoped she wouldn't no show on him, however, 11:30 came and went, and still no Dani. Dr. Peters asked his assistant to call and see if she was coming.

"No answer on her home and no answer on her cell," she reported back.

"Damn, I was afraid that would happen," he said, frustrated. All Dr. Peters could do was continue with his schedule and hope that Dani would come around. Throughout the day, he couldn't get his mind off Kathy. He picked up the phone and called her.

"Hello," said Kathy, her voice warm and inviting.

"Hello, Kathy, this is Steve. I wanted to make sure you have a ride tonight."

"Funny you should ask," she said. "I just got a call from Jackie of all people. She and I had a long talk on the phone, and she offered to pick me up. I can't believe I said yes, but I did, and she's supposed to be here around 6:30."

"Well, I'm really impressed," said Steve. "That is a huge step in the right direction."

"I'll be impressed if she not only shows up but shows up on time," Kathy said with a chuckle. "If for whatever reason I don't make it there tonight, I guess you'll know why."

"I look forward to seeing you around 6:30. Would you mind if I drove you home tonight?" Steve asked.

"I would love that. Thank you for offering," said Kathy.

"I really must get back to work," said Steve. "I can't keep my patients waiting."

"Okay, I'll see you tonight," said Kathy.

Jackie did show up on time, and both women arrived at the meeting promptly. Jackie talked the whole way there, so by the time they reached the clinic, Kathy was happy to see Jackie look elsewhere for the attention she needed.

Dr. Peters spotted Kathy in the room and came over to greet her. He held out his hand to shake Kathy's as he would any other patient. "How are you? Can I help you with your stuff?" he asked. Smiling at his sense of humor, Kathy played along.

"Yes, Dr. Peters, thank you," she said flirtatiously, handing him the items she carried in.

Right before the meeting began, the door opened. Dani stood hesitantly at the door, dressed in clothes that looked like she had been wearing them for days. Her hair was stringy and matted, as if it hadn't seen a brush in just as long. "C'mon in, Dani," said Dr. Peters. Everyone looked at her in amazement as she walked slowly into the room, arms crossed tightly over her chest.

Tammy stood up and waved her over. "There's a chair next to me. Come sit here," she said. Dani scanned the faces staring at her as she walked towards Tammy. She sat down, immediately dropping her head to avoid eye contact.

Dr. Peters began speaking to the group, diverting attention away from Dani. Tammy grabbed Dani's hand and squeezed it, offering silent reassurance. The group of attendees took turns discussing the issues they wanted to discuss. By the time the meeting was over, Dani had lifted her head and taken an interest in the others' stories.

As Dr. Peters excused the group, Kathy got out of her chair and approached Dani. "Girl, I was so worried about you. Are you alright?" she asked compassionately. Dani nodded but didn't say anything else. "If there's anything I can do to help you Dani," Kathy continued.

"No, I'm going to be okay. I'm going to start attending AA meetings along with coming to these meetings. I think I've hit bottom, and I don't ever want to go back to where I was the last couple of days."

"That's awesome to hear, Dani," said Kathy.

Jackie looked over at them just as Dani hugged Kathy. "Well, it sure is nice to see you getting back to normal," Jackie blurted out. Dani tried to ignore her, but Jackie continued as she walked over to them. "I thought you were going to die. Seeing you lay there as messed up..."

Kathy interrupted. "Well, that doesn't matter. What really matters is that she is with us now and on the road to getting better."

"Well, let's hope she keeps her word because she won't be around long if she continues to lead that kind of lifestyle," Jackie retorted.

"It would be a lot easier on her if you didn't instigate her to drink with you just because you have no one else that will." Kathy argued.

Kathy grew extremely angry with Jackie knowing that if she left Dani alone; Dani would have a better chance of getting better.

"Why don't we just drop this before it gets out of hand," Tammy said, her voice tight with frustration.

"You can't blame me for Dani's weakness." Jackie said with an attitude.

Dr. Peters walked up and asked,

"Is everything okay?"

"Yes, everything is fine," Jackie replied quickly. Dr. Peters took Dani's hand and in a sincere tone, said,

"It's nice to see you here, Dani. I'm glad you made it." Dani smiled, though her embarrassment was evident.

"Thank you, Dr. Peters. I'm sorry I didn't show up today."

"No worries, you made it tonight." He smiled warmly. "Did I hear you mention you're going to be attending AA meetings."?

"Yes," Dani nodded. "I haven't attended one yet, but I know of one tomorrow that I plan on going to."

"That's fantastic, Dani. I'm glad to hear that," Dr. Peters said, giving her a supportive side hug. "Please make arrangements to see me in my office this week." he said kindly.

"I will," Dani promised.

Dr. Peters walked away towards the back of the room where the group was eating cookies and socializing.

"I better help clean up," Kathy said.

"No, you shouldn't be doing anything on your feet. I'll help clean up," said Dani. "You just sit down and rest. Oh, and do you have a ride home tonight?" she asked.

"Yes, thank you for asking," said Kathy. As Dani walked away, Kathy turned to Jackie. "I won't be needing a ride home but thank you for the ride here."

"Really?" asked Jackie, surprised. "Well, I guess I better be moving along then."

Kathy sat back down and waited for Dr. Peters to finish clearing the room. When everyone had left except for Tammy, Dr. Peters walked over to where Kathy was sitting. "Are you ready to go?" he asked. Tammy looked over from across the room, watching as Dr. Peters picked up Kathy's belongings and helped her up from the chair.

"Well, I guess I'm done here," said Tammy. "Do you need a ride home, Kathy?" Tammy asked knowing that she would most likely get a ride with Dr. Peters. Tammy was suspecting something was going on with them and wanted to get confirmation.

"No, I'm good, but thank you anyway," replied Kathy.

Tammy left the room, hesitating at the door as she watched Kathy and Dr. Peters interact.

"Do you think she suspects something?" Steve asked once Tammy was out of the room.

"I don't know, but there really isn't anything going on now, is there?" Kathy asked, her face serious.

Steve looked at Kathy curiously, unsure how to interpret her expression. Kathy broke into a smile, easing his concern.

After helping Kathy into his car, Steve suggested, "How about we grab a bite to eat?"

"I thought that would be against the rules," said Kathy, raising an eyebrow.

"Well, I am hungry, and since I'm taking you home, I thought I'd invite you to join me," he replied with a smile.

"Actually I already had dinner, and I don't really like to eat this late, but I'd be happy to join you and maybe have a cup of tea or a slice of pie," Kathy said.

Steve drove into the parking lot of a dinner house. "How does this look?" he asked.

"Actually, this is a really good place to eat. This is one of the last places I ate before my accident," Kathy replied.

As they got out of the car and headed toward the door of the restaurant, Steve put his arm around Kathy. Realizing the awkwardness due to her crutches, he quickly removed his arm before reaching for the door. He opened the door for her and checked in with the host for seating while Kathy stood behind, watching.

"Follow me," said the host as she led them to a secluded booth towards the back. As the server approached, she offered wine or a drink before dinner. "No, not us," said Steve, glancing at Kathy for approval.

"Yeah, I think we're more in the mood for a nice hot cup of tea or something," said Kathy.

"Okay, I'll give you a few minutes to look over the menu and be right back with your tea," the server said.

"So, what do you suggest?" asked Steve.

"Just about anything on the menu is good," Kathy replied.

"I feel like having Prime Rib. Are you sure you don't want to order anything?"

"I think I'm going to be really bad and order the Tiramisu. It's to die for," said Kathy.

"Hmm, maybe I'll skip dinner and join you for dessert," Steve chuckled. "Actually, if I wasn't so hungry, I would, but I haven't eaten since this morning before I left my house."

The server returned with their tea and took their order. As they waited for their food, they made small talk about the meeting before the conversation turned to Dani.

"I'm really excited to see her get to a point where she wants to change her life," said Kathy.

"Yes, that would be nice if she follows through with it," Steve replied.

"You don't sound too optimistic," said Kathy.

"It's too early to tell. We hope for the best for these people, but we can expect just about anything from them," Steve said. Kathy looked at him in amazement, she was a bit disappointed in his comment.

"Let's talk about you. Tell me about yourself," Steve suggested.

"What would you like to know?" Kathy asked.

"Everything," he said, looking at her seriously.

"Oh, I don't know about that. I'd probably bore you to tears," she chuckled.

"Try me," Steve said.

Kathy began to tell him about her family, school background, and career.

"What about ex-husbands, children?" he asked.

"There aren't any," said Kathy. "I've had a couple of men in my life that I was serious about, but my career seemed to keep me from taking the relationships to the next level. I've always liked the idea of being in control of my own life, and I felt that the only way to do that was to work hard and provide for myself, so I didn't have to answer to anyone."

"So, are you happy with that decision?" asked Steve.

"Well, it's worked for me so far," replied Kathy.

The server returned to the table with Steves dinner and an extra plate. "I thought you might like an extra plate in case you decided to share your Prime Rib," she said. "I can bring your dessert after you eat your meal if you like."

"No, actually, I already ate dinner, and I would like my dessert now as he eats his meal," Kathy said firmly.

"I'm sorry. I will be right back with that," said the server apologetically.

"Woo, a little pushy, are we?" Steve asked with a playful grin.

"I didn't mean to be," Kathy replied, a hint of concern in her voice. "Was I out of line?"

"No, no, I'm just kidding with you," said Steve, smiling to reassure her.

The server came back with the dessert, placing it in front of Kathy. "Will there be anything else I can get you?" she asked.

"No, we're fine, thank you," Steve answered.

As they ate, they chatted about their lives and the paths they had chosen. Steve found himself becoming more and more intrigued with Kathy. He listened intently as she spoke about her family, her career, and her past relationships.

Kathy took a bite of her tiramisu, savoring the rich flavor. "This is just as good as I remembered," she said, smiling. Steve chuckled.

"I'm glad you're enjoying it." "So, tell me more about you," Kathy asked, leaning forward slightly. "What made you choose this path?"

Steve paused, considering her question. "I grew up in a tough environment," he began. "My parents struggled with alcohol and drug abuse, and I went through a lot as a kid. I decided early on that I wanted to help people avoid the pain I experienced. It's been a challenging journey, but I wouldn't trade it for anything." Kathy nodded, her eyes reflecting empathy. "That's incredibly inspiring. It takes a lot of strength to turn such a difficult experience into something positive." "Thank you," Steve said softly. "I think we all have the capacity to find strength in our struggles." They continued their conversation, sharing stories and experiences. Steve was captivated by Kathy's determination and resilience, while Kathy was struck by Steve's compassion and dedication. As the evening progressed, they both realized they had found a connection that went beyond the professional. There was mutual respect and admiration growing between them, setting the stage for a deeper relationship.

25 - Ignored

Jackie drove up the long driveway to her house, noticing how dark it was. She wondered if her husband was even home. Pulling into the garage, she saw Richard's car. As she gathered her belongings from the car, she expected her husband to greet her at any moment. Entering the house, it was quiet. She turned on the lights, noting everything was as she had left it.

She walked up the stairs, seeing the light on in the office. She entered and found Richard at his computer, working. He didn't look up, but she knew he was aware of her presence. She walked over and kissed him on the forehead, trying to start a conversation, but he ignored her, focused on his screen. She rubbed his back and shoulders, seeking his attention, but he only mumbled, "Uh-huh," as if he were listening. Jackie sat on the corner of his desk, gazing at the computer screen, trying to understand what he was working on.

"Well, I'm going to take a bath," she said, receiving no response as she walked out of his office.

After taking a bath she hoped that Richard would be waiting for her in bed only to find that he had not come up to the room yet. Jackie had gotten use to the routine over the years and blamed her promiscuity on Richard's lack of attention. In her mind, being ignored by Richard justified her being promiscuous. She pulled back the covers on the bed and climbed in falling asleep by herself.

In the morning Jackie woke up in bed alone as usual. Her husband Richard had already gone to work, leaving her in the big house all by herself. She put on her bathrobe and went downstairs to get some coffee and a bite to eat. As she sat at the kitchen table, she could hear the landscaper running the blower in the backyard. She went to the patio door and watched him work, while she held her coffee. When he finished, Jackie went outside to offer him some coffee or water. Though he wasn't the most attractive person, she was intrigued by the interaction. He tried to be respectful, avoiding prolonged eye contact. when she offered him something to drink. Jackie didn't want to take no for an answer, hoping for more attention. She made small talk until he finally said, "I really need to be getting along. I have other houses to maintain." Jackie walked back into the house, frustrated that she didn't get the response she was hoping for.

26 - Hope in AA

At 8:30 am, Dani woke up feeling tired and a little depressed. Being home alone was something she felt she could never get used to. She dragged herself out of bed and went into the kitchen to make some coffee. As she poured herself a cup, the phone rang. It was Dr. Peters.

"Hello, Dani, it's Dr. Peters. How are you doing?" he asked.

"I guess I'm okay," Dani replied in a tired voice.

"Do you think you could make it into my office today?"

"I don't know, Dr. Peters. I'm feeling so tired, and I'm supposed to go to the AA meeting at 11:00."

"Well, maybe you can come afterward. Can I put you down for 2:00?" asked Dr. Peters.

"Uh, okay, I'll try to be there," said Dani hesitantly.

"I would prefer it if you made a commitment. It is for your benefit."

"I will be there, Dr. Peters," Dani said.

"Perfect. I will see you at 2:00," said Dr. Peters.

Dani hung up the phone and flopped herself on the couch. She began to think about Paul and what he was doing. Grabbing the blanket on the couch, she covered herself and clutched a pillow, tears streaming down her face.

Meanwhile, Kathy had already cleaned her house and wanted to go outside so she could check on her plants. By 9:00, she was getting bored and decided to call Dani to see how she was doing.

She called Dani's house and got the recorded message. She began to leave a message: "Hey, Dani, it's Kathy. I was sitting here thinking about you and thought I'd give you a call. Call me when you get a chance, okay." Dani heard the message and debated whether to pick up the phone. Finally, just before Kathy hung up, Dani picked up.

"Hey, Kathy. I'm here. What's up?" she asked quietly.

Oh, you are there. How are you doing?" Kathy asked.

"I don't know. I guess I'm alright," replied Dani in a somber tone. "What do you have planned for the day?" asked Kathy.

"I was planning on attending the AA meeting at 11:00, but I'm feeling really tired," said Dani. "Oh, well, you got to snap out of it. You have to go to that meeting," Kathy said eagerly.

"Dr. Peters called me and wants me to see him at 2:00. I don't really know if I want to do that either."

"Why would you not want to? I don't understand. There are people reaching out to help you, and you're not in the mood?" Kathy's voice was filled with concern.

"Hey, I'm getting another call, I have to go." Dani said in order to get off the phone.

"Okay but call me back later and let me know how you're doing," said Kathy. "Yeah, sure," replied Dani.

Dani hung up the phone and continued to lay on the couch, sinking deeper into her depression. She finally forced herself up at 10:00 and took a shower. By the time she got out of the shower and dressed, she felt a little better.

As Dani walked up the short stairs to the building, she hesitated at the double door, holding one of the handrails. "Excuse me," said a woman who had walked up behind her. "Are you going to go in?"

"I was thinking about it," said Dani. The woman reached out her hand.

"Hello, I'm Betty. Is this your first time at a meeting?"

"Yes, it is," replied Dani.

"Why don't you come in with me? I promise I don't bite," Betty said with a friendly smile.

"Okay," said Dani, following Betty into the building.

They walked down a long hallway until they reached the room where the AA meeting was held. "C'mon, it's in here," said Betty. Dani slowed down as she entered the room, noticing the variety of people chatting.

"This reminds me of my therapy group," Dani said to Betty. Betty found a couple of chairs and suggested Dani sit next to her. Dani was relieved to have run into Betty, as she was feeling more comfortable with being there. When the meeting started, Dani watched as people introduced themselves and admitted they were alcoholics. When it was her turn, she nervously said,

"Um, hi, my name is Dani, and this is my first meeting. I don't know what to say, so I'll just sit down." The group welcomed her with claps and simultaneous "Welcome, Dani," which made her feel a little awkward but quickly comforted.

After the meeting, Betty asked "Dani would like me to be your sponsor until you find someone else."

"I'm not really sure what that means but sure." Dani replied.

"Well, there are a few books that are good that you will need to read. One is called the Big Book. It's "our bible" if you will, of Alcoholics Anonymous. There are a few others but let's start there." Dani was not really paying attention to Betty at this point because she could only focus on her own nervousness.

Dani was excited about the meeting she attended and could hardly wait for her appointment to tell Dr. Peters about her experience. As she walked into the office, she was greeted warmly by the receptionist. "It is so nice to see you here. How are you doing?" the receptionist asked.

"I am happy to be here," replied Dani enthusiastically. "And I'm doing great!"

"I wish all our patients could be more like you," the receptionist said joyfully.

Dani grabbed a gossip magazine and started thumbing through it, commenting out loud on the stories.

"Can you imagine the lives of these people? Their biggest problem of the day is where they're going to go shopping." The receptionist listened but didn't comment, continuing with her work.

The door to Dr. Peters' office opened, and a nurse called out Dani's name.

"Oh man, I was right in the middle of this great story," Dani joked as she put down the magazine and walked through the door. Dani was led to Dr. Peters' office, where he stood up and shook her hand, welcoming her and asking her to take a seat. He could tell by her energy that she was in a good mood.

"It's great to see you like this, Dani," he said.

"Yes, I don't remember the last time I felt this good," she replied.

"I've been very concerned about you, Dani," Dr. Peters said.

"I know I haven't been handling things right lately," Dani admitted. "But I feel like I have a new mission in life. I feel like I've been given another chance and want to make the best of it."

"Did you attend the AA meeting like you said you would?" he asked.

"Yes, I did. I was so scared to go in, but I met this lady at the door named Betty. She introduced me to people, and I sat next to her. Afterward, she asked if I wanted her to be my sponsor until I met someone else. I don't exactly know what that means, but I agreed, and we exchanged numbers."

"That's fantastic, Dani. I'm very pleased to hear that. You are definitely on the right track. Let me ask you this, have you been taking your medication regularly?" asked Dr. Peters.

"No, not really, but I plan on starting fresh tomorrow," said Dani.

Dr. Peters frowned. "I know you just started going to AA, but it's important to talk about the abuse you've put your body through with drinking and drugs."

"I know, Dr. Peters. I can't change the past, but I can work on now and the future. I plan on going home and lining up my medication so it will be right in front of me every morning when I wake up. And I'm going to clear out all the alcohol from my cupboards."

"Great," said Dr. Peters. "That's a great start." "I feel good about the change I'm seeing in you, Dani," Dr. Gifford said. "A word of caution though, sometimes the excitement doesn't last forever. When you start taking your meds, the first dose takes about two weeks to begin showing effects. This is why it's especially important to take your meds on time, every day. When you take your medication consistently, it stays in your system and works more effectively than if you take it inconsistently."

When the appointment was over Dani walked out of the doctor's office, she noticed the magazine she had been reading, still sitting where she left it. Glancing around to make sure the receptionist wasn't looking, she picked it up and slipped it into her purse.

When Dani arrived home, she immediately called Kathy.

"Hello," said Kathy.

"Kathy, it's Dani. I had such a great day! I went to the meeting, and it was great! I met a woman who said she would be my sponsor!"

"That's fantastic, Dani," said Kathy. "I don't know what that means, but it sounds like a good thing."

"Then I went to see Dr. Peters, and that was a good session too. He was proud of me for attending the AA meeting. I feel so good. I can't remember ever being this excited."

"That's great, Dani. It's so good to see you like this," replied Kathy. Kathy continued to listen as Dani exuberantly talked about her day and her plans. Though Dani kept talking over her, Kathy put the phone on speaker and continued with her chores, occasionally nodding and murmuring affirmations.

"Okay, I have to let you go now. I promised my sponsor that I would call her after the doctor's appointment," said Dani.

"Alright. Congratulations on the successful day," Kathy began, but Dani had already hung up. Kathy shook her head and chuckled quietly.

Dani immediately called Betty, her new sponsor. "Hello, Betty. It's Dani. We met at the AA meeting today."

"Yes, Dani, I remember. How are you doing?" Betty asked.

"I'm so excited! I went to my doctor's appointment, and he was so glad to see me," Dani said, barely pausing for breath. After listening to Dani for a few moments, Betty interrupted,

"Dani, did you pick up the Big Book or any of the other books today?"

"Books? I don't remember talking about any books," replied Dani.

"Yes, there are books in AA that help us stay focused on sobriety. It's a 12-step book. "I guess I didn't pick up on that. I don't really like to read; it makes me tired," Dani admitted.

"I used to be the same way," said Betty. But as you go through the program, the Big Book becomes your bible. It's something you won't want to put down.

Dani got quiet, listening to Betty. "Uh, yeah," she said, less enthusiastically. "You should go to the meeting tonight," Betty suggested.

"Tonight?" Dani hesitated. "I don't know about tonight."

"You need to attend as many meetings as possible within the first 30 days,". We suggest 30/30. Thirty meetings in 30 days. Betty insisted. "Besides, what else is more important than your sobriety?"

Dani hesitated again. "Well, I don't have any plans for tonight I suppose I could go."

"Great It starts at 6:00," said Betty.

"Are you going" asked Dani?

No, not tonight," replied Betty. "But you'll be fine. Everyone will welcome you like they did this morning. Feel free to call me after the meeting to check in."

"Okay, I will," said Dani. "I better get going so I can do something productive today."

"Alright, talk to you later," said Betty.

27 - BBQ Hang-Out

Dani hung up the phone, her earlier enthusiasm was leaving her. She sat back on the couch, put her feet up, and stared into space, feeling a sense of emptiness. Suddenly, the phone rang. Dani picked it up to hear Jackie at the other end.

"Hey, Jackie. How's it going?" she asked.

"I'm calling to check in on you. I've been worried about you."

"I'm doing okay, I guess," said Dani. "What's up with you?"

"I am just home alone, hanging out by the pool and relaxing. I thought you might want to come over and have dinner and swim with me." Jackie said.

"Wow, that sounds wonderful, but I just committed to going to an AA meeting for the second time today," said Dani.

"What are you doing that for?" Jackie asked, as if it were a terrible thing. "You already went to a meeting once today. Why would you go to another? That sounds like overkill to me."

"I was encouraged to go, and I found a woman who wants to be my sponsor. It is cool," said Dani.

"Well, if you already went once, why not skip the second one? I think you would have more fun hanging out with me. My husband is on a business trip, and I have this big place all to myself. C'mon, it will be fun."

Dani hesitated. "Okay, I guess it won't hurt. I can always go to a meeting tomorrow." "Great! "You won't regret it," said Jackie.

As Dani hung up the phone, she imagined what it would be like at Jackie's. What should she wear? Should she bring anything? She picked up the phone and called Jackie back.

"Hey, it's me again," said Dani. "Do you want me to bring anything?"

"No, just yourself," said Jackie.

"Are you sure?" asked Dani.

"Positive. Now get your sweet little ass in your car and come over here," Jackie demanded playfully.

"Okay, okay. I'll see you in a few," said Dani.

When Dani arrived at Jackie's, the gate was open. She pulled up to the house as Jackie came out in a white bikini, holding a glass of wine in one hand and a cigarette in the other. "I'm so glad you could make it," Jackie said as she walked closer to Dani's car.

"Damn, girl, did your bathing suit get left in the dryer a little too long?" Dani joked.

"Ha ha, funny," said Jackie. "You just wish you had a body like this."

"Yes, I do, but I think I'd wear something that fit a little better," said Dani.

"C'mon, let's go inside. I'll get you something to drink, and we can relax by the pool," Jackie said.

Dani followed Jackie into the kitchen. "Do you want anything to eat or wait until later?" asked Jackie.

"I'm fine. Just a drink would be nice," said Dani. "Iced tea, lemonade, or whatever you want?" Jackie asked.

"I'm on the wagon. I better stick with lemonade," said Dani.

"That's no fun, but I understand," Jackie said as she poured the lemonade. "Did you bring your bathing suit?"

"No, I didn't think I'd be swimming," said Dani.

"It's okay, let's go outside," Jackie said.

As they walked out, Dani admired the beautiful home and its furnishings. Jackie led her to the custom-made chaise lounges by the pool. "Have a seat and relax," said Jackie.

"This is so nice. If I lived here, I'd never want to leave," said Dani.

"Yes, it's nice, but it gets lonely being here alone a lot of the time," Jackie replied.

"Where's your husband?" asked Dani.

"He's at a convention in DC and won't be home for a week," said Jackie.

"Why don't you go with him?" asked Dani.

"Are you kidding? Been there, done that. Corporate meetings and dinner parties with people I don't like. I'd rather stay home and do my own thing," Jackie said.

After some small talk, Jackie reached over to the coffee table and opened a box. She pulled out a pipe, matches, and some weed. "Since you can't drink, I don't suppose you can smoke either"? Jackie asked.

"You're making it hard for me to be here," said Dani.

Jackie lit the bowl, taking a few hits before passing it to Dani. Without hesitation, Dani grabbed the pipe and hit it too.

The pipe went back and forth as the women got high, laughing, and sharing emotional stories about their lives.

Jackie got up from the chaise to get some refills on the drinks.

"Want some more lemonade?" she asked.

"Sure, but do you have any vodka to go in it?" Dani asked

"Of course I do. Are you sure?"

"Fuck yeah, I'm sure." Dani said with excitement.

Jackie came back minutes later carrying the drinks. "I took out a couple of steaks earlier so that I could BBQ them. Are you getting hungry?" she asked.

"Yes, just a bit," replied Dani. "I would really like to go for a swim, but I didn't bring my suit."

"Don't be shy, just take your clothes off and jump in. It's not like I have neighbors looking over fences," Jackie chuckled.

Dani took a drink of her lemonade, then began to strip off her clothes until she was naked. She jumped into the pool and swam back and forth until she saw Jackie sitting on the edge of the pool with another pipe load.

"Hey, what do you have there?" she asked. "Do you mind if I join you?"

After sitting for a while Jackie stood up and removed her skimpy bathing suit. Dani watched, shocked, as Jackie dove into the pool.

"Don't get any ideas," Dani said once Jackie resurfaced. Jackie swam over to the edge of the pool where Dani was hanging on to the side.

"What are you afraid of?" Jackie asked.

"Just don't fucking try anything with me because I don't go that way."

"I'm just more comfortable naked than I am with clothing on," replied Jackie.

Jackie jumped out of the pool, turning her body to sit on the ledge again. "I'm going to get the steaks started. Can I get you anything?" she asked.

"No, I am fine. "Do you want any help with anything?" Dani asked.

"No, everything is already taken care of." Jackie stood up, completely unashamed of her nakedness, and walked into the house.

Dani swam a couple more laps, then got out of the pool, wrapped herself in a towel, and sat back down on the chaise, grabbing her drink. She saw the pipe and the box with the marijuana and helped herself to a few hits.

Jackie walked outside, wearing just an apron. Seeing Dani making herself comfortable, she took a hit as well.

"Where the hell is the music?" asked Dani. "You got everything else." Jackie went back into the house, and this time Dani followed.

"We have a great selection of music if you want to go through it and pick something out," said Jackie. "You can also connect your phone to the speakers and play your own music if you want."

Dani used her phone to queue up some hard rock from the '80s and danced around as she browsed through the rest of the collection. Meanwhile, Jackie headed back outside to cook the steaks.

A little while later, Jackie's voice rang out from the patio, "The steaks are done!" as she came back into the house.

"Do you mind if I make myself another lemonade?" asked Dani.

"No, not at all. Make yourself at home," said Jackie. Dani poured half lemonade and the rest vodka.

"No wonder you get so fucked up," said Jackie. "Slow down, girl. It will be there later."

"If I'm going to drink, I'm going to drink. I'm not a pansy ass," Dani replied with a laugh.

After dinner, they went back to the lounge chairs by the pool and chilled for a while, taking periodic hits on the pipe. They were both feeling the high from the pot and the alcohol. A song came on that Dani liked, and she jumped up and started dancing. Jackie watched with a big smile on her face. She soon got the feeling and joined Dani in dancing.

Dani still had the towel around her body, but as she danced, it kept falling off. "Just leave it off," said Jackie. "Live a little!" Dani kicked the towel closer to the lounge and continued to dance naked. One song after another played, keeping them dancing. Dani got really hot and grabbed Jackie by the arm, pulling her into the pool with her. Jackie screamed as she was dragged into the water. When they surfaced, both were laughing hysterically.

"OMG! You caught me totally off guard," said Jackie. They swam to the edge and rested along the side of the pool. Dani got out, grabbed her drink and towel, dried off, and laid down on the lounge. She continued conversing while Jackie stayed in the pool.

"I love this song," Jackie said, heading toward the stairs of the pool. She began dancing erotically, moving closer to Dani. Dani laughed, thinking Jackie was just playing around. But Jackie was really into the moment, touching her breast and giving Dani a look that suggested she wanted her. Dani continued to laugh nervously not knowing what to expect out of Jackie. Continuing her provocative dance, Dani just lay there as Jackie continued with a lap dance, occasionally rubbing her body against Dani.

"You're fucked up," Dani said when the song was over. "Yes, but you liked it. "C'mon, admit it, Dani," said Jackie. "Hell, woman, I'm not admitting anything," said Dani. "C'mon, let's dance some more," Jackie said, pulling Dani off the lounge. "I was just fucking with you" she laughed.

Jackie and Dani continued to dance naked on the patio by the pool. Dani drank three times the amount of alcohol that Jackie drank and was starting to get really messed up. Dani slipped a couple of times and almost fell while Jackie grabbed her and helped her gain her balance. Both women laughed as they continued to dance and drink.

After several minutes, the mood changed for Dani. "How did I get this way?" asked Dani, almost crying.

"Don't worry about it, you're fine," said Jackie, encouraging Dani to continue to dance.

"I am not fine. I stopped drinking for a couple of days, and then you tricked me into coming over here so you wouldn't be alone." cried Dani.

"Oh, Dani, you're drunk. Stop worrying about it, just enjoy yourself." said Jackie.

"Damn! I was supposed to get sober! Bitch!" Dani shouted at Jackie.

"Why are you blaming me for this?" Jackie shouted back. "I didn't hold the drink up to you and make you drink, dumbass."

"Well, you didn't help me by offering it to me either, bitch," Dani slurred.

"What difference does it make if you stop drinking tomorrow instead?" asked Jackie. "Just plan on not drinking tomorrow, and everything will be fine."

Dani laid on the lounge moaning from time to time, not making any sense. She would close her eyes as if she were asleep and then open them suddenly, to complain about being tricked. Jackie, tired of listening to her, began picking up the clothes scattered around the pool deck. She took them into the house and went up to her room, leaving Dani in the lounge, passed out.

Jackie took a shower and got ready for bed while Dani lay on the lounge. She knew Dani was too drunk to drive home, so she prepared a spot for her to sleep in one of the guest bedrooms. She went down to the pool area again and tried to wake Dani up, but she was out cold. Jackie didn't want to leave her there, but she figured Dani would eventually wake up and come inside.

Jackie covered her with an oversized beach towel and went back into the house, leaving lights on to light the path in case Dani did wake up and come in. She left the lights off in the living areas to deter Dani from going into those rooms. She turned on a light in the guest bedroom downstairs, hoping it would encourage Dani to spend the night. Jackie then went into her bedroom and went to bed.

During the night, Dani woke, not sure where she was at first. She sat up in the lounge and realized she was still by the pool. She got up, realizing she was naked, and looked around for her clothes. When she didn't see them, she thought Jackie was playing a trick on her. She stumbled into the house, looking around for her clothes, but didn't see them anywhere. She followed the path of the light as Jackie had hoped, stumbling into walls along the way. When she got close to the stairs, she saw the light on in the downstairs guest bedroom and went inside. She saw the covers pulled back and her undergarments sitting on a nightstand beside the bed. Realizing Jackie intended for her to spend the night, Dani wasn't thrilled but knew she was in no condition to drive. She crawled into the bed, pulling the covers over her body, and fell asleep as soon as her head hit the pillow.

28 - The Date and Sleepover

Kathy sat in her backyard, reading a book, and enjoying the quietness of the day, when the phone rang. "Hello," she said.

"Hey beautiful, would you like to have dinner with a handsome and brilliant doctor?" Steve asked.

"Well, I do not know. My mother always told me to stay away from doctors," Kathy replied with a laugh.

"How has your day been?" he asked.

"Very nice and quiet," Kathy replied.

"How about I swing by around 7pm and pick you up for a nice steak dinner at Waynes' Steak House?" he suggested.

"Okay, 7 it is. I'll be ready," Kathy agreed.

"Great, see you then," Steve said as he hung up.

With a smile on her face, Kathy put the phone down and gazed off into her garden. She sat for a couple more hours reading her book uninterrupted, enjoying the sound of the birds and the trees swaying. She glanced at her watch and stood up, using her crutches to navigate back into the house.

In her bedroom, Kathy stood in her walk-in closet, feeling a rare sense of indecision. It had been so long since she had prepared for a date. She held up skirts and dresses, but nothing seemed right, especially with the cast and crutches complicating things. Finally, she found a broomstick skirt she had overlooked earlier. Holding it up against her body, she realized it would be perfect to hide her cast. She paired it with a knit tank top adorned with embroidered flowers and a few rhinestones.

Removing her clothes was a struggle, but she managed to get into the shower. She had a chair in the shower and used a removable shower head to make things easier, though she still had to cover her cast with a waterproof bag. Despite the hassle, Kathy did not mind—she was excited about her date with Steve.

When she finished her shower, Kathy sat at her vanity, wrapped in towels, applying her makeup, and fixing her hair. She constantly fantasized what her evening with Steve would be like. When she finished dressing, she threw a sweater over her shoulders and made her way to the living room, where she sat watching TV, anxiously waiting for Steve to arrive.

When the headlights flashed in her window, Kathy knew Steve had arrived. She stood up, gathered her crutches and belongings, and waited for him to approach the door. Hearing the knock, she slowly made her way to greet him. As she opened the door, she saw his big smile and felt her own excitement mirrored in his eyes. He reached over to hug her, kissing her on the cheek.

"You look beautiful," he said. What's the occasion?"

Kathy chuckled, "Do you want to come in, or should we just head out?" she asked.

"I'm ready and starving," said Steve. "Do you have everything you need?" Steve Asked.

"I just need to grab my purse and sweater from the table," Kathy said.

"I'll get that for you," Steve said, while walking over to the table and picking up her things.

As they left the house, Steve extended his hand for the keys. "May I lock the door for you?" he asked. Kathy appreciated his gentlemanly behavior but felt a bit awkward as she handed over the keys.

"Thank you," she said softly.

Steve locked the door and then guided her to the car, opening the door and ensuring she was comfortable before closing it. Kathy watched him through the window as he walked to the driver's side, feeling a mix of gratitude and unease at his attentive care.

At the restaurant, once they were seated, Steve talked a little about his day before confessing, "I have to be honest with you. I have thought about you all day, and I could hardly wait to see you tonight."

Kathy's face lit up with enthusiasm, though she was reluctant to let him know she had been feeling the same way. He reached out his hand, motioning to hold hers. She placed her hand in his, and he pulled it close, kissing it several times before resting their hands on the table. Kathy smiled and looked into his eyes.

"I've been thinking about you a lot too. I haven't felt this way in a very long time." she admitted.

They held each other's gaze until Steve leaned over the table, and Kathy met him halfway for a kiss. They sat back, with a warm feeling spreading between them, however, the moment was interrupted by the waiter.

"Have you decided what you're having?" the waiter asked. Steve gestured to Kathy. "Ladies first."

"I'll have the Angus steak, medium, with a baked potato and blue cheese on the salad," Kathy said, smiling.

Steve ordered the prime rib, medium, with steak fries and ranch dressing. After the waiter left, Steve asked, "What do you think about going away with me for a weekend?"

Stunned, Kathy replied, "What about the rules of your job?"

"I've thought about that," he said, holding up his fingers as he explained. "We have a few choices: One, we don't tell anyone; two, I can assign you to another doctor; or three, you can stop attending the class and not get your driver's license back."

Kathy chuckled. "Option three isn't really an option for me, and I don't want to see any other doctor."

"Well, then it is settled. This will be just between you and me," Steve said. Kathy smiled, feeling like she was doing something wrong but not caring.

"So, is that a yes?" Steve asked.

"Where are you thinking of going?" Kathy asked.

"We could go to Lake Tahoe and stay at a bed and breakfast right on the lake," Steve suggested.

Kathy had been to Lake Tahoe several times with friends or family over the years and had always fantasized about how it would be a wonderful place for a romantic getaway.

"So, is that a yes?" Steve asked again. Kathy smiled and, without hesitation, said, "Yes."

"Fantastic," Steve said. "You do not have to worry about a thing. I will take care of everything."

"I don't know how much fun I can be in a cast," Kathy said.

"Don't worry. Even if we just sit around and talk about how beautiful the lake is all day, as long as I'm with you, I'll be happy." Steve said.

When they got back to Kathy's house, she invited him in.

"What can I get you to drink?" she asked.

"I'm good. I don't need anything."

"Well, let's sit on the couch then," Kathy suggested.

They sat down, and without making small talk, Steve turned towards her and began kissing her. They embraced, hugging, kissing, and caressing.

"Will you spend the night with me?" Kathy asked, looking into his eyes.

"I would love to," he said, while softly putting his hand on her face and gently kissing her. He pulled back slightly and said, "I just so happen to have a change of clothes in my trunk."

"Look at you, all prepared," Kathy teased. They embraced and began kissing again.

"Why don't you go get your stuff out of your car and bring it into the house?" Kathy suggested. When Steve returned, Kathy asked him to put his clothes on the bed or in the closet in the extra bedroom. He walked directly to the room and put the items away. When he came back, she said, "don't worry, I'm not going to make you sleep in there."

"I would hope not, after the steak dinner I bought you" he said with a chuckle, returning to the couch he kissed Kathy again.

"What do you think about moving this to the bedroom?" Kathy asked with a soft tender voice.

"I was thinking the same thing," Steve replied.

He helped Kathy get up and followed her as she turned off the lights and headed to the bedroom. When they reached her bedroom, she turned towards him, "I'm not sure how this is going to work", tossing one of the crutches on the bed. "What a time to finally meet someone," Kathy said.

"Don't worry about it, Kathy. We can work around this. If all we do is hold each other, that is alright with me. It's temporary anyway," he said, continuing to kiss her as he led her to the bed. She sat down and he took the crutch she still had and placed it on the floor next to the bed, then grabbed the other crutch from the bed and put it with the first.

He laid down beside her and continued kissing her, their lips exploring each other with growing passion. Slowly, they began to undress each other, laughing at the struggle of making love for the first time. Kathy had to get out of bed to remove all her clothes, so Steve followed suit.

Once they were both naked, they turned to each other and embraced. Steve caressed her body as she stood, his touch sending shivers down her spine. As they passionately kissed, their bodies pressed together awkwardly The warmth of their connection intensified as they slowly laid on the bed, becoming entwined, savoring the beginning of their intimate journey together.

In the morning, Steve woke up and gently kissed Kathy on the lips. Kathy quickly smiled as she realized it was Steve. He got out of bed while she watched his naked form walk into the bathroom. Kathy struggled to get out of bed and grab her crutches from the floor. When Steve walked out of the bathroom, he saw her struggling, he said,

"Let me help you with that."

"I'm okay, really," she said, standing naked and holding her crutches. Steve reached over and kissed her gently on the lips. She wrapped one arm around his neck, as they began to embrace Donna said, "I could get used to this". Steve agreed.

Kathy made her way to the kitchen after showing Steve the shower and supplies. The early morning light streamed through the windows as she began brewing coffee and preparing a quick breakfast, the aroma of freshly ground coffee beans filling the room.

A few minutes later, Steve walked into the kitchen, freshly showered, and dressed, looking relaxed and content. Without a word, he came up behind Kathy, wrapping his arms around her waist and pressing his lips to her neck. She let out a soft sigh, leaning into his touch as he continued to kiss her, the warmth of his breath sending a pleasant shiver down her spine.

"You smell amazing," he murmured against her skin, his voice low and affectionate.

Kathy chuckled, turning slightly to look at him. "I could say the same about you," she replied, her eyes sparkling with affection.

Steve grinned, planting one last kiss on her neck before pulling back slightly. "What's for breakfast?"

"Just something quick," Kathy said, nodding toward the stove where eggs were sizzling in a pan. "Coffee's almost ready too."

"Perfect," Steve said, still holding her close. He watched her for a moment, a contented smile playing on his lips as he admired the way she moved around the kitchen. It was a simple, domestic moment, but it filled him with a deep sense of contentment.

As they worked together to finish preparing breakfast, their conversation flowed easily, filled with laughter and light teasing. It was clear that their connection extended beyond the physical, rooted in a growing affection and comfort with one another.

When the food was ready, they sat down at the kitchen table, enjoying their meal and each other's company. The sun continued to rise outside, casting a warm, golden glow over the room, adding to the cozy atmosphere of the morning.

For Kathy, it was a moment of peace and fulfillment, one that she wanted to hold on to for as long as possible. Steve's presence made her feel cherished and cared for, and as they sat together, she couldn't help but feel that maybe, just maybe, this was the beginning of something more.

As they finished their breakfast, Steve reached across the table, taking her hand in his. "I could get used to mornings like this," he said softly, his eyes full of sincerity.

"Me too," Kathy replied, squeezing his hand gently.

They sat there for a moment, just enjoying the comfortable silence, both of them knowing that whatever came next, they would face it together.

"You are coming to the group session tonight, aren't you?" he asked, his tone casual but with a hint of concern.

"Well, of course. I wouldn't want to lose my license," she chuckled, trying to lighten the mood.

"Let me know if you need a ride. I can come back and pick you up," he offered, his voice genuine.

She appreciated the gesture but wanted to maintain her independence. "I will get there one way or another. You don't have to worry about me," she assured him with a smile.

"Alright, just making sure," he replied, still looking at her with a hint of concern in his eyes.

"I'll be fine," she added, her smile growing. "See you tonight."

"See you tonight," he echoed, giving her a kiss before heading out.

As he left, she couldn't help but feel warmth from his concern. It was nice to have someone who cared, but she was determined to show up on her own terms, confident that she could handle whatever life brought.

Kathy sat for a moment, fantasizing their beautiful relationship and where it was going. "I should call Nancy and let her know what going on" she thought. Nancy didn't answer. Kathy sat thinking of who else she could call and share her excitement.

She knew she could not tell Dani about her relationship with Dr. Peters, but at least she could talk and maybe catch a ride to the meeting that night. Dani's phone rang and continued to ring with no answer. "That's odd," she thought, Dani should be answering her phone." For a moment Kathy was growing concerned. She considered calling Dr. Peters but decided she might be overreacting. Instead, she called Tammy, hoping she might be a good listener.

Tammy answered on the first ring. "What a pleasant surprise hearing from you, Kathy!" she said. How are you doing?

"Thank you, I am feeling so much better these days. Things seem to be falling in place." Kathy replied with a smile in her voice.

After the exchange of welcoming, Kathy's expression shifted to one of concern. "I'm curious if you've heard from Dani. I've tried calling her house a few times, and she doesn't answer," Kathy asked, her voice tinged with worry.

Tammy looked thoughtful for a moment before responding, sensing Kathy's unease.

"Wow, no, I haven't talked to her," Tammy replied, her brow furrowing slightly. "She could be sleeping, in the shower, or maybe she went to an AA meeting first thing this morning. You just never know with that girl," Tammy chuckled, trying to ease the tension.

"I understand your concern, though," Tammy continued, her tone softening with genuine care. "I've been with this group for a long time, and it's hard not to get attached to some of the patients. We're all in this together, and it's only natural to care about each other."

Tammy's warm concern was comforting, a reminder that in their shared struggles, they had formed bonds that went beyond just attending meetings.

"Why do you hang out with the group?" Kathy asked curiously. "You seem about as normal as can be."

"Well, it would take a sit-down session to explain how I got here, but the bottom line is I feel more comfortable helping with the group than anything else. I've tried to control my Tourette's," Tammy explained.

"Tourette's? You?" Kathy, interrupted.

"Yes, sweet lil ol' me," Tammy said. "With medication, I can control the tics and outbursts.

"I've heard some crazy things about Tourette's, but I don't think I've ever met anyone with it. I thought it was predominantly a male disorder," Kathy said, her voice curious and thoughtful. Tammy nodded, understanding the common misconception.

"You're right, it is more common in males," she replied. "But it can affect women too, just less frequently. It's one of those disorders that people often misunderstand, and it can be challenging to live with, especially when people don't know much about it."

Kathy listened intently, appreciating Tammy's willingness to share. "I can imagine," said Kathy. "It must be hard to explain to people who just don't get it". Tammy was grateful for Kathy's empathy. "Yes, it can be. But having a supportive environment, like this group, really helps. It's a place where you don't have to explain yourself all the time, where people just accept you for who you are." Tammy explained with compassion. "One of these days, we'll have to get together for a girl talk." Said Tammy

"I'd like that very much," Kathy replied. "Well, listen, if

you hear anything from Dani, have her call me, please. I want to see if she can give me a ride to tonight's meeting," asked Kathy.

" You got it," Tammy responded. "If you get stuck without a ride, call me. I'd be happy to come and pick you up."

"I appreciate that very much," Kathy said. "I may just take you up on that offer because at least I know I'll make it to the meeting on time".

"Sure, what time would you like me to pick you up?" Tammy asked.
"Why don't you come at 6:30," Kathy suggested. "

"6:30 it is," Tammy agreed. "I'll see you then. Tammy hung up the phone and immediately called Dani's house. She, too, became concerned as the phone continued to ring with no answer.

29 - Liar! Liar!

Jackie awoke alone in her bed as usual. She quickly remembered she had a house guest when there was a knock on her bedroom door. "Jackie, can I come in?" asked Dani.

"Sure, come in," replied Jackie, unsure what to expect. Dani entered the bedroom, wearing only her undergarments, her hair matted. "I feel like I was hit by a truck. Do you know where my clothes are?" she asked.

Jackie chuckled. "Yes, they're right over there on the chair next to the window. I was afraid you'd try to drive home last night, so I hid them. Did you finally come in and sleep on the bed I made for you?"

"Yes," said Dani. "Thanks for leaving me out there to fend off the mosquitoes."

"Hey, I tried to wake you, but you were out cold. I knew if you got cold, you'd come in and look for a warm place. So, see, I took good care of you," said Jackie with a smile.

"I need some coffee," said Dani, "or my head will explode."

Jackie got out of bed, wearing sexy babydoll lingerie. "Me too. Let's go downstairs and make some," she said.

"Do you always dress like that when you go to bed?" Dani asked curiously.

"Well, yes, of course. You never know when you're going to get lucky," Jackie replied with a laugh.

"Don't get any ideas with me," Dani said defensively. "No, I don't think that would happen," Jackie chuckled.

The women headed downstairs to the kitchen, where Jackie began making coffee. "Ah, that's what I'm talking about," said Dani.

"Yes, there's nothing like the smell of coffee or the first cup of coffee in the morning," replied Jackie, savoring the warmth of the mug in her hands. "Let's sit on the front porch. I'll bring some breakfast muffins. The view is to die for, especially in the morning."

Jackie moved through the kitchen, grabbing a tray for the muffins and coffee. The aroma of the warmed muffins filled the air, mingling with the rich scent of coffee.

They stepped outside onto the porch, the cool morning air greeting them gently. The view stretched out before them, a picturesque landscape bathed in soft sunlight, dew glistening on the grass. Jackie handed over a muffin, taking a seat in one of the cushioned chairs, and sighed contentedly.

"Isn't this just perfect?" Jackie asked, taking a bite of her muffin and glancing at the scenery. "Mornings like this make everything feel right with the world." The peacefulness of the moment wrapped around them as they settled into the comfort of the morning, savoring both the food and the view.

After a few minutes of taking it all in, Jackie commented, "You get pretty mean when you're drunk." Dani sat quietly, not responding to Jackie's comment. "I was a bit in fear, I thought I was going to have to use force with you last night," Jackie said.

Dani looked puzzled. "What are you talking about?" she asked.

Jackie laughed. "Don't tell me you don't remember."

"Remember what? What did I do?"

"You tried to have sex with me," said Jackie, bursting into laughter, her eyes sparkling with amusement.

The unexpected accusation, delivered with such playful humor, caught Dani off guard. She looked at her, wide-eyed for a moment, before breaking into a sheepish grin.

"Did I?" Dani asked, feigning innocence, though the corners of her mouth twitched with barely suppressed laughter. "I must have been drunk out of my mind."

Jackie continued to giggle, clearly enjoying the teasing. "You sure were. But nice try," she said, giving Dani a light, playful nudge.

"Bullshit," said Dani. "I did not. If anything, you were the horny bitch coming on to me. Dancing over my chair like a striper."

As they looked out at the view Dani said, "I don't believe you. You are lying right now"!

"Well, don't worry about it. It'll be our little secret," Jackie said, winking at Dani.

"Bitch," Dani muttered with a smirk. The exchange left both of them laughing, the tension between them dissolving into easy, playful banter. It was moments like this that reminded Jackie of how much she enjoyed their dynamic—light, fun, and female companion.

30 - Ungrateful Selfishness

Tammy and Kathy were the first to arrive at the group meeting. Kathy insisted on helping Tammy set up, even though Tammy told her she did not need to. As they worked, the room started filling up with patients.

Dr. Peters came in and saw Kathy helping with the setup. "Hello, ladies," he said. "Looks like you have a helper, Tammy."

"Yes, I tried to get her to sit and rest, but she insisted on helping me," Tammy replied pretending to be frustrated.

"It's just my style," said Kathy.

Dr. Peters smiled at Kathy. "Shall we get started?"

The three of them walked over to the circle and joined the rest of the group. Dr. Peters looked around while taking attendance. Shortly after, the door opened, and Dani and Jackie walked in, being excessively loud and chummy. Most of the group looked up and watched them, but Dr. Peters continued to focus on the meeting, not letting the interruption sidetrack him. Due to their late arrival, Jackie and Dani had to sit in chairs apart from each other, which Jackie loudly commented on.

"Well, if you got here when you were supposed to, maybe you two little lovebirds could find seats next to each other," Kathy commented with sarcasm. Both women looked at Kathy, Dani with a half-smile and Jackie with a "whatever" attitude.

At the end of the meeting, Tammy and Kathy rushed over to Dani. "We were so worried about you! Why weren't you answering your phone?" Tammy asked with deep concern.

"Oh my God! Since when did you two become my mother?" Dani replied, her voice tinged with mock exasperation as she rolled her eyes.

"This instantly angered Kathy, even though Dani said it with humor and sarcasm.

"Why do I bother," Kathy said, turning to walk away.

"I'm just kidding!" shouted Dani remorsefully.

Kathy continued to walk to the back of the room to get some punch.

"What crawled up her ass and died?" Dani whispered to Tammy as she laughed quietly.

"We were both just worried about you. We care about you and want to make sure you're okay," Tammy said softly with compassion. Dani, humbled by that comment, got up to walk over to Kathy, with Tammy following.

"Kathy, wait up," said Dani. Kathy slowly turned around and saw Dani reaching out her arm to hug her. "I'm so sorry," Dani said. "I'm glad you care, and I shouldn't be so rude. Please forgive me," I really do value your friendship, she cried. The three ladies continued walking to the back where the punch was. Tammy poured them all some punch and handed it to them.

Dani was anxious to tell them about her night. As they stood and talked Dani began by "So, I went over to Jackie's house for dinner and a swim last night. It got late, and I stayed the night and hung out with her most of the day."

"That explains the buddy-buddy act coming in the door," said Kathy with her negative overtone.

"You don't like her very much, do you?" asked Dani. Kathy looked at Dani with a smug expression but didn't respond. "If looks could kill," said Dani.

"I'm glad you're okay," said Kathy. They continued to chat until the room started to clear out. Tammy began to clean up, and Kathy and Dani helped a little.

"I think it would be great if the four of us could meet at Jackie's house for dinner and hang out. If you got to know her, you would see she's really not that bad," Dani said enthusiastically.

Kathy tried to change the subject by asking how Dani's sobriety was going. "I guess I'm going to have to start over today," Dani replied shamefully.

"Oh no, what happened?" asked Tammy.

"I guess you could say I got carried away last night at Jackie's," replied Dani.

Almost in concert, Kathy and Tammy said, "What! You're kidding!" Tammy said it with compassion, while Kathy sounded extremely angry.

Jackie heard the comments and turned to see what was going on. She walked over to where the ladies were and asked, "What is all the ruckus about?

Kathy was fuming. "Why in the hell would you give alcohol to someone who is trying to get sober?" she asked angrily.

"That is really none of your business," replied Jackie harshly. "Besides, she is a big girl and capable of making her own decisions."

Dani spoke up. "I knew what I was doing. I know I should have stayed away from the alcohol, but I figured one last night of partying with my friend wouldn't hurt."

"That is no friend," replied Kathy angerly as she stormed off.

"Who does she think she is?" Jackie commented to Dani and Tammy.

"I think she is just trying to be a true friend to us," said Tammy, rushing off to follow Kathy.

"Whatever," replied Jackie.

Tammy followed Kathy, calling out to her. Kathy picked up her belongings and scuffed toward the door. Dr. Peters noticed and became concerned. He followed Kathy to the door too.

"What is going on?" he asked.

"I've got to get out of here," replied Kathy.

"Well, can you tell me what is going on?" he asked.

In frustration, Kathy answered, "I can't stand the drama any longer."

She walked out, leaving Dr. Peters wondering what she was so upset about. Tammy, unsure what to do, continued to follow Kathy.

"Kathy, can I at least give you a ride home?" Tammy asked.

"No, thank you anyway," replied Kathy. "Just let me be. I can fend for myself, really," she said as she walked toward the elevator. Tammy stopped and watched as Kathy got on the elevator.

Dr. Peters came running out. "Where did she go?" he asked with great concern.

"She wouldn't take a ride from me. I offered," said Tammy. He saw the numbers above the elevator going down.

"Can you please help with the folks inside?" he asked Tammy as he ran toward the stairs.

Tammy, confused by what she had witnessed, went back into the room where most people were leaving. She noticed Dani and Jackie still talking. She touched base with a few patients and began to clean up. Tammy could hear Jackie and Dani laughing and carrying on as if what had happened was a big joke. She began to get concerned about their lack of empathy for Kathy.

"What is so funny?" she responded angerly. Jackie and Dani looked at her, surprised. Tammy was usually like a mouse around others, never voicing her opinions or being defensive, but this situation was obviously bothering her.

Dani walked over to Tammy and said, "Tammy, there is really nothing to be so upset about. Kathy is overreacting. She'll get over it."

"Actually, there is a lot to be upset about. This is what happens when people care about you more than you care about yourself. They get hurt by your actions, and you don't even realize it or care," Tammy said angerly.

Dani tried to laugh it off, but Tammy, like Kathy, didn't see the humor in Dani's behavior. Tammy continued to clean up and get out as soon as she could.

Dani turned back to Jackie. "What is everyone's problem around here?" she asked naively.

"Who knows. They just take life way too seriously," Jackie responded casually.

"I got to get out of here," Dani said with deep frustration.

"I'll walk out with you," Jackie replied.

Dr. Peters caught up with Kathy downstairs as she was using her phone to call a cab. "What are you doing?" he asked. Kathy ignored him and listened as the cab company answered the phone. "I need to get a cab, please." Dr. Peters reached out, grabbing her cell phone, and hung up the call.

"What are you doing?" he asked again.

"What does it look like I'm doing?" replied Kathy. "I'm getting a cab ride home."

"Why? I can give you a ride. Calm down. Why are you so upset?" he asked.

Kathy turned to him and said, "I don't know how you do it." "Do what?" he asked curiously.

"How do you pour your heart and soul out to these people who couldn't care less about your feelings, let along their own?" she asked with tears in her eyes.

He turned her face to his and replied, "I am not in it to be loved back. I am here to reach out and help those who will let me, to offer even one person a better life. Some will, some won't. Along the way, you lose some, but the ones that do get help are the reason I keep pouring my heart and soul into this job. There are rewards, but not 100% are going to get better. This is my calling. This is what I do." Kathy looked at him with tears in her eyes.

"I don't know if I can handle this. I don't want to be around people who don't take control of their lives and push towards a better life. I can't understand why they don't just stop! Why can't they see what they are doing to themselves?"

Dr. Peters reached out his arms and embraced Kathy just as Jackie and Dani were coming out of the elevator.

"Ooh, what is going on here?" Jackie asked sarcastically.

"Hello, ladies. Kathy and I were just talking about some personal things she is dealing with," Dr. Peters said.

"It looks serious," said Dani. "Do you need a ride home Kathy?" she asked with compassion.

Kathy stayed quiet and didn't make eye contact with either of the women.

"Kathy has a ride home, but thanks for asking, ladies. You go ahead and take off, and we will see you at the next meeting," Dr. Peters said. Both women looked confused and put out by being encouraged to leave. They looked at each other with concern, something neither was used to showing, and walked away, leaving Dr. Peters to tend to Kathy.

"So, what do you think her problem is?" Jackie asked, her tone tinged with curiosity and just a hint of skepticism.

"I'm not sure," Dani replied thoughtfully. "She always seems fine when I talk to her. I don't think it's boyfriend problems—she doesn't even have one."

"I can see why, as mean as she is," Jackie remarked, her voice dripping with sarcasm.

Dani glanced at Jackie, a small frown forming on her face. "She really isn't that bad," she replied, a hint of defensiveness in her tone. "You just have to get to know her. Jackie shrugged as they walked out of the building, the moonlight hitting them as they stepped outside. "Maybe. But she sure doesn't make it easy." Jackie said.

Dr. Peters looked back at Kathy. He put his arm around her shoulder. "I understand this is difficult and a different lifestyle than you're used to. Let me give you a ride home, and we can talk about it some more." Kathy looked up at him with tears in her eyes. "Do you mind waiting for me for just a few moments while I run back upstairs to check that everything is alright?" he asked.

He led Kathy toward the waiting area of the lobby. "Ya, sure. "I'll just sit here on this couch if you don't mind," said Kathy. Once Kathy was comfortable, Dr. Peters went back to wait for the elevator. When it opened, Tammy was standing in it alone. "Tammy, I was just going back upstairs to check on things before I left," he said, surprised.

"No worries, Dr. Peters. I have taken care of everything and closed up," Tammy replied.

"Thank you so much! I appreciate your help," he said, walking with her back to the building's entrance.

Tammy spotted Kathy sitting on the couch. "Kathy, what are you doing here?" she asked with concern. Dr. Peters answered for her.

"She has had a rough evening, and I'm giving her a ride home."

"Are you sure?" Tammy asked. "I don't mind at all."

"No, I'm heading in her direction, so it's no problem," he said. Kathy stood up, and the three of them walked out of the building. "Good night, everyone. I hope you're okay, Kathy,"

Tammy said as she went off in the direction of her car. Dr. Peters helped Kathy get into his car, he leaned over and kissed her on the side of her head. He then proceeded to get in on the driver 's side.

31 - After the meeting

Tammy arrived home, her aging parents were both asleep in the family room, her dad in his chair and her mom on the couch with the television blasting. "What are you guys doing up?" Tammy shouted. Both parents awoke, startled.

"You know you're supposed to go to bed when the alarm goes off, not sit out here and fall asleep with the TV blasting! Now come on, let's get you up and get to your beds," she said angrily.

Despite the patience and kindness Tammy showed to the group and others, she was the polar opposite with her parents, almost to the point of being abusive. As an only child born to parents in their mid-forties, she had spent most of her life ashamed of their age and inability to attend her events. Her mother, Flora, never wanted any children, and it showed, especially when Tammy's father was away from home. Tammy was a daddy's girl, which only fueled her mother's jealousy. When her father was diagnosed with Alzheimer's during her high school years, it became even harder for Flora to be present for her. Tammy harbored a lot of resentment, which eventually turned into a deep-seated anger she never shared or addressed.

"Come on, Dad, get up," she shouted as her father helplessly looked at her, not recognizing her or understanding what she was saying. She pulled him up from his chair, leading him by the arm into his bedroom.

"Mom, why didn't you put him to bed? I told you it's a lot harder when he's this tired." Tammy shouted.

"I'm sorry, I tried, but he got angry and almost fell. I couldn't get him to cooperate and was afraid of hurting myself, so I let him be. I guess I must have fallen asleep waiting for you to come home and help me," her mother said softly.

Tammy put her dad to bed and cleared his room to prevent any accidents. They set an alarm on the bedroom door so that if he opened it, the alarm would go off and wake someone to check on him. Her mother went to bed, leaving Tammy to clean up the day's mess and turn off the lights. Finally, Tammy went to her room to unwind and watch a little TV before nodding off.

Dani went home after the meeting to the empty house that she once shared with the love of her life. As she entered, a wave of depression and worthlessness washed over her. She looked around, seeing pictures of Paul and herself in happier times. She sank into the couch and turned on the TV, only to be bombarded with news of killings, bank robberies, rapes, embezzlement, and accidents "Depressing," she thought, flipping channels to find something more positive.

Dani got excited when she noticed the message light blinking on her recorder. Maybe, just maybe Paul called and left her a message. She hurried to the phone to hear the message. Upon pressing the button, she heard, "Dani, this is Betty. Where are you? I have been trying to get in touch with you since last night. I am worried about you. Call me when you get home, no matter what time it is. Just call me."

Dani sat for a moment, debating whether to call her sponsor and admit she had slipped and drank again. She thought, "Do I really want to be harped on again?"—this time by a lady she barely knew. Leaning back on the couch, she decided against making the call and closed her eyes, trying to shut out her thoughts.

Meanwhile, Steve and Kathy drove to a coffee shop near the hospital upon leaving the clinic. As they sat and talked, Kathy shared her frustration about being in the group with a bunch of people she wouldn't normally socialize with if not for the mandatory classes to get her driver's license back.

"Tammy is the only one who seems somewhat normal out of the whole group. But even she is a bit strange. Who in their right mind would attend these group meetings just to fix coffee and arrange cookies for a bunch of crazy people?" Kathy complained.

Steve chuckled. "Kathy, sometimes people need to feel needed and find little ways to contribute to something good." Kathy raised her eyebrows, looking at Steve skeptically.

"I'm just so frustrated trying to be a friend to Dani. Pouring my heart and soul into worrying about her, only to watch her destroy herself and not give a damn about how people feel. And then there's Jackie. Oh My God, she is a classic piece of work if there ever was one. Dani was sober for one day. She went to an AA meeting, got a sponsor, and was planning on attending another meeting that night until Jackie called her to come over. Jackie talked Dani into starting her sobriety the next day. Who does that?" If Jackie had just left her alone, she might still be sober. Jackie does not care about her. She just needs a friend and uses Dani to fill her void." Steve listened as Kathy unloaded on him, understanding her frustration but viewing the situation from a medical perspective.

"Kathy, you must remember that you are powerless over someone else. Over what they say or do." Steve continued, "I once knew a couple that struggled so much because the husband was always saying things that made his wife cringe, especially in public. After attending Alanon, she learned that she could not be responsible for anything that came out of his mouth. And she would let people know it when she needed to. She would say, "I am not responsible for whatever comes out of his mouth." People would chuckle but she was dead serious. "You only have a few more weeks of mandatory attendance, and then you're free to stop attending," he reminded her. "It can't come soon enough," Kathy said with enthusiasm.

32 - Reality of Differences

The next meeting brought a new face. An attractive man named Benjamin, still in his hospital gown, he looked worn out, unshaven, and tried to keep to himself. Tammy, familiar with him, introduced him to the group as a former patient of Dr. Gifford.

Most everyone tried to reach out to the newcomer, except for Kathy. She was becoming increasingly bitter and wanted nothing to do with him or anyone else. She patiently waited for the meeting to end so she could leave as soon as possible. Kathy had never been particularly vocal in group meetings, but she had reached a point where she barely paid attention to the members when they spoke.

She brought her crossword puzzle book and filled in the blanks throughout most of the meeting, a silent rebellion against the camaraderie forming around her. But when Dr. Peters spoke, she put her book down and listened, captivated by his tenderness and caring spirit. His words seemed to penetrate her bitterness, momentarily dissolving the walls she had built around herself.

When the meeting ended, Dani and Jackie introduced themselves to Benjamin. He seemed more interested in getting out of the room than socializing with them. He made eye contact for a second with Kathy and smiled. Kathy did not respond, instead putting her head down, focusing on her crossword puzzle.

Jackie and Dani gave up trying to befriend Benjamin and headed to the back of the room.

Kathy found herself sitting alone, waiting for the room to clear out while she waited for Dr. Peters to finish up. As she glanced away from her crossword puzzle, she noticed Benjamin looking at her. "What happened to your leg?" he asked.

"I was in a bad car accident," she replied.

"Wow, that must have been some accident," Benjamin said.

"Yes, it sure was. They thought I was dead at the accident scene," Kathy said. "But I fooled them," she said, with a smile.

"So how long ago was the accident?" asked Benjamin.

"It seems like it was yesterday, but it's been a couple of months already," said Kathy.

"When do you get the cast off?" he asked.

Kathy smiled. "Not soon enough," she replied. "This is very uncomfortable."

"I bet it is," replied Benjamin.

"So, are you doing okay?" Kathy asked hesitantly.

"I am now," replied Benjamin. He hesitated, then continued, "I got addicted to pain pills from an accident I had ten years ago. I could not alleviate the pain with prescriptions and soon became addicted to illegal drugs, eventually heroin and alcohol. I nearly died a couple of nights ago," he said, lowering his head in shame.

"Wow! You will find there are other people in the same boat here, so at least you are in the right place," said Kathy companionably.

A male nurse came to the meeting room to escort Benjamin back to his room. As Benjamin looked up, he said, "Well, I'd best be getting back to my room. Sorry for not being more presentable, but these are the only clothes I have right now."

Kathy chuckled. "I hate to disappoint you, but you're not the first to show up in their PJs." This brought a smile to Benjamin's face.

As he stood up, he walked over to Kathy and reached out his hand to shake hers. "I didn't catch your name," he said. "Kathy. My name is Kathy."

"Nice to meet you, Kathy," he said. "I'll see you again here, I imagine."

"Yes, unfortunately, I'll be here for a while longer," replied Kathy. They both smiled as Benjamin walked away. Kathy was amazed at herself for being so compassionate with him.

Jackie and Dani had noticed Kathy talking to Benjamin and watched as she shook his hand. "What do you suppose that was all about?" Dani asked Jackie.

"I'm not sure, but she probably was a bitch to him too," Jackie replied. Dani chuckled.

"Come on, Kathy is really a nice person," she said.

"Let's go get a drink," said Jackie. "Oh, wait. You can't do that anymore," Jackie said, catching herself.

Dani smiled, a hint of resignation in her eyes. "Well, I can go with you, and I'll have a soda or tea or something boring like that," she replied, trying to keep her tone light.

Jackie gave her a sympathetic look. "I did not mean to rub it in. I know it must be tough."

Dani shrugged, still smiling. "It's okay. I'm getting used to it. Besides, it's not about what I drink—it's about the company."

Jackie nodded, appreciating Dani's effort to stay positive.

"Well, I'll make sure the company is worth it then."

As the room cleared, Tammy saw Kathy sitting alone, working on her crossword puzzle. "Kathy, you're still here? Do you need a ride home?" she asked.

"Uh, no, actually I have a ride home, but thank you for offering," Kathy replied.

Tammy looked around and saw that Dr. Peters was one of the few people left in the room. "Is Dr. Peters giving you a ride again?" Tammy asked curiously.

Kathy was surprised by Tammy's boldness. "Yes, Tammy, he is. Is there a problem with that?" Kathy asked.

"No, no," Tammy said shyly. "I was just curious, that's all." "Okay, well, I'll see you in a few days. Have a good night," Tammy said as she turned and walked towards the doors.

Kathy could no longer sit patiently as Dr. Peters continued his conversation with a couple of his patients. The urge to leave grew stronger with each passing minute. Finally, unable to wait any longer, she got up and began gathering her things.

Dr. Peters noticed her movement out of the corner of his eye and tried to excuse himself from the conversation. However, one of the patients kept talking, not picking up on his subtle cues.

Determined not to let Kathy leave without a word, Dr. Peters gently interrupted the ongoing conversation and walked over to her.

"Kathy, I'm sorry to keep you waiting," he said, his tone apologetic. He turned to the patient and said, "It was really nice to meet you. I hope you found the meeting helpful and that you'll consider coming back for the next one."

Dr. Peters handed the patient a business card, noticing the patient behind him still trying to catch his attention. "Here's my card. I am sorry but I have to close up the room now. If you have time during the day, feel free to call me, and we can schedule some time to talk more in-depth," he offered.

The second patient nodded, taking the card. "I will," she said, though she felt a bit rushed.

"I'm glad you came tonight," Dr. Peters added, giving them one last reassuring smile before he turned back to Kathy.

Kathy couldn't shake the feeling of being caught in between his patients and her own needs, but she also felt a sense of determination to get home and to be more comfortable in her own surroundings.

As Kathy and Dr. Peters approached her house, she began to express her discomfort. "It's starting to get a little uncomfortable for me, and I think we need to take a step back," she said.

"What would make you feel that way?" he asked with deep concern.

"These people that you work with are a part of your everyday world. I don't understand them, nor do I want to. I realize I have a problem that brought me to the group, but surely, it's nowhere near what the other patients' problems are," Kathy explained. Dr. Peters looked at her sadly.

"I realize that you feel like you don't fit in, but I really care about you, and I don't want to lose you," he said.

Dr. Peters pulled into Kathy's driveway he turned off the car and looked at her. "Kathy, I don't want to lose you," he repeated. Kathy continued to look forward, not saying anything. Dr. Peters gently turned her face towards him. "Kathy, I don't want to lose you," he said again. Kathy could say nothing as she stared into his eyes, feeling torn. She knew how difficult it had been in her past to maintain a relationship with a man. There was never enough time due to her career, school, or personal ambitions. Now, she had met her match with a man that was busy with his career and possibly wouldn't have the time for her. As she looked at Dr. Peters, a new thought crept in: Could she be changing? Could she be falling for this man sitting next to her? The uncertainty gripped her, making her heart race. She felt a mix of fear and excitement, unsure of what the future might hold but suddenly willing to consider possibilities she had long since dismissed.

33 - Benjamin's Story

The next morning, Dr. Peters made his rounds at the hospital. He stopped to check on Benjamin and found him sitting up, talking to his nurse. "I see you're in good spirits, Benjamin," said Dr. Peters.

"I feel great now," Benjamin replied. "This nice nurse just gave me something to make me feel better."

"Good thing for those nurses," Dr. Peters joked.

The nurse smiled as she excused herself and left the room. Dr. Peters checked Benjamin's chart. "So, it looks like you're doing a lot better than when you came in," he said.

"I don't even remember coming in," Benjamin said.

"I'm glad you made it to the meeting last night," Dr. Peters said while continuing to read his chart.

"I really didn't want to. It was hard to muster up the courage, but I did," Benjamin admitted. And I enjoyed meeting a couple of the people."

"So, let's talk about you and how you got to where you are today," Dr. Peters said gently. Benjamin looked up, off into the distance, and hesitated before he spoke. Taking a deep breath, he began telling Dr. Peters about his past. "I was once a very strong man. I had a family and worked long hours in construction. One night, I was on my way home from work when an unlicensed drunk driver hit me. It nearly took my life but left me with a broken back, out of work, and in constant pain. I didn't have insurance, and the bills kept piling up."

He paused; his voice was thick with emotion. "Eventually, my marriage failed, and I struggled to get visitation with my children. My wife remarried and moved the family to another state. I got government assistance, which helped pay for my medical expenses and provided a small amount for living expenses. The doctors gave me Vicodin for pain relief, which I eventually became immune to. Then they put me on Oxycodone, but that stopped working too. A friend introduced me to heroin, which I swore I would never use, but the pain was so intense that I tried it."

Benjamin's eyes filled with tears as he continued. "After a few trials with heroin, I was hooked and lived with the addiction for years. Eventually, I was down and out, living on the streets. One night, I was attacked by some young punks who beat me unconscious. When a passerby found me, I was nearly dead. For the most part, the injuries from the beating were superficial, but my overall condition was poor due to the level of addiction I had."

Dr. Peters listened intently, his heart aching for Benjamin's struggles. "You've been through so much, Benjamin. But you're here now, and that's a start." Benjamin nodded, wiping his eyes. "I want to get better. I'm tired of living like this." "We're here to help you," Dr. Peters said. "It's going to be a tough journey, but you don't have to do it alone."

Dr. Peters shook his head in amazement after listening to the story. He had heard similar stories many times before. It starts small, and then in no time, it engulfs a person and takes over their whole life. "Have you ever tried to go through a recovery program?" Dr. Peters asked.

"No, I haven't," said Benjamin. "I don't have the resources to go through a program."
"What do you want for your life?" asked Dr. Peters.

"I want something I know I can never have again. I want my family back," Benjamin said, tears in his eyes.

"You realize that you won't get your wife back, but you can strive to see your children again," replied Dr. Peters.

"My children have been so brainwashed," Benjamin shouted. "They are never going to want to see me again!"

"Okay, well, let's start with you. Do you want to get clean? If I can put you into a detox center and then into a sober living environment at no cost to you, would you be willing to do whatever it takes to work the program?" Dr. Peters asked.

Benjamin put his face into his hands and cried uncontrollably. Dr. Peters comforted him by placing his hand on his shoulder until he was able to control himself.

34 - Betty Tried

Dani was about to fall asleep when the phone rang. She looked at the phone and saw it was Betty calling. She watched the phone, letting it ring, until she heard Betty begin to leave a message. "Dani, if you're home, please pick-up. I really need to talk to you," she said.

Dani hesitated until the very last moment, then finally answered. "Hi, Betty. Sorry I missed you. I've had a lot going on." "That's understandable," said Betty. "Have you been doing alright? I wanted to see if you were able to go to the AA meeting the other night."

"No, actually. But I did attend my group therapy session and saw a few friends. It's all good," Dani responded.

"Have you been able to stay sober?" Betty asked curiously.

"Oh yes, one day at a time" Dani lied. It wasn't easy, though. There have been a few times when I wanted to throw in the towel. I went to hang out with a friend, and I drank iced tea while she had wine.

"Awe...those are called slippery situations. It is best not to put yourself in them or around people who make it too easy for you. Especially in the beginning of your sobriety," Betty pleaded.

"Dani, you should call me when you feel that way. I'm here for you, and that's the best time to pick up the phone and call," Betty said with deep compassion and concern.

"Yeah, well, I was just getting ready to go to bed. Do you mind if I call you in the morning?" Dani asked in order to get off the phone.

"Better yet, how about you meet me at the meeting in the morning at 7:00?" Betty suggested

"Wow, that's early," Dani replied. I will see what I can do. I'll check my schedule and get back to you." As Dani hung up the phone she whispered, "I have no intention of getting up in the morning, especially so early to be at an AA meeting."

35-Don't let the dots disappear

At the next group meeting, Dr. Peters was pleased to see the attendance had increased. They went around the circle in the usual way, asking if anyone wanted to share. Benjamin, still dressed in his hospital clothing, raised his hand. "Go ahead," said Dr. Peters.

Benjamin began to speak slowly, all eyes on him. "I know you don't know much about me, but since I've been in the hospital, I've been able to look at my life differently than I have over the last couple of years. This is the clearest my head has been in a while. I've struggled with pain for so many years, which led me to become addicted to some very bad stuff. To even function, I'm on heavy doses of drugs, prescribed to keep my body from going into withdrawals that could kill me.

I don't want to be like this anymore. I wish I could go back to the day this all began, but I can't," he said, his voice cracking. With tears in his eyes, he continued, "I'm a father. My kids don't know who I am. They don't want anything to do with me. My wife remarried and took my kids to another state. I want my life back. I hope and pray that somehow, I can stay clean. That somehow the intense pain I have will subside, or there will be a surgery or something that can help me. I'm not good at asking for help, but if there is a God, I pray he gets me through this."

You could have heard a pin drop as everyone continued to look at Benjamin, some with tears in their eyes, others sad and stunned by his story. Kathy pulled a tissue from her purse, wiping her eyes as Dr. Peters looked on, touched by Benjamin's story. Dr. Peters stood up and walked over to Benjamin, placing his hand on his shoulder.

"Thank you for sharing, Benjamin. You've already come a long way, and we look forward to being here for you. You will get through this."

"Sometimes, we have to push ourselves a bit harder than normal if we want to achieve something that appears to be out of our reach," Dr Peters said He moved a chalkboard closer to the group. He erased what was on the board and began to passionately talk about dreams and goals. On one side, he drew a circle and wrote "You" inside it. On the other side, he drew another circle and wrote "Dreams / Goals" inside it. Turning to Benjamin, he continued, "There is only one way to get here," he pointed to the dream circle. "But it doesn't just happen. You have to make it happen. All of you," he said, looking around the circle, making eye contact with everyone who was looking up. "We put a plan together for you. Some of you follow the plan, others don't," he said, again looking for eye contact. "When you follow the plan, you can go from here to here," he said, drawing a dotted line from "You" to "Dreams / Goals."

"What do you think these dots are?" he asked. After a moment, Tammy spoke up, "Those are the steps." "Exactly," said Dr. Peters. "In most cases, the first step represents your medications. Some of you need to put more dedication into taking your meds as recommended. It is crucial you take your meds on time, every day that you're supposed to."

He turned and began erasing some of the dots on the board leading to the dreams/goals. "What else?" he asked again, looking at the crowd. "Doctor appointments," he continued, erasing more dots. "Group therapy," he said, erasing even more dots.

He turned to the group again and asked, "If these dots are steppingstones, how are you going to reach the goal if your steps aren't there?"

He erased a part of the board and began writing in columns: Daily, Weekly, Bi-Weekly, Monthly, 6 Months, 1 Year. "Goals, people. You need to make some goals for yourselves. AA talks about one day at a time. Why is that"? He asked, watching the reactions of the patients.

Why is daily goal so important? Again, looking around the room.

"Because it is only one day" Dr. Peters said calmly. One day! 24 hours!

They add up, but we do not worry about that. We get through one day. When we get through 6 days, we get excited, it is almost a week! Yay! But what is it going to take to get to one week when you are at day 6? One day. Do you see the power of one day" he asked again looking around.

"The most important step is the first step." Several of the group members looked on with great interest, while others squirmed in their seats, avoiding eye contact. "Every single one of you has a plan that either me or Dr. Gifford put together for you. If you don't have a copy, please talk to me about it at your next one-on-one appointment, and I will make sure you get a copy." He closed the meeting by offering cookies and coffee at the back of the room.

36 - Daddys Missing

As Tammy arrived home, she saw the lights were still on in the house, a sign that it was going to be an effort to get her parents to bed. As she approached the front door, she realized it was open. Her heart skipped a beat, as she hurried inside to check on her parents, finding her mother sound asleep in her usual chair. She felt panic set in when she didn't see her dad. She scurried through the house, checking the bathroom, the bedroom, and the kitchen. She ran to the back door and looked around the backyard with no sign of her father. Desperation mounting, she ran back into the house and out the front door.

"Dad! Dad!" she called as she ran down the street, looking in neighboring yards as she passed them. As she reached the end of the street, she turned back, frantically running up the opposite side, shouting his name. One of the neighbors came outside and offered to help her search. Tammy ran back into her house to grab her cell phone.

"Mom! Mom!" she shouted. As her mother woke up, "Where is Dad?" With confusion and panic in her eyes, her mother glanced around the room, saying,

"I don't know. I must have fallen asleep."

Tammy dialed 911 as she continued to yell at her mom. "Dad is missing, Mom. You were supposed to watch him and put him to bed."!

While speaking to the 911 operator, she frantically explained what had happened as she rushed outside to continue her search for her father. Soon Tammy saw red lights heading up her street toward her house. She hung up the phone when the police arrived.

When the first police car arrived, the officer got out of the car, introduced himself as Officer Bennett, and began asking questions about her father. Shortly after, several other police cars drove up, all with their lights on, some using their spotlights to search while driving.

Officer Bennett filled in the other police about the situation, sending them off in different directions to look for Tammy's father.

"Is there anyone else here?" he asked.

"Just my mom," said Tammy, "she was supposed to be watching my dad."

"Let's go into the house where it's a bit quieter," said Officer Bennett.

"I don't think we can do that, sir," Tammy said nervously.

"My mother always refuses to let anyone come into her home. She believes she would be judged by the way she keeps her house, and she believes people don't need to know about her business. "My mother is a very private person. She has tons of stuff all over the house and she..."

The officer interrupted, "Ma'am, I have seen just about everything. I need to speak to your mother as well as you." He began walking toward the front door, and Tammy followed behind him, trying to convince him not to go in. As soon as Officer Bennett stepped into the house, he could tell they were hoarders. He looked around in astonishment and asked, "Where is your mother?"

Tammy led him into the family room where her mother was still sitting in her chair. The officer introduced himself to her, asking if she was okay. She just nodded in response. She didn't seem to be bothered that he was in the house.

As Officer Bennett talked to the ladies, there was a knock on the door. Tammy went to open it and saw another police officer, this time with a large dog.

"My name is Officer Gray. May I come in?" he asked.

Tammy hesitated for a moment, then said, "Sure."

Tammy led him over to where her mother and Officer Bennett were. "I need to collect something with your father's scent," he said. "Is there a bedroom I can walk my dog around and maybe pick up a shirt or something to help my dog focus on your father's smell?"

"Sure, follow me." Tammy led Officer Gray to her parents' room and let the dog sniff around. She grabbed the pillowcase off her father's pillow and handed it to Officer Gray.

As Officer Gray opened the door to leave the house, Tammy could hear a helicopter flying over her house. "Is that a helicopter searching for my father?" she asked Officer Bennett.

"Yes, ma'am, we are going to find your father one way or another." Tammy clasped her hands to her chest and gave a sigh of relief.

When Tammy went back into the family room, she looked at her mother and said, "See, Mother? If you had stayed awake long enough to put Daddy to bed, all these people wouldn't have to be out looking for him."

Officer Bennett was a little surprised by Tammy's abrupt comment to her mother. He could see the fear in Tammy's mother's eyes as Tammy continued to reprimand her.

"I know this is all my fault," Tammy's mother said. "I am so sorry," she continued to say over and over. Officer Bennett picked up on the tension between them and wondered if there could be more going on than just a disappearance.

Tammy heard another knock on the door. This time, it was an officer accompanied by a woman who introduced herself as Sarah. "I'm a medic. I'm here to assist with your father once our search and rescue team finds him. Is it okay if I hang out here with you while we wait?" Sarah asked.

"Yes, sure," said Tammy. Sarah introduced herself to Tammy's mom. "What's your name?"

Tammy spoke up, answering for her mother. "That's my mom, Flora. She fell asleep when she was supposed to be watching my dad and that's how my dad got out of the house."

Sarah asked Flora several more questions, trying to establish a rapport, but Tammy kept answering for her. Sensing Flora's distress, Sarah squatted down to Flora's level. "Is there anything you need?" Flora's eyes teared up a bit, but she shook her head no.

"My mom is fine. She doesn't need anything," Tammy interjected.

Sarah could tell Flora was terribly upset. "Don't worry about a thing. I have a police radio that we can listen to. As soon as they find your husband, we'll know." Flora nodded, relieved while wiping her eyes with a tissue.

Several hours passed with no news. Tammy paced back and forth, trying to relax but failing. She picked up her phone and scrolled through her contact list, hoping to find someone for comfort. She came across Dr. Peters' number and called him. The call went straight to voicemail. "Dr. Peters, this is Tammy. Can you please call me right away? It's very important." She hung up and scrolled through her numbers again, calling Dani next. Again, the phone rang and went to voicemail.

"Hey Dani, it's Tammy. I have a problem and need your help. Can you please call me as soon as you get this message?" Continuing to search through her contacts, she came across Kathy's number and dialed it. Kathy answered on the second ring.

"Hello," she said, her voice tired and raspy.

"Kathy, this is Tammy. I'm so sorry to wake you at such a late hour, but I've had a situation, and I don't know what to do! I've called Dr. Peters and Dani, but neither answered their phones."

Kathy sat up in bed, concerned as she heard the fear in Tammy's voice. "Tammy, what's the matter?"

Tammy explained, her voice trembling, "I'm scared, and I don't know what to do. I feel so alone."

"No worries, Tammy. Text me your address. I'll come over right away," Kathy said.

Tammy hesitated, knowing that if Kathy came to the house, she would see the mess and might judge her. "Um, Kathy, my house is a terrible mess."

"This is not the time to think about how your house looks, Tammy," Kathy insisted. Tammy felt relieved to finally have someone she could count on and consider a friend.

Kathy hung up and called Steve but got his voicemail. "Hey, give me a call as soon as you can. Tammy has a serious problem." Within moments, Kathy received a call back from Steve.

"What's going on?" he asked. "I got a call from Tammy as well." Kathy explained the situation and mentioned she would take a cab to Tammy's house. "Send me her address, and I'll get dressed and head over there," Dr. Peters said anxiously.

As Kathy arrived at Tammy's house, she was amazed at all the cars parked outside. She could see and hear the helicopter flying nearby. She got out of the car and walked to the door just as Tammy came out with open arms and tears in her eyes. "What the heck?" Kathy asked.

"I have never been so scared in my life. Thank you so much for coming over. Come in and we'll talk about it", Tammy cried. Without thinking about the state of her house, Tammy led Kathy inside. Kathy tried not to show her shock as she looked around and saw the filth and mass accumulation of stuff. Tammy led Kathy into the family room and introduced her to her mother, Flora, and Sarah. Kathy walked over to Flora and tried to comfort her, sensing her distress. She gently squeezed Flora's hand. "I got in touch with Dr. Peters. He's coming over, but it will take him a bit longer because he lives far away," Kathy said to Tammy.

Tammy began recounting the events to Kathy, her voice rising. She pointed out that it was her mother's fault for not watching her father and putting him to bed. Flora sat there, staring forward as if she were a young child being scolded.

"Tammy, I'm sure she didn't mean to fall asleep," Kathy said gently.

"I know, but it just makes me so mad," Tammy replied. "That's all I ask of her, and she can't even do that," she said sternly. Kathy was amazed at Tammy's harshness. This was a total contrast to the caring, serving, sweet person she had come to know in the meetings.

"Tammy, I understand you're upset, but blaming your mom isn't going to help right now," Kathy said softly, glancing at Flora, who looked even more distressed. Flora's eyes filled with tears as she mumbled,

"I'm so sorry. I didn't mean to fall asleep." Sarah stepped in, trying to ease the tension.

"Let's focus on finding your father. Sarah said, we're doing everything we can. He's our priority right now."

Tammy nodded, taking a deep breath. "I just hope they find him soon."

Kathy turned to Sarah, noticing the concern in her eyes over how Tammy was speaking to her mother. "I have a radio," said Sarah, changing the subject. "We're listening to it, so we'll know if the police search finds her father."

The three women sat for hours, anxiously waiting for an update. Flora kept falling asleep in her chair, only to wake up startled and find out there was nothing new. Sarah tried to get

Flora to go to her bed and rest, but Flora wouldn't have it. With each passing hour, Tammy became more and more agitated.

"I wish I could do something more," said Kathy. "If I didn't have this cast on, I'd be out there with the search team."

Around 4 a.m., Dr. Peters arrived at Tammy's house. Everyone, especially Tammy, was happy to see him. He too was surprised to see that the house Tammy lived in was that of a hoarder. He introduced himself to Sarah and Flora, then went outside to speak with one of the officers. As he was introducing himself, a call came over the radio from the helicopter pilot.

"It appears they may have found him," said the officer. Dr. Peters listened intently as the pilot spoke.

"Possible subject lying on the lawn at the park near the freeway." Several minutes later, another officer confirmed it wasn't him.

"What can I do to help?" asked Dr. Peters. "You can search if you want, but I really think your time would be more valuable being inside with the ladies," replied the officer. Dr. Peters thanked the officer and went back inside the house.

Hours passed with no news. "I really hate to leave, but I must be getting to work," said Dr. Peters. "If I didn't have commitments already, I would stay, but people are counting on me." As he left, Tammy watched him and Kathy interact, noticing the subtle signs of a relationship.

Trying to downplay it, Kathy said, "What? We've become good friends. I'm not in any position to be in a relationship. Look at me, I can barely get around. I can't expect someone to come into my life and be my caretaker right off the bat."

Tammy wasn't entirely convinced. "So, you guys are seeing each other?" she asked with enthusiasm. "It's okay if you are. I mean, it's not like I'm going to say anything." Kathy tried to play down the relationship, but Tammy was not buying it.

"We're just friends," Kathy insisted.

Nurse Sarah apologized as she told Tammy she too must leave, and they would be sending a replacement for her shortly. A good part of the morning passed as Tammy and Kathy sat waiting for any news. The two dozed off from time to time or got up to walk around.

At about 9:30 a.m., Tammy's phone rang. "Hello, this is Tammy."

"Hi Tammy, it's Dani. Your message sounded important. Is everything okay?"

"No, no, it's not okay," Tammy said.

"My dad went missing last night, and he is still not home. He has Dementia and gets very turned around. I've got an army of people out here looking for him. Kathy has been here all night."

"Wow," said Dani. "I hope he is okay. I would come by, but I already have plans and need to be somewhere." Tammy assured her she was fine and thanked her for calling.

Not even ten minutes had passed when there was a knock on the door. Tammy thought it would be Sarah's replacement, only to find Officer Bennett standing there. "Come in," she said. "Is everything alright?" she asked with deep concern.

"Can we go into the other room?" he asked. Tammy led him to where her mom and Kathy were sitting.

"Sit down," he said.

Tammy asked, "What's wrong? Did you find my dad?"

"We found your father down the street aways," Officer Bennett began, looking at Flora. "Unfortunately, he fell and hit his head. He was unable to get up and it appears that he had hypothermia."

"Where is he?" Tammy asked hysterically. "I'm sorry, he didn't survive," Officer Bennett said gently.

Tammy became very distraught, shouting hysterically, while trying to make her way to the door.

"Where is he? Where is he?" Flora looked on with tears in her eyes, more concerned about Tammy than herself for once in her life. Kathy got up to console Tammy, wrapping her arms around her as she wept hysterically.

To Kathy's surprise, Tammy made eye contact with her mother. She pulled away from Kathy's embrace and began yelling and crying at her mother. "This is all your fault. Daddy is dead because of you!" she shouted. Kathy and Officer Bennett tried to calm Tammy down, stepping in between her and her mother. She just cried and screamed continuously, "This is all your fault!"

As the new medical assistant Debra walked up to the house, she could hear loud crying and people talking inside. She walked in, following the voices, and saw Tammy very distraught. She stood back and observed for a moment until she realized Flora was sitting by herself, looking a bit flushed. As she approached Flora, Tammy turned to her and screamed, "Get away from her! She is the reason this happened."

Tammy broke loose from Kathy's embrace and tried to move towards her mother in a violent way. "She is the reason my daddy died!" yelled Tammy.

Officer Bennett saw the situation was getting out of control and knew he would have to separate the two women for a while. He stepped between Tammy and her mother, trying to maintain control of the volatile scene.

"Tammy, please, calm down. We need to get a hold of yourself," he said firmly. Debra began to walk Flora to a different room to give her space and to check on her well-being. Kathy stayed close to Tammy, trying to soothe her, though she was visibly shaken herself.

As Debra spoke to Flora, it was clear she was shaking and very nervous. "Oh, my goodness, your heart is beating so fast I think it's going to jump out of your chest," Debra said as she was taking Flora's blood pressure.

Debra quickly pulled out her radio, her voice steady as she contacted the ambulance personnel who were on standby outside. "We need paramedics here immediately," she said, her tone urgent but controlled.

Within moments, two paramedics entered the room, their faces focused as they assessed the situation. They moved swiftly to Flora's side, beginning to check her vitals and assess her condition with practiced efficiency.

In the other room, Tammy was pacing anxiously, struggling to stay calm as the paramedics worked. The fear of what could happen to her mother was nearly overwhelming.

She could hear the low, steady voices of the medics, but it did little to reassure her.

Kathy noticed Tammy's distress and approached her, placing a gentle hand on her shoulder. "Tammy, they know what they're doing," Kathy said softly, trying to soothe her friend. "Your mom is in good hands. You need to take a moment to calm down."

Tammy stopped pacing and looked at Kathy, her eyes wide with fear and worry. "I'm just so scared, Kathy. What if something happens to her?"

Kathy gave her shoulder a reassuring squeeze. "I know it's hard, but you must trust that they're doing everything they can. Panicking won't help your mom right now. Take a deep breath and try to focus on staying calm—for her and for yourself."

Tammy nodded, taking a shaky breath, and trying to steady herself. Kathy's calm presence was a small comfort during the chaos. She knew Kathy was right; she needed to keep it together for her mom's sake.

As the paramedics continued their work in the room where Flora was, Tammy stood by the doorway, watching closely but trying to follow Kathy's advice. She focused on breathing deeply and keeping her emotions in check, knowing that staying calm was the best thing she could do right now.

Tammy rushed into the room when she heard the paramedic say "Her blood pressure and heart rate are out of control. We need to get her to a hospital right away."

"What's going on?" Tammy asked, her voice trembling with concern for her mother. "Your mother is in shock and needs to go to the hospital for observation," Debra replied. Tammy stood with her hands over her face, overwhelmed with fear and anxiety.

"Is she going to be alright?" she asked.

"She has a better chance if we get her to the hospital right away," Debra said.

The paramedics helped Flora onto a gurney and secured her. Tammy answered their questions about Flora's health, then went to her mother's side, reassuring her that everything was going to be alright. Tears streamed down Tammy's face as she watched her mother being wheeled off to the ambulance.

Kathy stood nearby, feeling helpless and shocked by the events. She wanted to offer Tammy a ride to the hospital but knew she couldn't with her cast. Tammy turned to Kathy, her face a mixture of disbelief and exhaustion. "Can you believe this?" she asked. "I have to go to the hospital after all this."

"Yes, you do," Kathy said gently. "Do you want me to come with you?"

"No, you've done so much already. I can't expect you to come with me. Besides, my mother will be fine. They just need to observe her and then they'll probably release her. Let me call you a cab," Tammy insisted.

While Kathy waited for the cab, her mind was racing as she tried to process everything that had just happened. She watched as Tammy hurriedly gathered her and her mother's personal belongings, preparing to follow the ambulance to the hospital. The weight of the day's events hung heavily in the air, leaving Kathy feeling both exhausted and overwhelmed.

As Tammy finally drove off toward the hospital, Kathy felt a strong urge to reach out to Steve, to share the chaos and confusion that had unfolded. She needed to talk to Steve, to hear his voice and make sense of the whirlwind she had just experienced.

Once Tammy was out of sight, Kathy pulled out her phone and quickly dialed Steve's number. The phone rang only once before he picked up.

"Hey, Kathy," Steve answered, his tone warm and familiar with concern of the tragedy.

Without preamble, Kathy exclaimed, "You are not going to believe what just happened! In all my life, I have never seen such craziness."

Steve's tone shifted to concern. "What's going on? Are you okay?"

Kathy took a deep breath, still feeling the adrenaline coursing through her veins. "I'm fine, but Tammy's family… it's been a total nightmare. First, we found out her father laid in a terrible state, hypothermic, nonresponsive. Then Tammy completely lost it on her mom, yelling at her like I've never seen before. It was awful, Steve. And just when I thought it couldn't get any worse, her mom, Flora, had a medical emergency right in front of us."

Steve listened intently as Kathy recounted the entire incident, his occasional murmurs of sympathy and surprise encouraging her to continue.

"And now Flora's headed to the hospital," Kathy added, her voice tinged with disbelief. "It all happened so fast; I still can't wrap my head around it. One minute we were just talking, and the next, everything spiraled out of control."

Steve sighed on the other end of the line. "That sounds intense, Kathy. I can't imagine how hard that must have been for you to witness."

"Yes, it was," Kathy admitted, finally allowing herself to feel the weight of the situation. "I didn't know what to do. I just tried to be there for Tammy, but it was like watching a train wreck in slow motion."

Steve's voice softened with empathy. "You did the best you could, Kathy. It sounds like you were a good friend to Tammy when she needed you the most. Sometimes, that's all you can do." Kathy nodded, even though he couldn't see her. His words provided a small measure of comfort.

"Thanks, Steve. I really needed to hear that. It's just a lot to process." I honestly believe that if someone hadn't been there tonight, Tammy might have physically abused her mother."

"You may be right," Steve replied.

"Thanks for listening, Steve. It means a lot," Kathy said, her voice soft with gratitude.

"Anytime, Kathy," Steve replied, his voice warm and reassuring. "I'm here for you sweetheart. "Kathy smiled at the familiar term of endearment. It brought her a sense of comfort, reminding her that despite the craziness of the day, she had someone who genuinely cared about her. As she ended the call, Kathy felt a bit lighter. The conversation with Steve had helped ease the weight of the day's events, and she was grateful for his support. She took a deep breath, tucked her phone back into her bag, and waited for the cab to arrive, feeling more grounded and ready to move forward.

37 - Let's Go Shopping

Dani called Jackie first thing in the morning. "Hey, what's going on? Are we still on for today?" she asked.

"Of course," replied Jackie. "I'm just finishing up with my hair and makeup. I'll swing by and pick you up within an hour."

Dani poured herself a cup of coffee adding a shot of brandy and sipped it while she changed into her jeans and a silky floral blouse, pairing them with high heel stiletto shoes. She knew Jackie would probably outdress her, but she was okay with that. She applied her makeup a bit thicker, using darker colors than usual.

Jackie approached the house in her sports car with the top down, honking the horn as she pulled into the driveway. She wore a straw hat and dark oversized sunglasses, clearly sporting designer clothing with a plunging neckline. As Dani got in the car, she reached over and gave Jackie a hug and kiss on the cheek. Jackie could smell the alcohol on Dani's breath.

"'Oh, starting early with the cocktails, are we?" Jackie asked with a chuckle. Dani smiled but ignored her comment, buckling up. She was happy to have a girlfriend that would spend the day shopping with her.

Jackie was very familiar with their destination and knew Dani would enjoy it. When they arrived in the downtown shopping area, Jackie drove around the quaint tree-lined streets, showing Dani some of the boutique shops and restaurants she loved.

"Wow, I love this place," Dani said with excitement.

"I figured you would," said Jackie. "It's one of my favorite shopping destinations." Jackie parked the car, and the ladies got out, looking around in amazement at the beauty. "I'm going to take you to my favorite place to shop in the whole world," said Jackie, locking arms with Dani and leading her towards a boutique.

As they walked inside, Dani was in awe of the delightful items in every direction. She followed Jackie throughout the store, gasping at everything Jackie pointed out. Jackie was no stranger to the store; a couple of clerks approached her, asking how she had been and if they could help her with anything. As soon as Jackie had an item in her hand, a clerk was right there to take it and set up a dressing room for her. "Come on, Dani, aren't you finding anything you want to try on?" asked Jackie.

"Uh, yeah, sure," Dani replied, fumbling through items on the racks and tables.

Dani found a couple of items she liked and carried them around, hoping one of the clerks would give her the same treatment as Jackie. Approaching Jackie, she said, "What am I, chopped liver? "she chuckled. Jackie looked at her curiously, not understanding what she meant, and continued shopping.

Dani grew frustrated with the lack of attention and went to find a clerk.

"Can I get a fitting room?" she asked. The clerk pointed towards the fitting room but did not escort her. Dani, feeling even more frustrated, made her way to the fitting room on her own.

While Jackie and Dani tried on clothes, they came out to ask each other's opinions. Everything Jackie tried on was stunning, while Dani's choices were much more conservative. "You need to be a lot more adventurous," Jackie told Dani. She went back to the showroom and grabbed several daring items for Dani to try on. "Here, let's have some fun," said Jackie, handing the clothes to Dani.

"Oh my God, that is not my style. Are you kidding me?" Dani asked nervously.

"You are not that old. You need to have a little fun and explore," Jackie said in hopes of encouraging Dani.

Dani reluctantly tried on the clothes Jackie picked out. When she looked in the mirror, she was amazed at how beautiful and sexy she looked. She wanted every item Jackie selected for her. Jackie's attendant was enthusiastic, bringing accessories to complement the outfits. Dani loved the attention from both Jackie and the attendant. She didn't think about the money as she handed her credit card to the attendant. "I want everything, including the accessories." The attendant took all the items to the register to ring them up and package them while Dani changed back into her clothes.

Throughout the rest of the morning, the ladies visited several other boutiques. Dani continued to buy things, keeping up with Jackie's shopping spree as if she were in the same financial category.

"Hey, I don't know about you, but I'm starving," said Jackie. "I want to take you to one of my very favorite places to grab a bite to eat."

"You've got my attention. Do they serve cocktails?" Dani chuckled.

"Of course, they do," replied Jackie.

They walked back to Jackie's car and put the bags in the trunk. "We can walk there from here," said Jackie.

As they approached the restaurant, Jackie pointed out the garden area with the ponds and koi fish. Dani couldn't believe the beauty and elegance as she walked through the entry doors. Jackie directed the host to seat them in the garden area overlooking the ponds.

As they were seated, Dani asked, "Can we get some martinis?" The host chuckled and said, "Your server will be right with you."

When the server approached, he introduced himself and said, "I understand some martinis are in order?"

Jackie chuckled and said, "Yes, my friend here would really like to get a martini ASAP."

Jackie sipped her martini and looked over the menu while Dani downed hers and ordered a second one even before the waiter left the table. "The menu has so many amazing things, I can't decide," said Dani.

"Go with the salmon salad," claimed Jackie. "It's to die for."

Before the food was delivered, Dani ordered her third martini. While they waited, they talked and laughed about all the adventures they had since they met. Dani grew louder as time passed, but it didn't bother Jackie, who noticed they were getting attention because of it.

Once they finished their meal, Jackie asked "are you still interested in shopping or is there anything else you want to do.

Dani, wanting to please Jackie, said, "Oh, shopping, of course," even though she had already overspent on her credit card.

As the ladies began to leave, they walked past a bar, peeking inside. "Hey, for fun, let's go in and see if there are any hot guys in there," Jackie chuckled. The bar had few customers, but no one caught their attention, so they continued to leave. As they got to the doorway, several men in business attire entered, making eye contact first with Dani and then Jackie. A couple of the men watched them as they walked out, chuckling and saying words the girls couldn't make out.

"Dang, too bad they're coming in now," said Jackie.

"Yeah, too bad," said Dani.

The ladies continued to go in and out of different shops, occasionally buying something. As they walked out of the last shop, Dani pointed to a sports bar across the street. "Look, now we're talking. That's the kind of shopping I want to do now," she said. Jackie agreed.

As they walked into the sports bar, most heads turned, noticing them. "Should we grab a table?" Dani asked.

"Oh, no. I think it would be more interesting to sit at the bar," Jackie said, leading the way.

As they sat at the bar, a handsome young, well-built bartender wearing a tight sports bar T-shirt approached and asked what they would like to order.

"I wouldn't mind one of you," Jackie said with a smile. Dani was amused by her comment and laughed it off.

"I'm going to stick with a martini," Dani said. Jackie agreed.

Jackie introduced herself and Dani and learned the bartender's name was Braden. He was an aspiring actor, trying to land a big part in a movie during the day and bartending at night to pay the bills. Dani ordered herself a second martini as Jackie continued to sip on hers very slowly. The three of them talked and laughed, enjoying the atmosphere and the company.

The entry doors opened causing bright light from outside to light up the room. Braden looked up and greeted the new guests. Both Dani and Jackie naturally turned to see who was walking in. "OMG, it's those guys from the restaurant earlier," said Dani.

"You know these guys?" asked Braden.

"No, but I have a feeling we'll be meeting them soon," Jackie chuckled.

As the men approached the bar, they were a bit loud and intoxicated. One of them pointed out that the "hot chicks" from earlier were sitting at the bar.

Jackie laughed. "Did you hear him call us 'hot chicks?" The two ladies laughed hysterically as the men approached.

Two of the men who had been eyeing the women at the bar earlier sat closest to Dani. They ordered their drinks, and the man closest to Dani turned and asked, "Can we get you a drink as well?" Dani was excited and spoke up, "Hell yeah!" She was beginning to feel a buzz from her martinis.

Jackie smiled and said, "Sure, thank you."

This gave the men an open invitation to introduce themselves and get their names. Jackie, being on the end of the row of seats, strained to join the conversation, so she got out of her chair and positioned herself in the middle of the group standing as she spoke to them. Once their drinks arrived, they all toasted each other.

The guy sitting next to Dani introduced himself as David and carried on a conversation with her. Meanwhile, the other three men were now under the spell of the voluptuous Jackie. Dani wasn't bothered by Jackie's dominance until David, too, turned to join the conversation with everyone else. Dani watched as David reached out his hand to shake Jackie's, not letting go as he spoke to her. Jackie didn't notice Dani's growing irritation.

Shortly after, another round of drinks arrived. Dani thanked whoever had bought them, her voice slurring slightly. In an effort to divert attention from Jackie, she said, "I'm not sure if Jackie's husband would like to know men, we just met at a bar are buying his wife drinks." She laughed. "I don't have that problem," she continued, turning her back on all of them and sipping her martini, becoming more intoxicated.

Jackie was in her element, enjoying all the attention and not noticing Dani's withdrawal. She was still on her second martini, with another waiting on the bar for her. As she glanced over and saw Dani with her back to them, she called out to her to join the conversation. Dani ignored her.

Dani downed her martini and ordered another one. None of the guys noticed her order, nor did they offer to buy her drink.

"Excuse me," Jackie said to the men as she reached over the bar, grabbing the backup martini and placing it in front of Dani. Dani looked at Jackie, but Jackie was already back in the circle of men.

Dani got out of her chair with a slight stumble and walked to the bathroom. When she came back, she noticed the group had not even realized she was gone. The men were engrossed in Jackie's stories. Dani walked up to the group and rudely said, "Jackie, it's time to go." She repeated herself a couple of times as Jackie continued to ignore her.

Dani positioned herself between Jackie and the men, making it obvious that she was very intoxicated. "Dani, relax, I'm not ready to leave yet. Here, sit down and have another drink," Jackie said, leading her back to her chair and placing the drink in front of her.

Dani picked up the drink, took a sip, and stood up, positioning herself next to Jackie. She put her arm through Jackie's for support. She tried to keep up with the conversation but was swaying too much for Jackie to hold her. Jackie led her back to her chair again.

Dani sat hunched over, staring at her drink, feeling invisible and helpless. After a couple of hours, Jackie called out to Dani, but there was no response.

Jackie walked over to her. "Hey, are you okay?" she asked. "They want us to go to dinner with them." Dani looked up, her eyes rolling as she tried to focus.

"What?" she shouted with a growl.

"They want us to have dinner with them," Jackie repeated.

"They want you to have dinner with them. Not me! I'm fucking invisible," Dani shouted, putting her head back down on the bar.

"C'mon, Dani," Jackie urged.

Dani picked her head back up. "I'm not fucking hungry. I want to go home. I told you that a long time ago," she shouted.

Jackie was shocked at how wasted Dani was. "Do you want some coffee?" Jackie asked.

"No! I want to get the fuck out of here," Dani shouted again. "I just want to go home. Can't you just take me home?" Dani cried.

The men watched as Jackie struggled to deal with Dani.

"Is everything alright?" one of them asked.

Jackie laughed it off. "Oh, my friend had too much to drink. I'm going to have to take her home, unfortunately."

One of the men approached Dani, speaking softly, he asked, "Are you okay?" Dani didn't look up at him. "Can I help you to your car?" he offered.

"No, I don't need your fucking help!" Dani shouted.

Jackie looked at the man apologeticallyand embarrassed. "I'm sorry, she's had a bit too much to drink." She helped Dani out of her chair, guiding her towards the exit. As they walked past the men, Jackie smiled and said, "I'd love to have a rain check."

David handed Jackie his business card, hoping for a future encounter.

"We'll do this again sometime," Jackie said with a wink.

The drive home was long and quiet. Dani passed out until they were almost at her house. "Hey, princess, wake up,"

Jackie said, trying to rouse Dani. She repeated herself until she got a reaction. Dani sat up, looking around and realized they were close to home.

"What happened?" she asked.

"Looks like you had another blackout," said Jackie.

"Can you stop at the store? I need to buy a pack of cigarettes," Dani asked.

"Yes, sure," replied Jackie. She pulled over at the first convenience store and watched as Dani walked in, swaying and stumbling. What the hell was I thinking? Jackie thought as she watched Dani nearly fall down a couple of times on her way back to the car.

"So, is this how it's going to be when I go out with you?" Dani asked.

"What do you mean?" Jackie asked with concern.

"I become invisible, and you carry on like you're the only person that matters?"

"What? Are you kidding me?" Frustrated, Jackie didn't say another word until she pulled into Dani's driveway. She got out of the car and opened the trunk while Dani sat dazed.

"Come on," Jackie said. "You have a ton of stuff back here." Dani got out of the car, lit a cigarette, and stumbled to the back of the car.

"What the hell was I thinking?" she muttered.

Jackie laughed. "We had fun, and now you're going to look hot with all this new stuff." Jackie handed Dani bag after bag as Dani continued to smoke her cigarette. Dani was in no shape to understand the amount of money she had spent or how it would affect her finances.

"Come on, I'll help you carry this stuff in," Jackie said, grabbing a few items from Dani and walking towards the front door. Dani fumbled in her purse to find her keys, struggling with the bags. I'd invite you in, but I think I really should go to bed," Dani mumbled.

"Let me help you find your keys," Jackie offered.

"No, no, no. I got it," Dani shouted angerly, pulling the keys out of her purse and opening the door. "See, I'm capable of doing it."

Jackie walked into the house, put the items she was carrying on the couch, and turned to Dani to give her a hug. "I've got to go," she said. "I'll see you soon." Jackie left the house without looking back and thankful to be getting away from Dani.

Dani stumbled to the front door, leaned against it, tears welling up in her eyes. She felt a deep sense of loneliness and wondered if she was ever going to find a place where she truly belonged.

Dani watched, through the window, as Jackie left the driveway. She then went to the fridge and grabbed a beer. She stumbled over to the couch and sat down next to her bags. She was no longer impressed with the things she had bought, tossing them onto the floor to make room to lie across the couch. After a few moments and a few sips of her beer, she was out cold.

Once Jackie got home, she made herself a cup of tea and sat down at her kitchen table. She took out David's business card and stared at it, debating whether to call or text him. After a moment, against her better judgement, she decided to send a simple text.

"Hey David, it's Jackie. Nice meeting you today. Thanks for helping with Dani tonight. I had a good time despite the chaos. Maybe we can do something just the two of us sometime?" She hit send and waited for a reply, her mind racing with thoughts about Dani and her own life. A few minutes later, her phone buzzed with a reply from Peter. "Hi Jackie, I'm glad you got home safe. I'd love to see you again. Let's plan something soon. Hope your friend is okay."

In the morning, Dani woke up with a pounding headache. The living room was still a mess, with shopping bags tossed everywhere. She groaned, trying to piece together the events of the previous day. As she stood up, she felt the room spin and had to lean on the couch. "God, I need to get it together," she muttered, making her way to the kitchen to get some water.

As she drank the water, she noticed her phone blinking with missed calls and messages. One was from Tammy, and a few others were from numbers she didn't recognize. Ignoring the others, she called Tammy back.

"Hey, Tammy. Sorry I missed your call," Dani said, her voice rough from sleep and the lingering effects of alcohol. "Dani, I've been worried about you," Tammy replied, relief evident in her voice. "Are you okay?"

"Yes, I'm fine," Dani said, trying to sound convincing. "I just had a bit too much to drink yesterday. What's up?"

"I just wanted to check on you. A lot has been going on in my life, with my parents."

Dani began talking over her, not even letting Tammy

finish her sentence. "I know, I've just been... busy," Dani said, portraying a pang of guilt.

Tammy hung up feeling a bit disappointed that Dani did not even ask her if everything was okay with her. Dani was made aware that Tammy's dad went missing, but she did not know that he had passed away.

38 - He's Gone

Dr. Peters entered the clinic as he usually did, but immediately sensed something was wrong. The normally calm environment was replaced with a flurry of emergency activity, particularly in his department. His heart began to race as he noticed the tension and urgency in the air. Without hesitation, he hurried toward the commotion, anxiety building with each step.

"What's going on?" he asked frantically as he approached a cluster of nurses who were visibly shaken.

A nurse turned to him, her face pale and her voice trembling slightly. "Dr. Peters, it's Benjamin. He locked himself in the bathroom and he took his own life."

"What?" Dr. Peters exclaimed, his eyes widening in shock. "Benjamin? That's my patient! Why didn't anyone call me?" His voice filled with a mix of disbelief and deep concern.

"Sir, it literally just happened," the nurse responded, trying to maintain her composure during the chaos. "We've been in Code Blue stress mode. Housekeeping went in his room to empty the trash and saw blood on the floor coming from under the bathroom door. She immediately alerted us. We managed to get the door open, but by the time we reached him, he had already bled out..."

Dr. Peters felt as though the ground had shifted beneath him. He stood there, his mind reeling, trying to process the enormity of what had just occurred. Benjamin was his patient—someone he had been working with closely, someone he had been trying to help.

"How… how could this happen?" he muttered, more to himself than anyone else. He felt a wave of guilt and sorrow washing over him, the weight of it almost unbearable.

The nurse, seeing the pain in Dr. Peters' eyes, gently placed a hand on his arm. "I'm so sorry, Dr. Peters. We did everything we could…"

Dr. Peters nodded absently; his thoughts scattered. He knew the staff had acted quickly, but the knowledge did little to ease the ache in his chest. He felt a deep sense of responsibility for his patients, and losing one this way was a nightmare come true.

"I need to see him," Dr. Peters said, his voice hollow. "I need to… I just need to see him."

The nurse nodded, guiding him down the hallway toward the bathroom where Benjamin had been found. As they approached, Dr. Peters braced himself for what he was about to see, knowing it was something he would carry with him for the rest of his life.

When they reached the bathroom, Dr. Peters stood outside for a moment, gathering the strength to enter. He took a deep breath and pushed the door open, stepping inside. The scene before him was both devastating and surreal. He felt a deep sorrow settle into his bones, a heavy weight that he knew would be with him for a long time.

Dr. Peters stayed there for a moment, silently grieving for the life lost, before turning to the nurse. "We need to notify his family," he said, his voice steady but laced with emotion. "And I need to review his file… see if there was something we missed, something I missed…"

The nurse nodded, understanding the depth of his pain. "We'll take care of it, Dr. Peters," she assured him.

As he walked away, Dr. Peters knew that this tragedy would leave a lasting mark on him. He was left questioning everything—his decisions, his treatment plans, and most of all, his ability to save the people who relied on him. Dr. Peters could not shake the pain of losing his patient throughout the rest of the day. He could not help but want the day to be over so he could take a break from the reality of his work.

Steve called Kathy on his way home from work. As soon as she answered he was ready to hear her soft welcoming voice. "Hey, do you mind if I stop by on my way home," he asked.

"Absolutely, come on by," Kathy said, feeling something wasn't right. Steve entered Kathy's house, his shoulders slumped and his expression weary. He gave Kathy a brief, tight hug before they moved to sit down in the living room. Kathy could see the stress etched in his face and knew whatever had happened was serious.

"Kathy," he began, taking a deep breath, "we lost Benjamin today." Kathy's heart sank. "What happened?" she asked, her voice barely above a whisper. "He took his own life," Dr. Peters said, his voice heavy with sadness. "They found him in the bathroom. He had somehow gotten hold of a plastic knife and... well, he bled out before anyone could get to him."

Kathy's hand flew to her mouth. "Oh my God," she said, tears welling up in her eyes. "He seemed so...so determined to get better." Steve nodded.

"He did. But sometimes, the pain becomes too much. He had a lot of demons, and I think they just overwhelmed him."

Kathy reached out and took his hand, squeezing it gently. "I'm so sorry, Steve." Dr. Peters looked down, his eyes glistening with unshed tears.

"I should have seen it coming. I should have done more."

"Don't do that," Kathy said firmly. "You did everything you could. You can't save everyone, no matter how much you want to."

Steve nodded, but Kathy could see the guilt still weighing heavily on him. She pulled him into a hug, letting him lean on her for a moment.

"I just wish..." Steve began, his voice breaking.

"I know," Kathy whispered. "I know."

They sat in silence for a while, each lost in their own thoughts. Finally, Dr. Peters pulled back and wiped his eyes. "I need to get home," he said. "Thank you for letting me come over."

"Anytime," Kathy said, her heart aching for him. "And if you need to talk, or just need someone to be with, you know where to find me."

He nodded, giving her a small, grateful smile. "I'll keep that in mind."

As he left, Kathy closed the door and leaned against it, her thoughts racing. She felt a deep sadness for Benjamin and a growing worry for Dani. She hoped Dani wasn't spiraling further into her own destructive habits. She resolved to reach out to her friend, to check in and see how she was doing. Kathy went to bed that night with a heavy heart, praying that somehow, they could all find a way to heal.

The next morning, Kathy called Dani's house, but there was no answer. She left a message, hoping that Dani would return her call. Throughout the day, Kathy found herself distracted, her thoughts constantly returning to Benjamin and Dani. By late afternoon, she decided to take action. She called a cab and headed to Dani's house. When she arrived, she found the door slightly ajar. Concerned, she pushed it open and stepped inside.

"Dani?" she called out, her voice echoing in the quiet house. There was no response. Kathy moved through the house, checking each room until she found Dani passed out on the couch, surrounded by empty beer bottles and shopping bags. Kathy's heart ached at the sight. She gently shook Dani's shoulder, trying to rouse her. "Dani, wake up."   Dani groaned and slowly opened her eyes. "Kathy? What are you doing here?"

"I was worried about you," Kathy said softly. "You've got to stop this, Dani. You're hurting yourself."

Dani sat up; her eyes blurry. "I know," she said, her voice cracking. "I just. I don't know how."

"We'll figure it out together," Kathy said firmly. "But you have to want to get better." Dani nodded, tears streaming down her face. "I do, Kathy. I really do."

"Then let's start now," Kathy said passionately. "First, let's clean up this mess and get you some water. We'll take it one step at a time." Kathy felt a glimmer of hope knowing that Dani was open and willing to change. It wouldn't be easy, but she was determined to help Dani find her way back to a healthier, happier life.

39 - Starting To Get It

When the next meeting began, Dr. Peters started with a heavy heart. The group was smaller than usual, the absence of Benjamin weighing heavily on some that already knew. Tammy had also not attended for the first time ever. "Before we begin," he said, looking around the room, "I have some sad news to share. Benjamin, who many of you got to know through this group, is no longer with us. I cannot get into the details, but he went to be with the Lord. I want us to take a moment to remember him and reflect on how he affected your life and also on how we can support each other through our struggles."

The room fell silent, a somber mood settling over the group. Kathy glanced at Dani and Jackie, who looked genuinely shocked.

After the moment of silence, Dr. Peters continued. "I know this is difficult to hear, but it reinforces why we are here. Addiction and mental health issues are not battles we can fight alone. We need each other."

Dani, who had been subdued since she arrived, raised her hand. "Dr. Peters, I just want to say that I'm really sorry about Benjamin. I know I didn't know him well, but it's hard to think that someone so close to us was in so much pain."

"Thank you, Dani," Dr. Peters said. "It's a reminder that we need to be vigilant and supportive, even when things seem to be going well."

"Jackie nodded in agreement. "Yeah, it's a wake-up call for all of us. We need to check in on each other more often."

Kathy, still shaken by the news, felt a surge of resolve. She knew she needed to reach out to those around her, including Dani, Tammy and even Jackie.

After the meeting, Kathy approached Dani. "Hey, I just wanted to check on you. Are you doing okay?"

Dani looked tired, but she nodded. "I'm okay. It is just...a lot, you know?"

"Yeah, I know," Kathy said, placing a hand on Dani's arm. "Let's make sure we stay connected. We can get through this together."

The following day, Kathy decided to visit Tammy at her home. She knew Tammy would be struggling, not just with her father's death but also with the increased burden of caring for her mother. When she arrived, she found Tammy sitting on the front porch, looking exhausted and overwhelmed.

"Tammy," Kathy said softly, "I came to check on you. How are you holding up?"

Tammy looked up; her eyes red from crying. "I'm not doing well, Kathy. I feel like everything is falling apart."

Kathy sat down beside her, taking her hand. "I know it's hard. You are dealing with so much right now. But you do not have to do it alone. Let me help you."

Tammy shook her head, tears streaming down her face. "I don't know how to do this, Kathy. My father is gone, and my mother...she is so demanding. I feel like I'm losing myself."

"You're not losing yourself," Kathy said firmly. "You're just going through a rough time. It's okay to ask for help.

Tammy looked at Kathy, her expression a mixture of gratitude and despair. "Thank you, Kathy. I don't know what I would do without you."

"You don't have to find out," Kathy said, squeezing her hand softly. "We'll get through this together. One step at a time."

As they sat together, Kathy felt a sense of purpose. She knew the road ahead would be difficult, but she was determined to be there for Tammy, Dani, and the others. They were all in this together, and together, they would find a way to heal.

When Kathy left, Tammy decided to take a walk to clear her mind. She left her mother asleep in her recliner, making sure the door was locked behind her. As she walked through the quiet neighborhood, she thought about her father and the support he had always given her. She missed him terribly and felt the void his absence created.

She passed by a park and decided to sit on a bench for a while. The cool air was refreshing, she took long deep breaths, trying to calm her racing thoughts. She needed to find a way to cope with her feelings of resentment and guilt towards her mother. Suddenly, her phone buzzed with a text message. It was from Dr. Peters.

Dr. Peters: "Tammy, I just wanted to check in on you. How are you holding up"? Tammy felt a wave of gratitude. She began typing a reply.

Tammy: "I'm struggling, Dr. Peters. It's been really hard since my father passed. My mother needs so much care, and I'm not sure I can handle it".

She hesitated for a moment before sending, then hit 'send' and waited for a response. Within moments, her phone buzzed again.

Dr. Peters: "I understand, Tammy. It's important to take care of yourself, too. Is there any way I can help? Maybe we can meet and talk"? Tammy felt a glimmer of hope. Maybe talking to Dr. Peters would help her sort through her feelings.

Tammy: "That would be great. When are you available"?

Dr. Peters: "How about tomorrow afternoon? We can meet at my office or somewhere you feel comfortable".

Tammy: "Your office works. Thank you, Dr. Peters. I appreciate it".

Dr. Peters: "Anytime, Tammy. Remember, you're not alone".

The next day, Tammy found herself sitting in Dr. Peters' office. She felt nervous but also relieved to have someone to talk to. Dr. Peters sat across from her, his expression kind and attentive.

"Tammy, I'm glad you came today," he said. "Tell me what's been going on." Tammy took a deep breath and began to pour out her heart. She spoke about her father's death, her mother's increasing demands, and her feelings of resentment and guilt. Dr. Peters listened without interrupting, giving her the space to express herself fully.

"I just don't know what to do," Tammy said, tears streaming down her face. "I love my mother, but I also resent her. I feel like I'm drowning." Dr. Peters handed her a tissue and gave her a moment to compose herself.

"Tammy, it's completely natural to feel the way you do.

You've been through a lot, and it's important to acknowledge your feelings. It's okay to feel conflicted."

"But what can I do?" Tammy asked, her voice trembling "I feel so trapped."

"We need to find ways to give you support," Dr. Peters said gently. "Have you considered talking to a therapist? They can help you work through these emotions. I know a pretty good one." He said with a chuckle.

I've thought about it, but I don't know if I have the time," Tammy admitted.

"Making time for your mental health is crucial," Dr. Peters emphasized. "Have you ever heard "You can't pour from an empty cup". Let's work together to find a solution to help you navigate this difficult period."

Tammy nodded, feeling a sense of relief. "Okay, I'll do it. Thank you, Dr. Peters."

He smiled. "You're taking the first step towards healing, Tammy. Remember, you are not alone in this. We're all here to support you." As Tammy left Dr. Peters' office, she felt a renewed sense of hope. She knew the road ahead would be challenging, but she also knew she did not have to walk it alone. She had friends, support, and the determination to find her way through the darkness.

40 - Tammy's next session

"Good morning, Tammy," Dr. Peters said warmly as he entered the room. "Thank you for coming in. How are you feeling today?"

Tammy took a deep breath, trying to steady her nerves. "I'm... managing, Dr. Peters. It's been really hard, especially with my mother needing so much care and not easy to get along with.   Dr. Peters nodded; his expression sympathetic. "I understand. Caring for a parent, especially after such a significant loss, can be incredibly challenging. I wanted to talk to you today to see how we can support you better."

Tammy felt a lump in her throat as she struggled to find the right words. "It's just... my mother. She is so demanding and critical. It is like nothing I do is ever good enough for her. And since my father passed, it's been even worse. I feel like I'm drowning, Dr. Peters."

Dr. Peters leaned forward; his gaze compassionate. "Tammy, it's important that you take care of yourself, too. Have you thought about getting some additional help for your mother? Maybe in-home care or a respite care service?"

"I don't know if I can afford that," Tammy admitted. "And to be honest, I'm not sure how my mother would react to a stranger coming in to help."

"I understand your concerns," Dr. Peters replied. "But there are programs and resources available that might be able to assist you, both financially and with the care aspect. It could give you some much-needed relief and help you manage your own stress and well-being." Tammy nodded, though she still looked uncertain.

"I guess I just feel so guilty. Like I'm failing her."

"You're not failing her, Tammy," Dr. Peters said gently. "You're doing the best you can in a very difficult situation. But it's crucial to recognize when you need help. There's no shame in that. In fact, it's a sign of strength."

Tammy felt a tear slip down her cheek, she quickly wiped it away. "I don't know what to do, Dr. Peters. I'm so scared of making the wrong decision."

Dr. Peters reached out and gave her hand a reassuring squeeze. "Let's take it one step at a time. We can look into some support options together. And I think it would be beneficial for you to speak with a social worker, someone who can help you navigate these next steps in life."

Tammy nodded, feeling a small glimmer of hope. "Okay. I'll give it a try."

"Good," Dr. Peters said with a smile. "I'll have my assistant give you some information on local social workers and support services before you leave today. And Tammy, remember, you're not alone in this. We're here to help."

Later that afternoon, Dr. Peters called Kathy to check in on her. "Hi, Kathy. I just wanted to see how you're doing."

"Hi, Steve," Kathy said, her voice warm. "I'm doing okay. How are you holding up?" she asked.

"It's been a challenging week as you know," he admitted. "But I'm managing. I will get through this." "How about I pick you up after work and we get a bite to eat?" Steve asked. "That sounds amazing, I look forward to seeing you" Kathy said.

Kathy spent a good hour preparing for her night out to dinner with Steve. She chose a simple yet elegant dress, applied makeup with care, and even put on a pair of low heels, despite the slight discomfort.

Steve chose a quaint, upscale restaurant with a cozy ambiance. "Kathy, you look amazing!" he said, offering his arm as they walked inside.

"Thank you, Steve" Kathy replied with a bashful smile.

They were seated at a quiet corner table, away from the main dining area, which allowed for a more intimate setting. The restaurant was softly lit, with gentle music playing in the background. Kathy could feel the weight of the past months lifting off her shoulders as she relaxed into the evening.

As they ordered their meals, the conversation flowed effortlessly. They talked about Kathy's recovery, her plans for the future, and shared anecdotes about their lives outside the therapy sessions. It felt refreshing to connect on a personal level, beyond the confines of doctor and patient.

When their meals arrived, Steve raised his glass. "To new beginnings and to Kathy, for her strength and resilience."

"To new beginnings," Kathy echoed, clinking her glass against his as they enjoyed their meals,

Steve leaned in slightly, his tone more serious. "Kathy, I wanted to tell you how proud I am of you. You've come a long way since the accident, and your progress has been remarkable. You've shown incredible strength and determination."

Kathy felt a bit bashful, "Thank you, Steve. I couldn't have done it without your support and the therapy sessions. They've been a lifeline."

Steve and Kathy drove home holding hands as he drove. When they entered Kathy's house, she turned on a few lights, illuminating the cozy, welcoming space.

"Would you like some tea or coffee?" Kathy offered, gesturing toward the kitchen.

"Tea would be great," Steve replied. "I'm going to wait out here if its aright with you." He watched as she moved around, impressed by her tenacious persistence for independence.

While Kathy prepared the tea, Steve took a moment to look around her home with a bit more depth than in the past. It was tastefully decorated, with personal touches that spoke of a well-lived life. Family photos, artwork, and a collection of books filled the space with warmth and character. Steve viewing was interrupted when Kathy called out for him to bring the tea to the living room, where they sat down on the comfortable couch.

"I have never really been able to take the time to look around your home at your photos and artwork. I am impressed with what all I see."

Kathy put a big smile on her face, "Yes, I come from a great family, and I have had some really good, life-long friends."

"It shows" Steve said as he looked admiring her.

They continued to talk, sharing stories and experiences, and the atmosphere grew more relaxed. There was a comfortable silence between them as they sipped their tea, both lost in their thoughts.

Steve stood up, sensing it was time to leave. "I should get going. It's been a long day, and you need your rest." Kathy walked him to the door, secretly wishing she could ask him to stay but knew he needed to go home.
"Thank you for tonight, Steve. It was exactly what I needed. said Kathy

"You're welcome, Kathy. It was what I needed as well. As he left, Kathy felt a sense of peace and contentment. The evening had been a wonderful distraction from the challenges of the past months.

In the morning, Steve made sure his office staff reached out to Dani once more. This time, he instructed them to be persistent and to arrange a visit if she didn't respond. He felt a growing concern for her well-being and wanted to ensure she wasn't slipping further into despair. As the staff tried to contact Dani, Dr Peters prepared for another day of appointments and therapy sessions. He knew that the work he did was challenging, but seeing patients like Kathy and others recover and thrive made it all worthwhile. He hoped that, with the right support, Dani could find her way back too.

41 - There is help

Meanwhile, Tammy was having another rough morning. She had managed to get her mother up and dressed, but the daily routine was wearing her down. She found herself snapping at Flora over small things, and the guilt weighed heavily on her. Flora, sensing Tammy's frustration, tried to make things easier by staying quiet and compliant, but her presence alone seemed to be a trigger for Tammy's anger.

As the morning wore on, Tammy's phone rang. It was Kathy, checking in on her as promised. Tammy hesitated before answering, not wanting to burden Kathy with her problems, but she knew she needed someone to talk to.

"Hi, Kathy," Tammy said, trying to sound cheerful.

"Hey, Tammy. I Just wanted to see how you are doing today," Kathy asked cheerfully.

Tammy sighed, the facade slipping away. "I'll be honest with you, it's been tough. My mom is...difficult, and I'm struggling to keep it together."

Kathy listened, offering words of encouragement, and understanding. "You're doing the best you can, Tammy. It is okay to feel overwhelmed. Have you thought about getting some help? Maybe a caregiver to assist your mom?" Kathy asked.

Tammy shook her head, even though Kathy could not see her. "I don't know if we can afford it. And I feel like I should be able to manage this on my own"

"I'm pretty sure you don't have to handle this alone Tammy. There are public resources available and help that will come and spend time with your mom so you can get a break. I have had friends that have gotten help, so you should be able to also. "Let's talk to Dr. Peters and see what options we have," Kathy said, her voice filled with determination and a hint of urgency.

"Well actually, I already spoke to Dr. Peters when I went to my therapy. His office staff gave a sheet with phone numbers for social workers and programs." Tammy said with enthusiasm. I just have to make some phone calls." As they ended the call, Tammy felt grateful knowing she had friends who cared and were willing to help her through this difficult time.

42 - Isolation

Dani, on the other hand, continued to isolate herself. She ignored the calls from Dr. Peters' office, letting them go to voicemail. She felt disconnected from the world, her depression deepening with each passing day. Finally, Cloee one of Dr. Peters' staff made a visit to Dani's home. She knocked on her door repeatedly until Dani, groggy and barely able to communicate, finally answered.

"Hi Dani, I am Cloee from Dr. Peters office. We have been trying to reach you. Dr. Peters is very concerned about you," Cloee said gently.

Dani mumbled something incomprehensible, her eyes avoiding contact rolling about as if she was looking right through her.   "Can I come in and talk for a bit?" Cloee asked. "You don't have to go through this alone, Dani. We are here to help. Let's get you back to the clinic and see what we can do to support you," Cloee said, her voice full of compassion and energy.

"No, I am good." Dani mumbled. I just need to take a shower and wake up a bit." Dani began to close the door on Cloee, but Cloee put her foot in the doorway and tried to talk more.

"Dani please," Cloee pleaded. "We can recommend a recovery facility that can help you get better. If you need help paying for it, we can get you the help you need." Please Dani."

Dani stood in the doorway, unable to speak for a moment, her hair falling onto her face. "No, I am good. "Please go away and stop bothering me." she mumbled.

Cloee kept her foot in the door continuing to plead. Dani looked down at Cloee's foot. "Please move your foot or I am going to call the police" she said.

Using her foot, Dani pushed Cloee's foot out of the doorway, shutting the door firmly and locking it behind her. Cloee stood there for a moment, stunned, and hurt by Dani's abrupt dismissal. The rejection stung deeply, leaving her feeling helpless and unsure of what to do next.

With a heavy heart, Cloee turned and walked back to her car, trying to process what had just happened. She had only wanted to help, but now she was shut down

Once she reached her car, Cloee took a deep breath and pulled out her phone. She knew she needed to talk to Dr. Peters. With a broken spirit, she dialed his number, hoping he would pick up quickly.

After a few rings, Dr. Peters answered. "Hello, this is Dr. Peters."

"Dr. Peters, it's Cloee," she began, her voice shaky with emotion. "I just tried to check on Dani, but she... she pushed me out the door and locked it behind me. She told me to leave, and I don't know what to do. I'm really worried about her."

There was a brief pause on the other end of the line as Dr. Peters absorbed what Cloee was saying. "I'm sorry to hear that, Cloee," he responded, his tone calm and professional, yet filled with genuine concern. "It sounds like Dani is in a difficult place right now. But I'm glad you called me.

"What should I do?" Cloee asked, feeling lost. "I don't want to push her away further,
but I'm really worried she's not okay."

I understand your concern," Dr. Peters replied thoughtfully. "Sometimes, when people are going through a tough time, they push others away because they don't know how to handle what they're feeling, but it's important that she knows you're there for her even if she's not ready to accept your help right now. Cloee nodded, even though he couldn't see her.
"Is there something else I can do?" she asked.

"For now, I think it's best to give her some space," Dr. Peters advised. "You can send her a text message, letting her know that you're there when she's ready to talk, and then let's give her time to come around."

"Thank you, Dr. Peters," Cloee said, feeling grateful for his guidance. "I really appreciate it." After ending the call, Cloee sat in her car for a moment, taking a few deep breaths to steady herself. She knew it wasn't an easy situation, but with Dr. Peters' support, she felt a bit more prepared to navigate it. She typed out a brief text message to Dani, letting her know she was there if she needed anything, and then sent it, hoping that Dani would reach out when she was ready.

43 - Mail Man

Several days had passed since Cloee had made a visit to Dani. She had tried on numerous occasions to reach out to Dani via phone call with no success. Each time Cloee would report back to Dr. Peters the results.

"Maybe it's time to do a welfare check," he said. "We need to call the police and have them stop by her house just to make sure she is okey."

Cloee did not hesitate to pick up the phone and call the police. She had seen with her own eyes the shape Dani was in, and it was not good.

That morning, as the mail carrier walked up to Dani's house, he smelt a foul, nauseating odor, as if there was a dead animal somewhere nearby.

He began to put the mail in her mailbox, but realized it was overflowing, untouched for days. His eyes darted around, searching for the source of the stench. Maybe a dead rodent, he thought.

He knocked on the door several times, but there was no answer. Peering through the window, he saw no movement inside, only the reflection of the flicker of the TV and the glow of several lights.

Unease gnawed at him. Something wasn't right. He pulled out his cell phone and dialed 911, reporting a suspicious incident.

"The operator asked him if he could stay in the neighborhood until someone arrived at the scene. He agreed, but continued his rounds, dropping off mail at the neighboring houses, all the while casting anxious glances back at Dani's place.

When he saw the police arrive, he hurried back. "I'm the one who called," he told the officer. "There's a really bad smell, and the mail hasn't been collected for days."

The officer checked the door and peered through the windows, circling the house. At the back of the house, he stopped, his face shocked with the view. Through the glass, Dani's lifeless body sprawled on the floor.

The police officer radioed for backup, his voice steady despite the urgency of the situation. Within minutes, additional officers arrived on the scene, their presence lending an air of grim determination. Together, they forced the back door open, the wood splintering under pressure. As the door swung inward, a heavy rotting smell filled the air, one that seemed to grow thicker with each step they took inside.

The scene they encountered was tragic. Dani's lifeless body lay sprawled on the floor, her skin pale and her breathing stopped long before they arrived. The signs were unmistakable—she had drowned in her own vomit, a heartbreaking end to what must have been a desperate and lonely struggle.

One of the officers, his expression dark with sorrow, noticed a business card on the coffee table near Dani's body. He picked it up carefully, the name on it read "Dr. Peters, Psychiatrist, and his phone number." The sight of it only deepened the weight of the moment. It was clear that Dani had recently been in touch with her psychiatrist, perhaps hoping for a lifeline she couldn't grasp in time.

The news of Dani's death was conveyed to Dr. Peters by the hospital. As he listened to the person on the other end of the line, his face went pale, his breath slowing in depth. The shock of losing another patient, especially so soon after Benjamin's tragic suicide, hit him like a physical blow.

He sank into his chair, the phone still clutched in his hand, the words replayed in his mind. Dani was gone. Despite all his efforts, despite the support he had tried to offer, she had slipped through the cracks. The weight of it was unbearable—a crushing sense of failure and loss that left him reeling.

"How could this happen?" he whispered to himself; his voice barely audible in the quiet of his office. He had just spoken to Cloee, trying to offer her guidance on how to help Dani, but it hadn't been enough. The realization tore at him, a gnawing guilt settling deep in his chest.

He stared at his desk, the papers and files that had once seemed so important now nothing more than a blur. Two patients lost in such a short span of time—two lives that he couldn't save. The burden of those losses weighed heavily on him, bringing with it an overwhelming sense of responsibility.

Dr. Peters knew he had to inform the rest of the team at the clinic but for a moment, all he could do was sit there, grappling with the emotions that threatened to consume him. The profession he had devoted his life to was one of healing, yet here he was, facing the stark reality that sometimes, despite his best efforts, it wasn't enough.

Eventually, he forced himself to stand, taking a deep breath to steady himself. There were calls to make, people to inform, and reports to file. But beneath the surface, a question lingered—one that would haunt him for a long time to come: How could he have done better? What could he have done differently?

As Dr. Peters walked out of his office, the weight of Dani's death pressed down on him, a somber reminder of the fragility of the human spirit and the limits of his own ability to save those in his care.

Dr. Peters didn't want to call Kathy and let her know of the tragedy. Instead, he drove to her house wondering how she would take the news. When Steve arrived, Kathy greeted him at the door, her face a mask of concern. She had seen the anguish in his eyes the moment he stepped out of his car. As he approached, she asked, "What is it?" Her voice was urgent, filled with dread. He looked at her with deep sorrow.

"What is it?" she repeated, more insistent. "Is it Dani?"

He nodded; his expression pained. "Yes."

"No!" Kathy shouted, her voice cracking. "Is she okay? "What happened?"

Softly, he replied, "Dani... she drank herself to death."

"No! How can this be?" Kathy's voice was a mix of disbelief and guilt. "We should have gone by there last night! I felt something was wrong. I was right!" She clutched her head in her hands, her voice breaking. "Oh, my God."

Kathy stepped back into the house, overwhelmed, and sank onto the couch, tears streaming down her face. "She was a good woman. I can't believe this has happened."

Dr. Peters followed her inside, closing the door softly behind him. "Even if we had gone by there last night, it would have been too late. Dani had been dead for a couple of days," he said, his tone somber.

He walked over to where Kathy was sitting and sat down next to her gently placing his hand on her shoulder. "I'm so sorry," he said again, his voice heavy with regret.

Kathy looked up at him, her eyes red and swollen. "She was struggling, and we couldn't help her," she cried.

"We can't blame ourselves for this Kathy. It is the nature of the beast." They sat in silence, the weight of their shared grief settling around them. The room held its breath, the world outside a distant, uncaring place.

The funeral was sparsely attended. Dani's sister knew of her passing but refused to show up. Paul sat in the front row, though nobody knew who he was. Jackie, dressed in a beautiful all-black suit with a hat and black netting over her eyes, cried the whole time, carrying on as if they were best friends. Tammy and a few others from the group attended as well. At the end of the ceremony, the pastor asked if anyone had anything to say.

Dr. Peters walked up to the coffin, pausing for a moment before turning to address the crowd. "Dani was a good person," he began. "She had so many talents and gifts, but she was plagued with a condition—a mental illness—that, although we think we understand it, we will never quite grasp without walking in her shoes." He glanced around the room, his voice steady but filled with emotion. "'Get over it!' they say. Why can't you be like everyone else? Be thankful for what you have. Focus on the good. But that is not enough. It does not work that way. When someone is struggling with depression, bipolar disorder, or any other mental illness, you cannot just wish it away. Positive thoughts are not a cure.

Dr. Peters took a deep breath before continuing. There is something chemically off balance in the brain. Neurotransmitters might not connect correctly, hormones may be out of whack, or genetics may play a role. People need to be seen and treated by doctors. There is medication that can help if taken regularly. There is therapy if we can get patience to come to their appointments. But the problem, as with Dani and many others, is that they stop taking their medication. Maybe their prescriptions run out, they don't refill them, they don't want to be bothered, or they can't afford it." He paused, looking down for a moment. "Once they stop, the symptoms come back, sometimes with a vengeance. Some turn to alcohol or drugs because they are easier to get than seeing a doctor. Looking up he concluded; may God rest her soul.

There was complete silence, the weight of his words hanging in the air. Dr. Peters stepped back, his heart was heavy, hoping that Dani's story might help others understand the unseen battles so many face.

Stacy C. Kramer

THERE IS HELP FOR YOU

If you're having a medical emergency always dial **911**

For a psychiatric emergency dial **988**

National Alliance on Mental Illness 1-800-950-6264

NAMI   Text HelpLine to 62640

APPS To Get Help

Talkspace -

7 Cups